Lexical Inferencing in a First and Second Language

SECOND LANGUAGE ACQUISITION
Series Editor: Professor David Singleton, *Trinity College, Dublin, Ireland*

This series brings together titles dealing with a variety of aspects of language acquisition and processing in situations where a language or languages other than the native language is involved. Second language is thus interpreted in its broadest possible sense. The volumes included in the series all offer in their different ways, on the one hand, exposition and discussion of empirical findings and, on the other, some degree of theoretical reflection. In this latter connection, no particular theoretical stance is privileged in the series; nor is any relevant perspective – sociolinguistic, psycholinguistic, neurolinguistic, etc. – deemed out of place. The intended readership of the series includes final-year undergraduates working on second language acquisition projects, postgraduate students involved in second language acquisition research, and researchers and teachers in general whose interests include a second language acquisition component.

Full details of all the books in this series and of all our other publications can be found on http://www.multilingual-matters.com, or by writing to Multilingual Matters, St Nicholas House, 31-34 High Street, Bristol BS1 2AW, UK.

SECOND LANGUAGE ACQUISITION
Series Editor: David Singleton, *Trinity College, Dublin, Ireland*

Lexical Inferencing in a First and Second Language
Cross-linguistic Dimensions

Marjorie Bingham Wesche and T. Sima Paribakht

MULTILINGUAL MATTERS
Bristol • Buffalo • Toronto

Library of Congress Cataloging in Publication Data
A catalog record for this book is available from the Library of Congress.
Wesche, Marjorie Bingham
Lexical Inferencing in a First and Second Language: Cross-linguistic Dimensions/
Marjorie Bingham Wesche and T. Sima Paribakht.
Second Language Acquisition: 46
Includes bibliographical references and index.
1. Vocabulary--Study and teaching. 2. Second language acquisition. 3. Language and languages--Study and teaching. 4. Inference. I. Paribakht, Tahereh, – II. Title.
P53.9.W47 2009
418.0071–dc22 2009033461

British Library Cataloguing in Publication Data
A catalogue entry for this book is available from the British Library.

ISBN-13: 978-1-84769-223-8 (hbk)
ISBN-13: 978-1-84769-222-1 (pbk)

Multilingual Matters
UK: St Nicholas House, 31-34 High Street, Bristol BS1 2AW, UK.
USA: UTP, 2250 Military Road, Tonawanda, NY 14150, USA.
Canada: UTP, 5201 Dufferin Street, North York, Ontario M3H 5T8, Canada.

Copyright © 2010 Marjorie Bingham Wesche, T. Sima Paribakht and the co-author of Chapters 1 and 2.

All rights reserved. No part of this work may be reproduced in any form or by any means without permission in writing from the publisher.

The policy of Multilingual Matters/Channel View Publications is to use papers that are natural, renewable and recyclable products, made from wood grown in sustainable forests. In the manufacturing process of our books, and to further support our policy, preference is given to printers that have FSC and PEFC Chain of Custody certification. The FSC and/or PEFC logos will appear on those books where full certification has been granted to the printer concerned.

Typeset by Datapage International Ltd.
Printed and bound in Great Britain by Short Run Press Ltd.

Contents

List of Figures and Tables. vii
Acknowledgements ix
Preface xi

Part 1: Lexical Inferencing: A Research Review 1
1 Research on the Lexical Inferencing Process and its
   Outcomes 3
      What is Lexical Inferencing and How Does it Relate to
      Reading Comprehension and Lexical Development? 3
      What Factors Influence Lexical Inferencing and its
      Outcomes? 10
      What Processes are Involved in Lexical Inferencing and
      How Have They Been Conceptualized and Explained? 18
      Conclusion 29
2 Cross-linguistic Issues in Lexical Inferencing. 32
      First Language Influences in Second Language Lexical
      Inferencing 33
      The Importance of Typological Distance Between Languages . . . 34
      Conclusion 42

**Part 2: Trilingual Study of Lexical Inferencing in a First and
Second Language.** 45
3 Conceptualization and Methodology. 49
      Conceptualization 49
      Research Design 51
      Research Questions 52
      Methodology. 54
      Data Analyses 63
4 First Language Influences on Knowledge Source Use in
   Second Language Lexical Inferencing 67
      Issues 68
      Methodology. 74
      Findings 76
      Summary and Discussion 107

5 Inferencing Success and Initial Development of Word
   Knowledge 114
      Issues 115
      Methodology 116
      Findings 119
      Summary and Discussion 134
6 Trilingual Study Summary, Discussion and Implications 139
      Shared Cross-linguistic Aspects of Knowledge Source Use
      in First and Second Language Lexical Inferencing 140
      Overall First and Second Language Differences in Lexical
      Inferencing 144
      Persian and French First Language Influences on Second
      Language Lexical Inferencing Processes and Outcomes 146
      Differential Receptive Second Language Vocabulary
      Knowledge and Lexical Inferencing Outcomes for
      Persian and French Speakers 154
      What Have We Learned? 157
      A Final Word 161
      Research Issues 161
      Implications for Second Language Reading and Vocabulary
      Instruction 163

Appendices 168
   Appendix A 168
   Appendix B 170
   Appendix C 172
   Appendix D 173
   Appendix E 174
   Appendix F 175
   Appendix G 178
References 180
Index 190

List of Figures and Tables

Figures

3.1	VKS elicitation scale: Self-report categories	57
3.2	VKS scoring categories: Meaning of scores	58
4.1	Trilingual study taxonomy of KS use in L1 and L2 lexical inferencing	77
4.2	Examples of KSs from transcripts of English, French and Persian speakers reading L1 and L2 texts	78
5.1	Examples of fully and partially successful inferences	118
5.2	Success of Persian speakers in inferring meanings for lexicalized versus non-lexicalized L2 words	121
5.3	Success of French speakers in inferring meanings for lexicalized versus non-lexicalized L2 words	123
5.4	Pre-task to post-task gains in average VKS scores for all L2 target words by Persian and French speakers	124
5.5	Pre-task to post-task changes in knowledge of L2 target words: Persian speakers	126
5.6	Pre-task to post-task changes in knowledge of L2 target words: French speakers	127
5.7	Example of a Persian L2 reader's difficulties with a non-lexicalized word	133

Tables

3.1	Average English reading proficiency and receptive English vocabulary scores for the Persian and French speakers	55
3.2	Topics of English texts used for eliciting lexical inferencing	60

4.1	Readers' use of main KS types: Percentages of overall use in each condition	85
4.2	L2 readers' use of main KS types in English with lexicalized and non-lexicalized target words	89
4.3	L1 and L2 readers' use of *word* KSs in lexical inferencing	90
4.4	L1 and L2 readers' use of *sentence* KSs in lexical inferencing	92
4.5	L1 and L2 readers' use of *discourse* KSs in lexical inferencing	93
4.6	Synthesis of L1 and L2 readers' use of KS sub-types: Rankings within relative frequency bands	95
4.7	Number of different KSs used per inference in each condition	100
4.8	Relative frequency of initial and post-initial KS use in lexical inferencing	103
4.9	Average number of KSs per inference in each condition by word class	105
4.10	Frequency rankings of KS sub-type use by word class: English L1 and Persian L2 readers	106
5.1	L1 and L2 lexical inferencing success of English, Persian and French speakers	120
5.2	Success in inferring meanings for lexicalized versus non-lexicalized words by Persian and French speakers	122
5.3	Pre-task to post-task gains in average VKS scores for lexicalized L2 words by Persian and French speakers	125
5.4	Pre-task to post-task gains in average VKS scores for non-lexicalized L2 words by Persian and French speakers	125
5.5	Persian speakers' L2 receptive vocabulary knowledge, lexical inferencing success and gains in knowledge of target word meanings	129
5.6	French speakers' L2 receptive vocabulary knowledge, inferencing success and gains in knowledge of target word meanings	130

Acknowledgements

This book has come to fruition with the contributions and support of a number of institutions and individuals, for which we are grateful. The Social Sciences and Humanities Research Council of Canada funded the study reported here. The University of Ottawa's Faculty of Arts and our home department, the Official Languages and Bilingualism Institute (former Second Language Institute), provided financial and administrative support at different stages of our research and preparation of this publication. A Distinguished Scholar-in-Residence Grant awarded by the Journal, *Language Learning*, made possible an intensive work period with Kirsten Haastrup in Ottawa.

Our special appreciation goes to Kirsten Haastrup for her insightful and steady collaboration as co-author of the research review presented in Part 1 of the book, and for her pertinent comments on Part 2 at different stages of manuscript preparation.

We are grateful to our colleague, Marie-Claude Tréville, for her vital role in all aspects of the French sub-study, most critically in data collection and qualitative analysis.

We are particularly indebted to the Persian-, French- and English-speaking students from post-secondary institutions in Tehran and the Ottawa region, including the University of Ottawa, who participated in the study and shared their insights. Without these participants there would have been no study.

We thank all our research assistants, especially Shiva Sadeghi, who conducted interviews in Tehran and Ottawa, trained the French interviewers and worked on data analysis, and Nazmia Bengeleil, Danielle Higgins, Hélène Lamarche, Golda Tulung, Julita Kajzer, Karen Jesney, Shahla Shoeybi, Ali Abasi and Roozbeh Paribakht for their valuable assistance with different aspects of the project.

We thank Dr Akbar Mirhassani, who coordinated the recruitment of Persian-speaking participants for the study and facilitated data collection in Iran, and Geraldine Arbach, who carried out similar functions in Quebec.

Doreen Bayliss and her assistant Frederic Nolet, and Philip Nagy earned our gratitude for their patient work on statistical analyses.

Our thanks to Birgit Harley, who provided thoughtful and timely comments on an early version of Part 1, and to Rolf Wesche and Margaret Des Brisay who gave useful editorial feedback on different chapters of Part 2.

We benefited from the expertise and efficiency of Manon Labelle in the word processing and formatting of the manuscript and of Béatrice Magyar, who prepared the final tables and figures.

We also appreciate the collegial support of James Cummins and Alister Cumming. Sonia Wesche was an ongoing source of encouragement.

Finally, we express our deep gratitude to our spouses, Rolf Wesche and Alireza Shoamanesh, for their ongoing support, humor and steadfast faith in us and our lengthy project.

Preface

This volume includes two closely related parts: the first, a comprehensive review of research on the topic of lexical inferencing, and the second, presentation of a trilingual study of first language (L1) influences in second language (L2) lexical inferencing and other cross-linguistic dimensions of L1 and L2 lexical inferencing by Persian, French and English speakers. The trilingual study evolved from our previous studies of L2 lexical acquisition starting in the early 1990s and carried out within the larger context of an increasing research focus by applied linguists and language educators on lexical issues. Our mutual professional context at the University of Ottawa's Official Languages and Bilingualism Institute (formerly the Second Language Institute) and Education Graduate Studies involved participation in academic English L2 instruction and test development alongside graduate teaching and research.

The research journey we undertook together began with issues of lexical development through L2 reading and reading-related vocabulary instruction, leading over time to a primary focus on lexical inferencing. It built on our respective life experiences as language learners in varied contexts and as applied linguists and language educators; thus, in addition to theoretical considerations, language learners' perspectives and considerations of appropriate contexts and methodologies for language teaching were important in the conceptualization and interpretation of our studies of L2 vocabulary learning through reading. Paribakht brought to this work a research background in L2 communication strategies and comprehension-based language learning and instruction, while Wesche's previous research had centered on the nature of the language addressed to learners, L2 learning through content-based instruction in school immersion and post-secondary programs, and language testing.

A shared research journey

Our early joint studies evolved from issues facing the University in terms of its L2 instructional programs for Canadian and international student populations, and all of them have been at least partially grounded in the French/English context of the bilingual national capital region of Ottawa, Canada. Important to all our work has been frequent contact with North American and international colleagues involved in related issues, in person and through correspondence, particularly in the early years when both applied linguists and language educators were beginning to deal more comprehensively with L2 lexical issues after a long period in which vocabulary acquisition research had tended to be separate from lexical research in language education. Annual AAAL conferences and triennial World Congresses of Applied Linguistics (AILA) provided stimulating venues for the critical exchange of ideas and information in this area.

In 1996, at the 11th AILA Congress in Jyväskylä, Finland, we reported on our work in two symposia that – together with other Congress activities – recognized the increasing importance of lexical issues in second language acquisition (SLA) after a long period of relative neglect and the need to share research perspectives on vocabulary research across the fields of SLA and language education. One symposium, co-organized by Kirsten Haastrup and Åke Viberg (Haastrup & Viberg, 1998), offered multiple perspectives on lexical acquisition, including that of lexical input processing (Wesche & Paribakht, 1998). This led to our ongoing exchange of ideas with Kirsten on topics of common interest that culminated in her collaboration with us on the comprehensive review of lexical inferencing research that comprises Part 1 of this book. We, ourselves, co-organized the other symposium, on 'incidental' vocabulary acquisition (i.e. gains in vocabulary knowledge that occur as a 'by-product' when L2 readers are focused on comprehending text meaning rather than on the goal of learning new words). Several of its participants underscored the importance of lexical inferencing in reading comprehension and its frequent role as an initial stage in lexical acquisition. Papers from this symposium were published, with others, in a special issue of *Studies in Second Language Acquisition* on the same topic (Paribakht & Wesche, 1999; Wesche & Paribakht, 1999a, 1999b). This Congress and the resulting interactions with other researchers provided a vital stimulus to our work on L2 lexical issues.

The following brief account of the consecutive studies that led to the trilingual study of Persian, French and English speakers presented in Part 2 of this volume serves to contextualize this research, and may be of particular interest to readers not familiar with our previous work. The individual studies are outlined below.

Study I: Vocabulary learning in a comprehension-based L2 course

The first study (Paribakht & Wesche, 1993) responded to changes in a long-standing L2 graduation requirement at the University of Ottawa, an institution with a mandate to promote students' knowledge of both official languages of Canada. Undergraduate students enrolled in the faculties of Arts and Social Sciences were required to attain functional listening and reading proficiency in their second 'official' language, adequate for them to read textbooks or comprehend lectures in their respective fields. In reality, this L2 requirement in English or French represented a third (or later) language for many international students, whose study language was itself an L2. Due to difficulties in equitably enforcing this high-level, functional L2 proficiency requisite for graduation through formal testing, particularly with the University's increasing enrolment of international students, the requirement was modified to allow students the alternative of completing a series of four one-semester L2 courses that emphasized receptive skills (listening and reading comprehension). The Institute was mandated to develop and deliver these 'comprehension-based' courses in both English and French. The resulting teaching approach emphasized development of students' ability to comprehend challenging thematic content presented through authentic oral and written texts, with only a minimal focus on grammar and language production.

As faculty members involved in the design and delivery of these comprehension-based courses, we undertook evaluation of the reading-related learning outcomes of the advanced English as a second language (ESL) comprehension courses and an exploration of the role of comprehension in L2 development. In the 1993 study, we examined students' proficiency gains in receptive vocabulary and grammar over a period of one semester in the fourth-level ESL comprehension course, as compared with gains by students in a four-skills course at the same level, involving explicit grammatical instruction and both oral and written production. The vocabulary study evaluated and compared gains in target word knowledge by the two groups in terms of the word types (nouns or verbs versus discourse connectors) that were more readily acquired by each group, and explored whether different stages of word learning could be identified and measured. The comprehension-based group showed superior gains in vocabulary knowledge for all the word types studied, whereas the comparison group made greater gains in grammatical knowledge.

A major by-product of this research was an instrument that could capture certain initial stages in learning previously unknown L2 words. This instrument, the *Vocabulary Knowledge Scale* (VKS), has been useful in our subsequent studies of word learning through reading, including the present research (see Chapter 4; Paribakht & Wesche, 1996, 1997; Wesche & Paribakht, 1996), as well as to other researchers, including in an adapted form for oral language (e.g. Joe, 1995).

We developed the VKS for the purpose of documenting evidence of learners' knowledge of selected L2 words, to allow tracking and comparison of their knowledge gains in different contexts involving written texts. It uses both a self-report Elicitation Scale and confirmation tasks evaluated on a separate Scoring Scale to identify five kinds of target word knowledge that are widely considered to represent progressive stages in learning a given word. These range from recognition of the word form to the ability to use the word with both semantic and syntactic accuracy in a sentence. VKS scores offer a relatively efficient means of broadly characterizing a reader's knowledge of selected target words at a given point in time; they do not, however, provide detailed information on the process of learning individual words or a particular dimension of that process. Parallel and subsequent work for other purposes on the multiple dimensions of lexical development, 'depth' of vocabulary knowledge and the issues involved in determining developmental progressions has advanced understanding of what is needed for more precise theoretical characterizations of the word-learning process, but the development of measurement instruments for quantifying this remains a challenge (see, e.g. Haastrup & Henriksen, 1998; Henriksen, 1999, 2008).

Study II: Incidental versus instructed vocabulary learning

The findings of the first study incited us to further explore the nature of incidental vocabulary acquisition through reading in post-secondary educational contexts, given the relevance of this issue not only for theory, but also as a practical concern for learners studying through their L2. A follow-up comparative study (Paribakht & Wesche, 1997) investigated the vocabulary gains of a similar population of ESL students at the University of Ottawa under two experimental conditions: 'incidental' versus 'instructed' vocabulary acquisition. In the 'Reading Only' (incidental) condition, students read thematically related core and supplementary texts that together provided repeated exposure to unfamiliar target words, followed by a series of text-based comprehension questions. In the 'Reading Plus' (instructed) condition, reading of core texts was combined with systematic exposure to the target words through a series of text-based vocabulary exercises. An equal amount of time was spent on the two treatments.

Learners gained vocabulary knowledge under both conditions, but the gains were superior in the Reading Plus condition, both quantitatively (i.e. the number of words learned) and qualitatively (i.e. how well they were learned, as operationalized by the VKS). This research demonstrated the slow and unpredictable, even if measurable, nature of incidental L2 vocabulary learning through reading, and that it often leads only to a recognition level knowledge of target word forms. It also showed that instructional intervention involving manipulation and practice of words first encountered through reading enhances vocabulary-learning outcomes. In the course of this research, we developed a 'taxonomy of text-based vocabulary exercises/task types' for designing different word-learning exercises for selected words in texts (Paribakht & Wesche, 1996). These types roughly correspond to Gass' (1988) SLA stages (here applied to lexical acquisition), which are each, in turn, seen as requiring a higher level of cognitive activity, i.e. apperceived input (noticing), comprehended input, intake, integration and output.

The next, closely related, research phase involved two introspective studies with similar groups of intermediate ESL readers to further explore the processes underlying the differential vocabulary learning outcomes of the Reading Only and Reading Plus experimental conditions.

Study III: Reading Only

In the Reading Only introspective study (Paribakht & Wesche, 1999), the goal was to better understand how learners deal with unfamiliar words when reading and the strategies they use. Participants were required to read brief authentic texts and carry out two comprehension tasks. The first task required them to answer a series of text-related comprehension questions, while the second required them to orally summarize the main points in the text. Following each of the comprehension tasks, readers were asked to indicate any unfamiliar words they had encountered while reading the texts and doing the tasks, and how they had dealt with each of them.

Participants reported ignoring about half of the words they did not know, while for the other words, they used three strategies to find word meanings. Lexical inferencing was their main strategy, used 80% of the time, while in the other cases they either attempted word retrieval (repeating the word to see if it sounded familiar or to arouse any associations) or they used a dictionary. Our further analysis of the kinds of textual information and knowledge these L2 readers used in lexical inferencing led to a conceptualization of such inferencing as a search process through which learners attempt to identify constituents of the missing lemma, such as its grammatical category or conceptual elements (see Chapter 1; de Bot *et al.*, 1997).

Study IV: Reading Plus

The second introspective study, involving the Reading Plus instructional condition, sought insight into how text-based vocabulary tasks might contribute to learners' acquisition of vocabulary knowledge (Wesche & Paribakht, 2000). In addition, a separate task analysis, including both the instructionally intended and the learner derived goals and realizations of each comprehension task and the five exercise types in the two conditions, illuminated how given pedagogical activities may influence lexical processing. Differences were found between the two comprehension tasks as well as for each Reading Plus exercise. Additionally, divergence was found for at least some learners in each case between the instructional intention behind the task and what they actually did (Wesche & Paribakht, 1998). The comparative findings for the two treatments nonetheless confirmed notable overall differences between the comprehension task realizations in the Reading Only treatment and the more varied cumulative processing that occurred with the Reading Plus exercises. The latter together promoted both greater knowledge elaboration and practice of the target words. Participants furthermore reported greater confidence in their knowledge of the target words following the exercises. We interpreted these outcomes as an indication that the exercises had increased the salience of the target words and focused learners' attention on different aspects of word knowledge (e.g. formal, semantic and grammatical properties, relationships with other words). The exercises also provided opportunities for using the words in different contexts, thereby presumably requiring deeper levels of lexical processing. The findings helped explain the superior vocabulary learning outcomes of the Reading Plus condition and provided support for the claim that vocabulary learning is an incremental, iterative process, requiring multiple exposures to and use of given words in varied contexts.

Study V: Cross-linguistic study

Given the demonstrated importance of lexical inferencing in word and text comprehension, and its role as well as limitations in L2 vocabulary acquisition, we next embarked on the large-scale trilingual study reported in Chapters 3–6 of this book (also see Paribakht, 2005; Paribakht & Wesche, 2006; Paribakht & Tréville, 2007). This research has involved a much more comprehensive examination of the process and outcomes of lexical inferencing than the earlier studies. The rich data elicited from learners from three different L1 backgrounds inferring meanings for unfamiliar words in L1 and L2 texts have permitted a detailed examination of the complex cognitive strategy of lexical inferencing. They have also illuminated several factors that affect the process and its outcomes; most prominently, the influence of readers' L1 knowledge, their very high lexical proficiency in their L1 versus lesser lexical proficiency in their L2, and the typological distance between the L1 and the L2. The findings of the several sub-studies in this project have helped us to better understand not only lexical inferencing, but also the related processes of reading comprehension and initial vocabulary acquisition through reading. In addition, they have brought to light some of the specific problems that L2 readers from different L1 backgrounds encounter, and offer implications for reading and vocabulary instruction at advanced levels.

Organization of the book

Part 1 of this book, co-authored by Kirsten Haastrup, consists of two chapters that together provide an overview of the topics and introduce the empirical study reported in Part 2. The first chapter reviews lexical inferencing research since the early 1970s, synthesizing what is known about this complex cognitive phenomenon, its role in reading comprehension and vocabulary acquisition, factors that influence the inferencing process and its outcomes, and theoretical characterizations of it. Chapter 2 presents previous research findings relevant to the issues of L1 transfer in L2 lexical inferencing, including relative typological distance between L1 and L2, as background to the trilingual study reported in the remaining chapters.

Part 2 of the book reports on the trilingual study of L1 and L2 lexical inferencing outlined above under Study IV. Chapter 3 presents the conceptualization and methodology of the study. Chapter 4 reports on readers' use of different knowledge sources as these relate to their native languages and to L1 versus L2 conditions, and as they reveal L1 transfer effects in L2 lexical inferencing. Chapter 5 deals with lexical inferencing success and retention of new knowledge as these vary for the different language groups and in L1 versus L2 conditions as well as with readers' previous L2 lexical knowledge. Tentative relationships are drawn between the lexical inferencing process and initial retention of new word knowledge. Chapter 6 synthesizes the study findings, drawing conclusions with respect to commonalities across all conditions, L1 versus L2 lexical inferencing; L1 transfer in L2 inferencing, particularly as influenced by L1/L2 typological distance; the importance of previous L2 lexical knowledge in inferencing success and word learning, and other factors explaining differences between outcomes for the Persian and French speakers in English. Finally, implications are drawn for further research and for L2 reading and vocabulary instruction.

Part 1
Lexical Inferencing: A Research Review

Overview

Part 1 consists of two chapters that together provide an overview of the topic and introduce the empirical study reported in Part 2. Chapter 1 provides a comprehensive review of research on lexical inferencing in a second language (L2), beginning in the 1970s and stimulated in the 1980s by work on the topic of first language (L1) vocabulary acquisition through reading. The main work has been carried out over the past two decades, with an emphasis on L2 lexical inferencing in reading contexts. Lexical inferencing emerges as a complex cognitive process that plays an important role in both word and text comprehension, and at the same time can result in initial learning of new words or otherwise contribute to vocabulary development.

Chapter 2 deals with the seldom-studied question of L1 influences, or transfer, in L2 lexical inferencing, extending the research review while providing background information for the cross-linguistic study presented in the remainder of the book. It reviews research relevant to the issue of L1 transfer in L2 lexical inferencing and to cross-linguistic commonalities and L1/L2 differences in lexical inferencing. Particular emphasis is given to recent inferencing studies using L1 and L2 data from the same speakers and of readers whose L1s represent different typological relationships with English (L2).

Chapter 1
Research on the Lexical Inferencing Process and its Outcomes

with Kirsten Haastrup

In Chapter 1, we deal with three major issues. The first question is: what is lexical inferencing and how does it relate to reading comprehension and lexical development? We first present an overview of our understanding of lexical inferencing, followed by a brief description of early studies that established second language (L2) lexical inferencing as a significant research area with implications for both reading theory and vocabulary acquisition. The second question is: what factors influence lexical inferencing and its outcomes? Here, we provide a synthesis of shared findings from mainly descriptive empirical studies of lexical inferencing undertaken in the 1990s and early 2000s, organized around factors influencing different parts of the process and its outcomes. These include learners' decisions to attempt inferencing, factors promoting successful determination of appropriate word meanings and factors relating lexical inferencing to retention of new lexical knowledge. The third question is: what processes are involved in lexical inferencing and how have they been conceptualized and theoretically explained? Research findings are presented pertaining to the linguistic and other types of cues and knowledge used by readers in lexical inferencing, its procedural components and theoretical perspectives proposed to explain its different aspects.

What is Lexical Inferencing and How Does it Relate to Reading Comprehension and Lexical Development?

Language comprehension and vocabulary development are intertwined issues of primary importance in our understanding of language learning and use. In first language (L1) development, young children initially learn new word forms and their meanings through frequent exposure to them in oral language contexts, particularly the most common few thousand words. Later, as they master literacy skills, reading becomes an important context for continued vocabulary growth (Nagy *et al.*, 1985; Nation & Coady, 1988; Sternberg, 1987). In L2 development by older, literate learners, oral contexts remain important, but written texts are often a major source of exposure to new words, particularly in a foreign L2 (Huckin & Coady, 1999; Horst *et al.*, 1998). When a text presents unfamiliar words, readers often make informed guesses, or inferences, about their contextual meanings. 'Lexical inferencing', a term made prominent in the L2 literature by Haastrup (1991a), is a sub-type of the more general inferencing process that operates at all levels of text comprehension, involving the 'connections people make when attempting to reach an interpretation of what they read or hear' (Brown & Yule, 1983: 265). While the reader's primary goal is comprehension, attention to a particular word form and an effort to determine its intended meaning in the given context may also lead to retention of new lexical knowledge by initiating or pushing forward the lengthy, incremental process of learning that word. It is for this reason that lexical inferencing is seen as operating at the core of the relationship between reading comprehension and vocabulary development and is crucial to 'incidental' (non-intentional) word learning while reading. (For discussions of 'incidental' vocabulary learning see Haynes, 1998; Hulstijn, 2001; Wesche & Paribakht, 1999a: 176, 1999b.)

Reading comprehension in one's L1 involves ongoing inferencing at different text levels. At the word level, due to the existence of homonyms and homographs and because many words have multiple meanings, even fluent L1 readers must continually make semantic inferences to determine which meaning of a familiar word is contextually appropriate – or to infer an unknown additional meaning. Information from individual words interacts continuously with information from the larger context, the former contributing to construction of textual meaning, while the latter is necessary for accurate selection of the precise contextual meaning of a given word. In L2 reading, orthographic and underlying phonological word forms themselves may be unfamiliar, so that the reader must process the word form in addition to attempting to identify an appropriate meaning for it in the given context. In some cases, even the concept(s) underlying the word's meaning may be unknown to the L2 reader, particularly if the word has no lexical or phrasal equivalent in the reader's L1.

Identifying an appropriate meaning of a word in context involves finding useful cues from the word and the surrounding text and drawing on previous knowledge to generate an informed guess. An appropriate inference enhances the accuracy of text comprehension and interpretation, whereas a wrong inference may lead to miscomprehension. Readers who verify the contextual accuracy of their guesses, often passing through several cycles of trying and rejecting possible meanings, are more likely to arrive at appropriate meanings (Haynes, 1993). Most readers studying at secondary and post-secondary levels depend heavily on understanding complex written texts for academic success. Lexical inferencing ability can be a particularly important tool for readers who are studying through the medium of an L2 and thus face many more unfamiliar words than their fellow students reading in their L1. Effective inferencing ability will enhance not only their reading fluency, but will also support their academic learning. While a reader's primary purpose in attempting to comprehend a given word meaning is to aid in understanding the larger text, successful identification of a previously unknown word meaning may also lead to retention of new knowledge about that word.

The process of reading comprehension – and of lexical inferencing – is in many ways similar for readers in their L1 and an L2; however, studies comparing L1 and L2 reading or lexical inferencing consistently show a marked advantage for L1 readers. This native speaker advantage appears to relate to L1 readers' more efficient language processing skills in the text language as well as to their richer and more established linguistic – especially lexical – and cultural knowledge. Such knowledge and abilities are reflected in measures of reading proficiency and vocabulary knowledge in the text language. The persistence of such an advantage – even when L2 readers have very high levels of proficiency – suggests that subtle L1-related factors may continue to influence L2 users' performance over many years. Recent research on L2 word recognition and reading comprehension points to L1 influences (or transfer) relating to the typological distance between readers' L1 and L2, with specific outcomes traceable to features of the particular languages (Koda, 2005; Odlin, 2003; Paribakht, 2005), as well as to the persistent presence of the L1 in L2 processing, as opposed to 'monolingual' processing by native speakers in their L1. Research on these issues relating to L2 versus L1 lexical inferencing is only at an early stage, but is already providing insights into reading comprehension problems faced by L2 learners, including those specific to learners from given L1s. This book, reflecting the focus of the majority of studies to date, emphasizes inferencing by adolescent and adult L2 (English) readers at relatively advanced proficiency levels, many of them carrying out university studies through their L2.

Early studies of lexical inferencing

Carton (1971) was the first to publish an in-depth study in the foreign language learning literature of what was later called lexical inferencing. For him, 'inferencing' (a coined term) involving the use of 'attributes and contexts that are familiar... in recognizing what is *not* familiar', was a process that played an important role in 'the acquisition of new morphemes and vocables[1] in "natural" contexts' (Carton, 1971: 45). His research from the dual perspectives of psychological processing and 'language as an ecology in which [inferencing] can be manifested' (Carton, 1971: 56) focused on the types of cues to word meanings available to language learners in L2 texts and the different kinds of information these could provide to aid in learners' acquisition of new linguistic knowledge. His three-way categorization of main cue-types distinguished *intra-lingual* cues (from the L2, such as plural or tense markers that indicate word-class), *interlingual* cues (from the L1 or another language (Ln), such as cognates) and *extralingual* cues (world knowledge-based cues), for which he provided numerous examples for foreign language learners. He paid little attention, however, to the cognitive processes required for correct inferences to become acquired knowledge, a result that – as subsequent research has amply demonstrated – cannot be assumed, especially for L2 lexical inferencing. Nevertheless, this unique and substantive early work stimulated considerable interest among foreign language teaching professionals and scholars in the nascent field of L2 acquisition, not least for the attention Carton (1971: 57) drew to the 'complex intellectual processes' involved in language learning at a time when it was still viewed by many within a behavioristic perspective of skill learning.

In the early to mid-1980s, several studies suggested that children's dramatic increase in L1 vocabulary mastery during schooling might be largely attributed to incremental learning through extensive reading (Nagy & Anderson, 1984; Nagy *et al.*, 1985; Nagy & Herman, 1987; Sternberg, 1987). As a result, many L2 educators began to place high expectations on reading as a primary path to vocabulary development (see Krashen, 1989). This led to increasing research on L2 reading comprehension, vocabulary learning through reading, and lexical inferencing, generally independent from but at least indirectly influenced by the L1 studies.

In 1983, Bialystok, working in an L2 learning context and building on Carton's work, devised several experiments to test whether L2 learners, who lack the environmental cues that facilitate contextual language learning by L1 children, could be helped to infer word meanings more effectively while reading if provided with supplementary information. She was able to demonstrate that both supplementary information, such as a glossary of difficult words in the text, and 'procedural' instruction, such as a mini-lesson on inferencing, could improve L2 readers' inferencing for successful word comprehension.

The same year, Sternberg and Powell (1983), working from the disciplinary perspective of psychology, developed an explanatory framework for the general inferencing process that they saw as relevant to all kinds of contextual learning. Sternberg (1987), in a paper entitled *Most Vocabulary is Learned from Context*, reported more fully on the framework as it related to inferring L1 word meanings. His example was American high school students learning low-frequency L1 English words through reading. The framework posits three basic knowledge acquisition processes that allow meanings to be inferred from contextual cues: *selective encoding* (determining what information is relevant), *selective combination* (combining relevant information from different cues into a meaningful whole) and *selective comparison* (associating the new information with what one already knows) (Sternberg, 1987: 91). Each of these processes is seen as operating on a 'relatively stable set of cues provided by the context in which new words occur', of which eight types are proposed; these include *temporal cues* (e.g. regarding the frequency of or constraints on occurrence of the word), *spatial cues* (e.g. locations in which the word can be found), *class membership cues* (e.g. the word class to which it belongs) and *equivalence* (e.g. a meaning or antonym of the word). *Moderating variables* also play an important role, influencing how the three processes are applied. Examples given of such variables for vocabulary learning through inferencing include the frequency and apparent importance of a given word, the density of unknown words in the text, and the particular kinds of information available from cues surrounding the word. These three variables, among others, have received empirical verification in subsequent research. Sternberg's early work was well known among first language researchers and helped stimulate the interest of both L1 and L2 educators and researchers in 'incidental' vocabulary learning from reading. Sternberg (2003), in a recent book, revisited this procedural framework and further elaborated on word learning as a prototypical example of contextual learning.

Several other independent, largely descriptive studies of word-guessing by L2 students, inspired by work on incidental vocabulary learning in L1, were also carried out around this time. These included a widely cited paper by Bensoussan and Laufer (1984) that reported a high percentage of wrong guesses and resulting poor text comprehension among their low-proficiency English foreign language student population in Israel. Another study, by Liu and Nation (1985), described factors that influenced contextual guessing, and one by Li (1988) dealt with the adequacy and accessibility of cues in L2 reading texts in successful inferencing.

In 1991, Haastrup published an influential monograph on L2 lexical inferencing, which focused attention on this phenomenon within the field of L2 learning. Haastrup's definition of lexical inferencing, inspired by Færch's (1984) work, continues to be widely used:

> The process of lexical inferencing involves making informed guesses as to the meaning of a word in light of all available linguistic cues in combination with the learners' general knowledge of the world, her awareness of context and her relevant linguistic knowledge. (Haastrup, 1991a: 13)

In Haastrup's study, Danish secondary school learners at two grade levels, representing three and six years of formal English study, worked in pairs to determine the meanings of 25 unfamiliar words in a two-page English text and wrote their joint solution on the test sheet. They were asked to verbalize their thoughts aloud as they worked, producing introspective and subsequent retrospective verbal protocols for analysis (Haastrup, 1987; after Ericsson & Simon, 1984, 1987; Færch & Kasper, 1987). This methodological approach to lexical inferencing research has been used in many subsequent studies around the world. In her analysis of cue types, Haastrup built on Carton's (1971) work in her investigation of the types of cues her participants reported using in their efforts to infer the meanings of different types of words. These included linguistic cues from the target word itself and associated with linguistic knowledge of the L1, L2 or another known language (Ln), cues found in the surrounding text ('co-text') and readers' world knowledge. Haastrup also studied the level of inferencing success achieved by the two informant groups. Like Sternberg, Haastrup was interested in inferencing procedures, and the most innovative feature of her study was her framework for analysis of the procedural aspects of lexical inferencing, i.e. the actual processes that learners reflected upon in their verbal reports.

Approaches to the study of lexical inferencing

Starting in the 1990s, many empirical studies involving L2 lexical inferencing were carried out in the context of intensive or extensive L2 reading programs. One major line of research focused on L2 reading comprehension or incidental vocabulary learning while reading. The latter interest had been whetted by claims supporting L1 reading as a likely major engine of vocabulary growth during schooling (Nagy *et al.*, 1985; Saragi *et al.*, 1978; Sternberg, 1987) and by related work on L2 vocabulary learning from reading (Dupuy & Krashen, 1993; Elley & Mangubhai, 1983; Krashen, 1989; Pitts *et al.*, 1989). These and other studies, continuing through the early 2000s, have explored different aspects of the lexical inferencing process and its outcomes in a range of contexts (Bengeleil & Paribakht, 2004; Chern, 1993; de Bot *et al.*, 1997; Dubin & Olshtain, 1993; Fraser, 1999; Haynes, 1993; Hulstijn, 1992; Kim, 2003; Mondria & Witt-de Boer, 1991; Mori, 2002; Morrison, 1996; Nassaji, 2003, 2004; Paribakht & Wesche, 1999; Parry, 1993, 1997; Schouten van Parreren, 1989; Soria, 2001; Wesche & Paribakht, 1998).

The methodologies used in these studies have varied, one major distinction being between 'naturalistic' studies of lexical inferencing in L2 reading, in which readers recorded or recounted to researchers how they dealt with unfamiliar words and, when this involved inferencing, how they went about it (e.g. Fraser, 1999; Haynes, 1993; Kim, 2003; Paribakht & Wesche, 1999; Parry, 1993, 1997), and those – informed by naturalistic studies – in which researchers 'manipulated' inferencing contexts and set up tasks for readers to direct their attention to particular words and, in some cases, toward certain kinds of cognitive processing that might promote their retention of new lexical knowledge (e.g. Haastrup, 1991a; Hulstijn, 1992; Joe, 1995; Wesche & Paribakht, 1998, 2000). In addition to differences between naturalistic and manipulated contexts, and task variation, methodological factors have varied across studies of L2 lexical inferencing, for instance with respect to participants' native language, their age, literacy experience and level of L2 proficiency. Both introspective and retrospective verbal reporting have been primary means of data collection in the majority of studies of lexical inferencing, but studies have varied in terms of their use of supplementary observational and performance data collection. While both longitudinal case studies and cross-sectional group comparisons have been common, longitudinal group comparisons have only recently been contemplated.[2]

Most research to date has focused exclusively on L2 lexical inferencing, but several recent studies – including the trilingual study presented in this book – involve comparative L1 and L2 lexical inferencing by the same learners (see this chapter and Chapter 2; Haastrup, 2008; Paribakht & Wesche, 2006). Important new insights are emerging from these studies of L1 and L2 inferencing by learners representing different L1s, and it is becoming possible to be much more precise with regard to how far findings can be generalized.

What Factors Influence Lexical Inferencing and its Outcomes?

Studies of L2 inferencing when reading have tended to report both inferencing attempts and readers' success in identifying appropriate meanings in context in terms of a variety of predictive factors. Research on factors related to lexical inferencing attempts and success are summarized below, followed by a more detailed discussion of L2 proficiency – particularly vocabulary knowledge – in lexical inferencing success and learning outcomes, and of learner engagement in the task.

Lexical inferencing attempts

L2 readers often do not attempt to infer the meanings of unfamiliar words they encounter; in fact, they tend to ignore many of these words (Bensoussan & Laufer, 1984; Kim, 2003; Parry, 1993; Paribakht & Wesche, 1999). For example, in Paribakht and Wesche's 1999 study in which students were asked to read short texts and answer comprehension questions or provide summaries, they either made no reference to, or explicitly stated that they had not bothered with, approximately half the text words they had previously identified as unfamiliar. For the words that readers choose to deal with, they may request assistance or consult a dictionary if these options are available (Fraser, 1999; Hulstijn, 1993; Milton & Meara, 1995), with individuals varying considerably with respect to the use of either (Kim, 2003). While appealing to another individual or to a dictionary for help may be a feasible and preferable means of identifying specific word meanings for some individuals in given contexts, and an effective means of confirming an inferred meaning (Fraser, 1999; Hulstijn, 2001; Kim, 2003), these resources are not always readily available to learners.[3] Lexical inferencing may often be the only tool available to readers faced with unknown words. Thus, in spite of its uncertain outcomes, particularly for L2 readers, it tends to be the main means by which they try to resolve their vocabulary knowledge gaps as they seek to understand the text (de Bot et al., 1997; Fraser, 1999;

Harley & Hart, 2000; Huckin & Bloch, 1993; Huckin & Coady, 1999; Kim, 2003; Parry, 1993, 1997).

Many factors influence whether L2 readers will attempt to infer a word meaning. Major ones identified through research include text factors: for example, how difficult the text is perceived to be in terms of the density of unknown words (Sternberg, 1987). Certain word features are influential, including the word's salience in the text (Parry, 1993); the reader's perception of its general importance (Paribakht & Wesche, 1999), or its importance to text comprehension or task completion (Brown, 1993; Fraser, 1999; Kim, 2003; Paribakht & Wesche, 1999); whether it appears easy to guess (Bensoussan & Laufer, 1984); and its class, with nouns and verbs being more likely to attract inferencing attempts than other word classes (Paribakht & Wesche, 1999).

Lexical inferencing success

A substantial body of empirical research has identified factors that influence whether the process of L2 lexical inferencing is likely to lead to determination of an appropriate word meaning. When L2 readers do attempt lexical inferencing, success is far from assured. In spite of their pervasive attempts to infer the meanings of unfamiliar words when reading in an L2, learners frequently fail to generate appropriate meanings (Bensoussan & Laufer, 1984; Haastrup, 1991a; Fraser, 1999; Hulstijn, 2001; Kim, 2003; Laufer, 1997; Paribakht, 2005; Paribakht & Wesche, 1999, 2006; Paribakht & Tréville, 2007). This may sometimes be due to the lack of adequate textual cues; clear contextual cues are critical to word guessability (Dubin & Olshtain, 1993; Haynes, 1993; Li, 1988). Furthermore, as Li points out, for contextual cues to be of real help for inferring word meanings, they must not only offer the information needed by the reader, but this information must also 'be perceptually and conceptually familiar' to the reader (Li, 1988: 403). Cue location is also important; many researchers have noted the enhanced utility of cues either in the word itself or the immediate context. For example, English as a second language (ESL) readers in Haynes' (1993) study were more successful in guessing meanings for words for which clues were available in the word itself or in the adjacent text than for those requiring attention to more distant cues. Several studies have reported that the great majority of knowledge sources reported for both L1 and L2 lexical inferencing are within the same sentence as the target word or from the word itself (Haastrup, 1991a; Paribakht & Tréville, 2007; Paribakht & Wesche, 2006).

L2 readers may not be able to recognize the cues that are available due to poor comprehension of the surrounding words and text. Such problems are generally related to their inadequate proficiency in the text language for the given text (see below). Readers may also lack the conceptual knowledge to support an accurate guess. Obvious examples are cases where the text represents unfamiliar cultural patterns (Carrell, 1993) or when L2 readers are reading about unfamiliar topics through their L2 (Lessard-Clouston, 2005). This is likely an important but seldom noticed issue in many other circumstances as well. Learner factors beyond L2 proficiency and background knowledge that have been reported include relatively specific tendencies such as the attention they give to relevant details in the text and their ability and inclination to use the context effectively (Frantzen, 2003). A crucial but somewhat neglected factor in the research literature on lexical inferencing is learners' motivation to make a careful and sustained effort to identify an appropriate contextual meaning (Dörnyei, 1994; Laufer & Hulstijn, 2001). Laufer and Hulstijn (2001) have conceptualized this in terms of learners' involvement in carrying out a task as part of their discussion of task-induced learning (see below).

Second language proficiency

The importance of L2 proficiency in effective lexical inferencing has been amply demonstrated in studies comparing more and less proficient learners (e.g. Bengeleil & Paribakht, 2004; Haastrup, 1991a; Ittzés, 1991; Morrison, 1996). In her study of school age learners, Haastrup (1991b: 130) concluded that L2 proficiency is a decisive factor in lexical inferencing procedures and there definitely seems to be a threshold level of L2 proficiency that learners have to reach first before they are able to use effective inferencing procedures.

Evidence suggesting that proficiency makes a difference even at very high levels is seen in the widely documented difficulties of L2 readers when inferring meanings of unfamiliar words in texts as compared with the relative success of native language readers in arriving at appropriate meanings for unknown words in L1 texts.

While measures of general L2 proficiency and reading proficiency have predictive value for successful lexical inferencing (Haastrup, 1991a, 2008; Bengeleil & Paribakht, 2004; Paribakht, 2005; Paribakht & Tréville, 2007; Nassaji, 2004), measures of L2 vocabulary knowledge – themselves highly correlated with reading and general proficiency – are increasingly seen as reflecting the most essential component of L2 proficiency underlying successful lexical inferencing while reading (Henriksen et al., 2004).

Second language vocabulary knowledge

Research findings from varied sources indicate that success in inferring meanings for unknown words while reading depends on learners' ability to understand most of the other words in the text. Estimates of the percentage of words that readers must know in a text in order to read the text unassisted or to infer appropriate contextual meanings for those they don't know are very high, between 95% of the words in the text estimated in early studies (Hirsh & Nation, 1992; Laufer, 1988; Liu & Nation, 1985) and more recent studies estimating around 98% (Hazenberg & Hulstijn, 1996; Hu & Nation, 2000; Nation, 2006). Traditional vocabulary measures estimating the size (or 'breadth') of a reader's recognition vocabulary knowledge provide a broad characterization and a basis for comparison of individuals' vocabulary knowledge, which underlies a reader's ability to comprehend the vast majority of the words in the text surrounding unknown words. Not surprisingly, such measures show relatively high correlations with learners' success in inferring meanings for unknown words (Coady et al., 1993; Laufer, 1997; Paribakht, 2005; Albrechtsen et al., 2008). Recent research in L2 vocabulary acquisition has, however, emphasized the importance of the many aspects of word knowledge that are not tapped by breadth measures, elaborating the complex knowledge that constitutes an individual's full understanding of and ability to use a word (after Cronbach, 1942; e.g. Harley, 1995; Henriksen, 1999; Nation, 1990; Richards, 1976). Specific elements emphasized by recent researchers include development from 'partial to precise' knowledge of the referential meaning of words (Haastrup & Henriksen, 1998; Henriksen, 1999); development from receptive to productive use ability (Henriksen, 1999; Paribakht & Wesche, 1993; Wesche & Paribakht, 1996); and the development of an ever more complex network-based organization of the lexicon, or what Henriksen (1999) proposed as 'depth' of vocabulary knowledge. This includes a word's

> sense relations to other words in the vocabulary, such as paradigmatic (antonymy, synonymy, hyponymy, gradation) and syntagmatic relations (collocational restrictions)... [as well as] ...knowledge of the syntactic and morphological restrictions and features of a lexical item. (Henriksen, 1999: 305–306)

Recent years have seen several attempts to find ways of measuring the complex construct of vocabulary depth. One approach has been that of Read in the English *Word Association Test* (WAT), now available in several versions (Read, 1993, 1998, 2004). This test probes learners' ability to recognize paradigmatic and syntagmatic relations to a given word and to distinguish these from distractors. Thus, the test-taker's task in the following sample item from this test is to identify the words related to the stimulus word 'edit' (Read, 2000: 181)

edit
arithmetic   film   pole   publishing
revise   risk   surface   text

The stimulus words are selected from high-frequency academic vocabulary for their multiple meanings or range of use, and for their likely familiarity to a university ESL clientele. The WAT has proven to be a useful tool in inferencing research investigating the relationship of depth of vocabulary knowledge to successful L2 lexical inferencing.

Qian (1999) used the *Vocabulary Levels Test* (Nation, 1990) to measure the breadth of university ESL learners' recognition vocabulary in English, together with the WAT (Read, 1993). Scores on both tests correlated highly with measures of L2 reading comprehension ability. The WAT was, however, the stronger predictor, making a significant contribution beyond that shared with the vocabulary breadth measure. This finding reflects the importance of aspects of word knowledge other than primary referential meanings in readers' ability to comprehend L2 word meanings in context. In a subsequent study, Nassaji (2004) extended Qian's findings to lexical inferencing, confirming the relationship of L2 learners' WAT scores to their success in lexical inferencing while reading. Not only were L2 readers who had higher WAT scores more successful in inferring appropriate word meanings in written texts, but they also used certain depth-related inferencing procedures more effectively than those who demonstrated weaker depth of vocabulary knowledge. Nassaji (2004: 117) concluded that 'their richer lexical knowledge may make them better able to make use of the potential cues available in the text and co-text'.

A recent Danish study (Albrechtsen *et al.*, 2008) addressed the question of whether a relationship could be found between informants' lexical inferencing procedures and success in L2 and their vocabulary knowledge in L2. Both the size and the organization of declarative L2 lexical knowledge were tapped, the latter reflecting lexical network knowledge (Henriksen, 1999) as measured by a word association task.[4] The underlying assumption behind including the network component was that a large and well-structured lexicon functions as an important knowledge base for high-quality lexical inferencing. The results indicated a positive relationship between lexical inferencing success and vocabulary size, confirming earlier findings that L2 lexical knowledge is indeed a strong predictor of L2 lexical inferencing success. In addition to this was the important finding of a positive relationship between the measure of lexical network knowledge and lexical inferencing success, in line with Nassaji's (2004) finding of a significant relationship between depth of vocabulary knowledge and lexical inferencing success.

Lexicalization status of target words

An issue indirectly related to L2 learners' lexical proficiency concerns the lexicalization status of L2 words in a learner's L1. In some cases, L2 words do not have lexical equivalents (i.e. single or compound lexical items or lexical phrases, with similar meanings) in the L1.[5] Two recent studies on the influence of L1 'lexicalization' (versus non-lexicalization) of target words on L2 lexical inferencing success have revealed a strong positive effect for lexicalization (Paribakht, 2005; Paribakht & Tréville, 2007; Chapter 5). Both the Persian- and French-speaking participants, respectively, inferencing in their L2 (English) were more successful in inferring accurate meanings for lexicalized than for non-lexicalized target words. Paribakht's (2005) findings also revealed an interaction between lexicalization effects and readers' L2 receptive vocabulary knowledge while inferencing. In her study of university level Persian-speaking students of English, scores on the *Vocabulary Levels Test* (Nation, 1990) predicted their success in inferring meanings of target English words that had lexical equivalents in Persian. (It did not correlate significantly with readers' success in inferring the meanings of words without Persian lexical equivalents, presumably because of their extreme difficulty and the resulting very low success rate.)

The above findings provide empirical evidence for the important role of different aspects of L2 proficiency in lexical inferencing, particularly vocabulary knowledge, and support the view of lexical inferencing as a meaning construction process that is significantly influenced by the breadth and richness of the learner's pre-existing lexical knowledge.

Retention of new lexical knowledge after inferencing

Some of the studies of L2 reading as a potential agent for vocabulary acquisition, based on studies in the 1980s with L1 readers, have indeed shown links between extensive or intensive reading in an L2 and vocabulary acquisition (Elley & Mangubai, 1983; Horst & Meara, 1999; Krashen, 1989; Paribakht & Wesche, 1993, 1997; Parry, 1993), although progress is in small increments, and subsequent research suggests that at least six to ten encounters with a word are generally required to ensure retention of its meaning (Zahar *et al.*, 2001; Cobb, 2005). Cobb's (2005) research suggests that readers will not encounter many less common words often enough to learn them through reading.[6] Other studies have demonstrated vocabulary learning gains following reading-based lexical inferencing tasks (Paribakht & Wesche, 1999; Paribakht, 2005). The latter studies have, in general, tended to show readers' retention of word-form familiarity following several encounters with given words in a text followed by inferencing attempts, with a far lower tendency for them to be able to recall meanings for the words or use them productively. The possibility that the lexical inferencing process is a key mechanism that takes readers beyond exposure to comprehension and initial retention of meaning is nonetheless suggested by these results; it remains for the link between successful inferencing and retention to be made (see Chapter 5). A comparison of such 'incidental' vocabulary learning with studies of instructed, intentional and task-based vocabulary learning has supported Sternberg's (1987: 94) observation that the 'facts and framework do not imply... that learning from context is the fastest or most efficient way of learning specific vocabulary'. For example, in their comparative studies of the kinds of lexical processing underlying word learning through *reading only*, i.e. thematic reading involving multiple exposures to target words followed by comprehension questions (Paribakht & Wesche, 1997, 1999) versus *reading plus*, i.e. more limited reading plus text-based exercises involving manipulation of target words (Wesche & Paribakht, 1998, 2000), the researchers found that knowledge gains from reading followed by comprehension tasks tended to be limited to word-form familiarity or recognition knowledge of new words, while those involving other kinds of manipulation of words first encountered in reading, promoted retention of other aspects of word knowledge. (Also see discussion of 'input processing' theory below; Cobb, 2005.)

Finally, a small number of studies have demonstrated the often assumed relationship between learners' L2 vocabulary knowledge and subsequent learning of vocabulary through reading (Haynes & Baker, 1993; Parry, 1997; Pulido, 2003), supporting the observation that vocabulary learning through reading – and presumably the inferencing process that underlies it – will be more efficient for readers with more advanced lexical proficiency.

Related research has demonstrated that the nature of the cognitive effort involved in inferencing or related lexical processing tasks is related to learners' retention of new lexical knowledge (Fraser, 1999; Hulstijn, 2001; Laufer & Hulstijn, 2001; Joe, 1995; Wesche & Paribakht, 2000). Feedback has also been shown to support retention (Joe, 1995; Nation, 1990). Hulstijn (2001: 6), while noting the inability of cognitive researchers to provide 'adequate theoretical explanations of phenomena of human learning and memory in terms of quality (type) and quantity (duration and frequency) of information processing', observes that more elaborate processing of new lexical information will lead to higher retention than shallow processing. His examples of such elaborative processing include paying careful attention to the word's pronunciation, orthography, grammatical category, meaning and semantic relations to other words. In fact, all of these may – but will not necessarily – occur during a motivated and persistent inferencing attempt.

Based on findings such as those cited above, Laufer and Hulstijn (2001) proposed a theoretical construct of *task-induced involvement* to encapsulate the necessary conditions for vocabulary retention from initial incidental processing of lexical form-meaning relationships. In their view, such involvement includes both affect, expressed as learner *need* (to achieve, as manifested through motivation), and information processing, expressed as *search* (noticing/attending to the needed meaning or form and their relationship) and *evaluation* (or comparing/ testing word forms or meanings to determine what is appropriate in the context). The task-induced involvement construct integrates relevant concepts from cognitive theory in its narrow sense of information processing with affective aspects of cognition that may influence information processing through learner attention and effort. Through this construct, they believe that researchers will be able to operationalize sub-constructs, such as noticing, elaboration, motivation or need 'at the micro level of learning tasks' (Laufer & Hulstijn, 2001: 9), in order to investigate their effects on lexical processing and acquisition. They note that in addition to theory building, such research could lead to criteria for developing effective instructional tasks.

Most inferencing research that has tested students for retention has for practical reasons been limited to verification of retention immediately or shortly after inferred guesses are reported (e.g. Fraser, 1999; Paribakht, 2005; Paribakht & Wesche, 1999; Svensson, 2003). Some see this as a major limitation, among them Hulstijn (2001: 286), who emphasizes that even if there is immediate retention of new word meanings, '[n]ew information will seldom leave a lasting trace in memory if not frequently reactivated'.

Such reactivation can be accomplished for frequently occurring words through frequent use of the language in various modes and contexts, but for low-frequency words is likely to require deliberate review and practice. Thus, although immediate retention appears to be a necessary condition for vocabulary learning from inferencing, justifying its value as a research measure, it is not a sufficient basis on which to claim that learning has taken place.

What Processes are Involved in Lexical Inferencing and How Have They Been Conceptualized and Explained?

Through the various studies described above, researchers have adopted, adapted or created theoretical conceptualizations to frame their studies and to explain different aspects of the L2 inferencing process and its outcomes. In all of them, lexical inferencing – like inferencing in general – is understood as a multidimensional cognitive process, focused on meaning construction, which involves both declarative and procedural components. Several of the frameworks discussed below deal primarily with lexical inferencing in comprehension, while cognitive approaches and connectionism make the link between comprehension and acquisition. In the discussion, they are grouped according to their primary focus: lexical issues, comprehension processes, declarative and procedural knowledge, and cognitive processing in relation to comprehension and/or acquisition.

Lexically linked frameworks

The frameworks described here have to do with conceptualizing lexical knowledge as it may operate in lexical inferencing and in the acquisition of word meaning. They have been used in interpreting the findings of studies investigating learners' use of knowledge sources and learners' attempts at lemma construction in lexical inferencing. An account is also given of the way in which connectionism has been applied to the study of the acquisition of word meaning.

Knowledge sources

The kinds of knowledge sources – or the types of previous knowledge and information from the word and surrounding text – used by L2 readers inferring new word meanings, have been a primary focus of a number of studies, leading to descriptive taxonomies of knowledge source use by different groups of learners (Bengeleil & Paribakht, 2004; de Bot *et al.*, 1997; Paribakht & Wesche, 1999, 2006; Haastrup, 1991a;

Paribakht, 2005; Paribakht & Tréville, 2007). These taxonomies share the starting point of Carton's (1971) three major cue categories: interlingual, intralingual and extralingual. More specifically, knowledge sources include the learner's knowledge of the native and text language (or other languages) as well as his or her world knowledge, interacting with content and linguistic cues found in the L2 text at all levels of the linguistic system – from orthography to discourse patterns. Within the intra- and interlingual categories, Paribakht and Wesche have found it useful to classify linguistic cues according to the unit of the language system in which cues to a given word are identified; i.e. within or adjacent/related to the *word* itself (e.g. morphology, collocation, association); within the same *sentence* (e.g. meaning, syntax); beyond the sentence at the *discourse* level (e.g. cumulative meaning, formal schemata). It appears from analyses of learners' verbal reports on their inferencing attempts in English that some knowledge sources (such as word morphology or sentence meaning) are used frequently by most learners, reflecting their general availability and utility, whereas others (such as awareness of formal schemata or word collocations) are used rarely and only by some learners, yet appear useful in certain circumstances (Paribakht, 2005; Paribakht & Wesche, 2006).

Studies comparing groups of L2 readers with different native languages indicate that the L1 may also affect patterns of use of particular knowledge sources. For example, Persian speakers rarely use *word* cues in L1 inferencing, while French L1 speakers use them frequently, a difference that persists in English (L2) (Paribakht & Wesche, 2006; Paribakht & Tréville, 2007). Overall, it appears that meaning-oriented cues in the same sentence as the target word are of primary importance, suggesting that the immediate semantic context of an unfamiliar word is the first place both L1 and L2 readers look for information about unfamiliar words. In addition to L1 influences, patterns of knowledge source use also appear to relate to L2 proficiency, L2 text features and target word features (see Chapter 4). Furthermore, certain individuals show unique patterns of knowledge source use, probably reflecting their personal linguistic and educational histories.

Lemma construction

In a study focusing on different knowledge sources used in L2 inferencing by university level English learners from mixed L1 backgrounds, de Bot *et al.* (1997) conceptualized readers' meaning search in lexical inferencing in terms of 'lemma construction', linking the taxonomy of knowledge sources to the lexical knowledge components of

Levelt's (1989) lexically based speech production model. This model includes a detailed presentation of the hypothesized components and organization of the mental lexicon as these may function in speech processing, from the conceptual level (the speaker's intended meaning) to the meaning comprehended by the listener. The model has been adapted for bilingual processing (de Bot & Schreuder, 1993; Poulisse, 1993), for L2 listening comprehension (Green, 1993) and for L2 written text comprehension (de Bot *et al.*, 1997). As adapted for receptive language processing, it has potential as a theoretical framework for further study of how lexical inferencing in reading and listening contexts may lead to lexical development. The *lemma*[7] (Kempen & Huijbers, 1983), which specifies a word's semantic and syntactic information, is of particular interest as a framework for the study of knowledge sources in lexical inferencing. In Levelt's model, the lemma mediates between the speaker's pre-verbal concept and the corresponding phonological or orthographic word form, the *lexeme*, that is heard or read by the receiver and represents its phonological and morphological information. In the model's adaptations for reading (and listening), the process begins with the lexeme, which may awaken a lemma or elements of one in the reader's (listener's) mental lexicon as an indicator of the writer's (speaker's) intended meaning. The reader's initial attention to the form of an unfamiliar word may lead to creation of an 'empty knowledge structure for a new lemma' (de Bot *et al.*, 1997: 317). Lexical inferencing can be viewed within this framework as the process of attempting to fill this knowledge structure for a new word or meaning for a known word. Identification and assemblage of lemma information involves finding and using various knowledge sources from textual cues and previous knowledge, guided by lemma specifications representing the word information components of the mental lexicon. Whereas experienced L2 readers may infer syntactic information with relative ease, semantic inference is much more open-ended, involving interaction among cumulative textual meaning, other textual cues and the learner's conceptual system. The lemma search may activate an existing lemma in the reader's L1, L2 (or Ln) mental lexicon that she or he may then associate with the new lexeme, such as that of a near L2 synonym, or a presumed lexical equivalent in the learner's L1 or another known language. In such cases, even a partially appropriate lemma will facilitate comprehension. If the word has no lexical equivalent in the learner's L1 or other known languages, the process is necessarily more one of construction from existing concepts than identification, and according to evidence presented for the *lexicalization hypothesis* (Paribakht, 2005), the word is unlikely to be successfully understood, or at best, only parts of its meaning will be identified in an initial lemma construction process.

The lexeme/lemma distinction also helps clarify the relationship between the reader's perception of the new word form (its orthographic representation and underlying morphophonological features) and comprehension of a new word's meaning through inferencing. Identification, in context, of a word's semantic and syntactic information can, of itself, serve for purposes of word and text comprehension – the primary motivation for lexical inferencing. Beyond this, mapping between the word meaning and its form is a crucial early step in word learning. For these reasons, research relating successful lexical inferencing in context with retention must take account not only of the lemma, but also of the lexeme.

Connectionism

One early criticism of the Levelt model and other functional models of the lexicon that use a dictionary entry type metaphor, noted by Seidenberg (1995), as discussed by Hulstijn (2001), was that their basis in a dictionary metaphor evokes the image of an integrated lexical entry stored in one place, all of whose features become available upon access. This appears to conflict with connectionist theory (also known as associative networks or parallel distributive processing theory), a now widely accepted explanation of the basic cognitive mechanism underlying the accessing and development of knowledge. In connectionist models, access to knowledge involves parallel, simultaneous activation by multiple processors; there can also be partial activation with respect to aspects of a 'lexical entry' (e.g. meanings, pronunciations) because knowledge of a word is represented in a distributed way, accessible as patterns of activation at the level of sub-lexical features rather than as a unified lexical entry.

Applied to vocabulary acquisition, connectionism assumes that formfunction co-occurrences (e.g. linguistic forms and meaning-making functions) are accessible to learners in language input, and become internalized over repeated activation in the form of network activation patterns rather than as symbolic entities (MacWhinney & Bates, 1989; Koda, 2005: 17). Progress or performance improvement is explained through practice or experience during which the network adjusts the processing connections among associative networks. Connectionism is seen as applicable to motor aspects of articulation and to the perceptual aspects of acquiring new words (N. Ellis, 1994, 2002). The latter point presumably helps explain the gradual familiarization with lexemes through repeated exposures to given words and the findings in some lexical inferencing studies linking retention of new word knowledge to overall (as opposed to within text) word frequency (e.g. Brown *et al.*, 1999). It also provides a powerful explanation for certain observations in L2 reading development, such as the long-lasting influence of L1 form-function mapping procedures during L2 lexical processing (Koda, 2005: 18). Acquisition of word meanings, however, appears to require explicit learning (i.e. learner attention) as part of 'a more conscious operation where the individual makes and tests hypotheses in a search for structure' at the semantic and conceptual levels (N. Ellis, 1994: 1–2), as in lexical inferencing.

More recently, a number of scholars concerned with lexical acquisition have accepted the feasibility of reconciling a connectionist perspective with a symbolist view (e.g. Hulstijn, 2002; Singleton, 1999). Henriksen (2008), likewise adopting a unified, hybrid model of cognitive representation and processing, sees these as operating with both lower-order elements of a more connectionist kind as well as higher-order elements in the form of symbols. In her study of lexical networks, she investigates the links between the various lexical items in her informants' lexical store using a word association format for one of her tasks (see Note 4). In her view of how networks appear to be acquired and activated,

> [the] creation of links between the various lexical items is a continuous process of expansion and restructuring as words occur in different contexts and new items are added to the lexical store. Some associative links gain a canonical status (Murphy, 2003), whereas others may be weakened by lack of activation."..."This is why we [expect to] see a shifting pattern in response behavior in word association studies. (Henriksen, 2008: 28)

The recently completed Danish project, jointly published by researchers Albrechtsen *et al.* (2008), includes a study of the relationship between participants' lexical knowledge and their lexical inferencing skills, discussed below.

Comprehension-oriented frameworks

Reading theory

The conceptual basis for Haastrup's (1991a) earlier study drew largely from a view of reading comprehension as a meaning construction process that operates at discourse, sentence, clausal and lexical levels of organization, as readers strive to interpret what they are reading

(Kintsch, 1998). Just as general inferencing ability is regarded as essential for text comprehension and the reading process, lexical inferencing is crucial for word comprehension. From this perspective, lexical inferencing is viewed as a sub-category of text inferencing. Haastrup distinguished between two macro types of processing: *holistic processing*, based exclusively on contextual cues, and *analytic processing* that includes the informants' activation of linguistic word-level cues. For the latter macro type, she introduced a cross-talk continuum processing framework that included a scale of seven observed processing types, with the higher-level types relating to processing that required interaction and integration between contextual and, where available, linguistic cues to meaning. Processing that includes interaction between contextual and linguistic cues to meaning is referred to as *interactional processing*.

A major difference between the low- and high-proficiency learners of the study was that the latter used a much wider repertoire of potentially successful processing types, including interactional processing; moreover, these learners were able to adapt their processing according to word type and available cues, thus demonstrating 'flexibility' of processing, a construct that Haastrup has elaborated in subsequent research. Overall, Haastrup's (1991a) findings demonstrated the importance of L2 proficiency for lexical inferencing success and its relationship to lexical processing patterns. Her processing framework, taxonomy of cue types, and use of think-aloud verbal protocols form the theoretical basis of her recent study of L1 and L2 lexical inferencing (Haastrup, 2008), discussed below.

A cognitive processing framework

In an early, exploratory case study, Huckin and Bloch (1993) sought to link the procedural and knowledge components underlying lexical inferencing. They developed a cognitive processing framework to represent the results of their lexical inferencing study of three young adult Chinese intermediate level ESL readers. The framework consists of two major parts, a *generator/evaluator* component and a *metalinguistic control* component. In it, the first component employs knowledge modules (e.g. morphological knowledge) to generate and verify hypotheses about a word's meaning, while the second provides a series of both sequential and parallel procedures to guide the learner's decision making while seeking information and making and evaluating inferences, for example, when and how to seek help from the context or other sources of knowledge. Through this framework, Huckin and Bloch characterized their learners' use of different knowledge sources and cognitive strategies while inferencing, the degree to which these knowledge and procedural components were used and how they related to the students' lexical inferencing success. Nassaji (2003) later drew on this framework in a study of intermediate ESL readers with diverse L1s, exploring their use of specific knowledge sources and cognitive procedures in successful lexical inferencing. While inadequate English proficiency for the task appeared more influential in explaining learners' low success, the study confirmed learners' use of both procedural and knowledge components, as well as links between these and lexical inferencing success (Nassaji, 2003).

Cognitive theory in comprehension and acquisition outcomes of lexical inferencing

Researchers interested in lexical inferencing have drawn heavily on cognitive theory as it relates both to language comprehension and acquisition. Why is it, for example, that some unfamiliar words in a text may go unnoticed, while others are perceived only at the formal level, and others, through inferencing, are (at least partially) understood in context? And why are formal and meaning elements of some of them at least temporarily retained in memory? One useful perspective has been that of *input processing* (Chaudron, 1985a, 1985b; Faerch & Kasper, 1986; Gass, 1988, 1999; Wesche, 1994), and as applied to lexical processing (Paribakht & Wesche, 1996, 1999). Gass' (1988, 1997) input processing framework, originally formulated to characterize stages in the acquisition of new syntactic knowledge, also provides a useful perspective for lexical acquisition, from the learner's exposure to a new word as part of ambient language use to storage of information about it in memory. This framework has proven useful in situating the lexical inferencing process in relation to word and text comprehension and to post-inferencing retention of new knowledge, as well as to clarify relationships between given lexical tasks and word learning outcomes (Paribakht & Wesche, 1996; Wesche & Paribakht, 2000). As applied to word learning through reading, the framework traces learners' 'input processing' from the initial *apperception* (or noticing) of a new word form in the L2 data they read and its association with prior knowledge, through the *comprehension* of a meaning for it in the given context (a process that may involve lexical inferencing), to *intake/assimilation* of some mental representation of the word form and its associated meaning (as limited by the quality of analysis during initial comprehension), to the possible *integration* of all or part of this representation into existing knowledge structures. Eventual internalized availability of the new knowledge representation for recall and active use by the learner may itself aid in the conversion of further comprehended input to intake.[8]

Initial attention to a word-form in a text, or noticing it as significant, depends on many factors. Aside from having one's attention drawn to it by an instructor, it may be salient in a text owing to its frequency of appearance, perceived importance in the text or its importance in general, or for other reasons. It may meet a need, or *gap*, felt by the learner with respect to a word form that corresponds to a given concept (Brown et al., 1999). Learner attention to a word and the kind of processing he or she undertakes – such as lexical inferencing – is also strongly influenced by task demands (Hulstijn, 2001; Laufer & Hulstijn, 2001) as these are perceived by learners (Wesche & Paribakht, 1998). In inferencing, successful comprehension of an appropriate word meaning in context is, as already noted, not to be assumed, and in addition to ability factors, contextual support and task demands, will be mediated by individual differences in the effort that learners are ready to expend in generating and verifying possible meanings (Huckin & Coady, 1999; Joe, 1995; Laufer & Hulstijn, 2001; Newton, 1995; Parry, 1993, 1997; Wesche & Paribakht, 1998). The inferencing process may stop at comprehension without leading to detectable learning outcomes. It may, however, result in at least temporary or partial retention of new associations for a familiar word or of a new word form or meaning as a crucial step in the complex and incremental process of learning a new word.

There is broad support for the position that the intake and integration of new lexical knowledge depends on the amount and kinds of cognitive processing it undergoes during initial and subsequent exposures. As summarized by Hulstijn (2001: 275),

> It is the quality and frequency of the information processing activities (i.e., elaboration on aspects of a word's form and meaning, plus rehearsal) which determine retention of new information, far more than the question of whether they process lexical information without or with the intention to commit it to memory.

During repeated experiences with the word involving intake and integration of new lexical knowledge, the learner develops an increasingly detailed mental representation of the word's phonological and orthographic form, its meaning(s), its syntactic constraints, its network links with other words, and other kinds of knowledge about it, as well as increasingly fluent access to it in comprehension and production. As Henriksen (1999: 309) points out,

Acquiring word meaning involves... two interrelated processes of (1) adding to the lexical store via a process of labeling and packaging (i.e., creating extensional links) and (2) reordering or changing the lexical store via a process of network building. ...There has... been a tendency in L2 vocabulary acquisition research to focus on the first aspect (i.e., mapping meaning onto form) and to disregard the second aspect (i.e., network building).

In recent years, the concept of vocabulary network knowledge and closely related constructs, such as organizational knowledge and depth of vocabulary knowledge, have proven valuable in lexical research and have enriched our understanding of the mental lexicon and how it develops.

Lexical inferencing viewed as interaction between declarative and procedural knowledge

The recent Danish research (Albrechtsen et al., 2008) is a comprehensive project incorporating a major study of lexical inferencing, which will be discussed in some detail, given its relevance to both previous work and as a complement to the study reported in Chapters 3 to 6. The theoretical framework used in this study, which views lexical inferencing as a comprehension process, draws on the notions of declarative and procedural knowledge, as conceived by Færch and Kasper (1983, 1985) and Wolff (1994). These authors view declarative knowledge ('knowing that') as encompassing a wide range of different knowledge aspects, of which the most relevant ones in this context are knowledge of the world, discourse knowledge and lexical knowledge. Procedural knowledge ('knowing how') includes language learners' mastery of a number of different procedural aspects, notably reception and production processes in language use, as well as learning procedures. Of these, the receptive processes most pertinent to our discussion include reading processes, among which text inferencing ability is an essential constituent. According to Albrechtsen et al. (2008), lexical inferencing involves both declarative and procedural knowledge and represents the interaction between these two types of knowledge in lexical problem solving, as will be exemplified below.

The larger research project by Albrechtsen et al. (2008) linked three studies examining different aspects of the same informants' communicative competence: their lexical knowledge, lexical inferencing procedures and writing processes. A major aim of the overall project was to determine whether significant correlations could be established between

learner abilities in these three domains. The informants were Danish learners of English from three educational levels (grades 7, 10^9 and first year university students), who carried out a large number of tasks in both English and Danish. Focus here will be exclusively on the L2 data and the study of lexical inferencing (Haastrup, 2008), as supported by the study on declarative lexical knowledge by Henriksen (2008).

The inferencing study was based on the processing framework for describing lexical inferencing processes, developed by Haastrup (1991a) in an earlier study. The following example from the L2 inferencing task is offered in order to make explicit what is meant by viewing lexical inferencing as interaction between procedural and declarative knowledge. From a continuum describing eight types of processing, it illustrates use of one of the *higher-level processes* (top-ruled processing with integration of linguistic cues to meaning). It relates to the target word 'indiscriminately' that appears in the following context (Haastrup, 2008: 208):

> In order to help the plants to grow, families were shown how to place animal dung in holes in the ground instead of spreading it indiscriminately.

A higher-level process requires from the informant both analysis and synthesis skills. Such abilities are set out below in order to clarify to the reader what the author believes it takes to carry out interactive processing; their presentation as a list is not intended to imply sequence (seriality).

- Focusing at word level, the informant would need the ability to spot anything in the target word that might help. This involves paying attention to word form, or more specifically the ability to identify and select relevant components of the target word, i.e. word analysis skills; in this case the word stem *'discriminate'*, the prefix /in-/ and the suffix –/-ly/.
- To such procedural word analysis skills must be added the ability to assign meaning to the selected words, word stems and affixes, by putting to use declarative lexical knowledge of the selected words, word stems and affixes.
- The word analysis skills must, moreover, be supplemented by the ability to integrate the identified linguistic cues into a coherent whole at the word level.
- The result of this process must, furthermore, be integrated into the conceptual framework of the text of which the target word is

part, i.e. the proposal for word meaning must make sense in the context. The ability required adheres to the principle of top-ruled processing.

Synthesis and integration skills are thus required from a lexical perspective as well as from a text comprehension perspective, implying that the informant has to master a double integration process. The described processing type is referred to as advanced processing, since it requires maximum interaction between an informant's declarative and procedural knowledge.

Haastrup's evolving model of *high-quality lexical inferencing* includes three components: learners' use of *advanced processing*, their *adaptability*[10] in the use of appropriate processing types for different word types,[11] and the related component of their *success* in identifying accurate word meanings in context. This complex model, based so far on cross-sectional data in L1 and L2 from the same learners, offers a firm basis for theory building with respect to lexical inferencing procedures.

A main research question addressed by the lexical inferencing study was whether a difference would be found between the lexical inferencing processes used and the level of inferencing success achieved by informants at the three educational levels. The findings were as expected. The quality of lexical inferencing, including both process and outcome, increased with rising educational level.[12] Not surprisingly, advanced processing was found to be far beyond the capacity of the youngest informants in the L2 context, since many of the required abilities described in the example above are dependent on a high level of foreign language proficiency, not least the informants' vocabulary knowledge and reading skills.

In an attempt to situate the coding framework described above as a processing continuum including eight processing types, interesting parallels from adjoining research disciplines will be discussed briefly. The first parallel is with Sternberg's (2003) work, adding a psychologist's perspective on lexical inferencing. Sternberg uses the inferencing process as a prototypical example of problem solving with insight, which for him is constituted by three separate psychological processes (Sternberg, 2003: 183–187): *selective encoding, selective combination* and *selective comparison* (also see reference to Sternberg, 1987, above). Haastrup views these processes as precise parallels to what in her terms are *spotting the relevant cues* (selective encoding), *using interactive processing* (selective combination) and *using world knowledge to check whether your guess makes sense in the context* (selective comparison). The second parallel comes from insights into L2 reading reported by Koda (2005). A key factor in the Danish processing framework is *word analysis skills*, i.e. spotting the relevant cues in a word such as 'indiscriminately' (as described above), an ability that is a necessary pre-requisite for carrying out advanced processing. Haastrup sees word analysis skills as closely linked to Koda's construct of *segmental understanding*, which is at the core of Koda's broader notion of *intra-word awareness* (Koda, 2005: 76, Figure 5.1). For Koda, intra-word awareness is a major factor behind the development of word knowledge. In our view, this underpins the claim that advanced processing is regarded as a hallmark of high-quality lexical inferencing.

Conclusion

The research literature reviewed above from the 1970s through the early years of this new century is rich and varied. Because of the multitude of perspectives on the phenomenon of lexical inferencing from written texts, it is difficult to do justice to the many lines of inquiry that have been pursued – not to mention the work of individual researchers. Furthermore, the diverse methodological variations on a number of parameters likewise make comparisons and synthesis of findings across studies extremely difficult, even while common principles appear to underlie successful lexical inferencing in its many contexts.

What does the available body of research from the last century tell us? What can we all agree on? Lexical inferencing from written texts is now widely understood as a complex meaning determination process that may occur when readers encounter words whose meanings, and often the corresponding forms, are not known or when a known meaning is not appropriate to the context. The reader's goal is word comprehension, as needed for text comprehension. Not all unknown words lead to inferencing; many are ignored, or readers try other means of finding meanings, such as appealing to others or using a dictionary. Attempts at inferencing or confirmation of guesses may also benefit from such other sources. As readers try to understand the meaning of a new word in a given context, they seek cues in the word itself and the surrounding text, identify some as relevant, and use these in light of their cumulative understanding of the text and general knowledge in attempting to generate an informed guess about the word meaning. If correct, an inferred meaning will aid their text comprehension; if not, understanding may be impaired or mistaken.

The lexical inferencing process is often neither smooth nor successful. Research has clarified the many potential hurdles that readers face between their initial exposure to a new word in context and some level of comprehension of its meaning, and between such comprehension and longer-term retention of new lexical knowledge. Research has also revealed the long duration, complexity, uncertainty and iterative nature of the process of learning new words from their use in context (Hulstijn, 2002; Schmitt, 1998). In the case of L2 learners, it appears that successful lexical inferencing in naturalistic reading contexts cannot be assumed as a likely outcome of most encounters with unfamiliar words while reading, and that – when successful – its word learning outcomes at best are usually limited to retention of some aspects of word form and initial word meaning connections. This knowledge generally requires subsequent exposures and consolidation for long-term retention.

While research has over time led to much greater shared understanding of L2 lexical inferencing, an integrated theoretical explanation of this process and its outcomes remains an elusive goal, one that will continue to draw from ongoing research on L2 comprehension and vocabulary acquisition studies, as well as explicit research on lexical inferencing itself.

Notes

1. 'Vocable' appears to be used here in its larger sense, 'word form', given Carton's concern with cues to word meanings, rather than the alternative narrower meaning of word as a group of sounds or letters.
2. The research project by Albrechtsen *et al.* (2008) was designed to include both a cross-sectional and a longitudinal dimension. As yet, the data from the longitudinal study has not been analyzed; however, findings based on these data are expected to throw further light on lexical inferencing in L1 (Danish) and L2 (English).
3. It should be mentioned that on-line and hand-held electronic dictionaries are increasingly available as a resource for readers.
4. Henriksen's word association task used a traditional productive word association format. Forty-eight high-frequency nouns and adjectives were read aloud to her informants at 15-second intervals. When a word had been read out, the informants had to write down the first two words that came to mind in response to the stimulus word (Henriksen, 2008: 40).
5. Cross-linguistic equivalents are at best approximate; it seems more likely, as Brown (1998: 36) has discussed in detail, that even speakers of the same language do not share 'equivalent' dictionary-like representations of words, but rather each has a somewhat different network of experience accessed by a given word. The issue in communication is one of 'identifying the relevant part of that network in a particular context of use'.
6. Krashen (1989, 2003) maintains his early stance that lexical growth through extensive reading is generally underestimated, as the measures typically used cannot account for partial learning. Those that can, such as the

Vocabulary Knowledge Scale, for reasons of feasibility are only applicable for the study of a relatively small number of selected words (Wesche & Paribakht, 1996). Work by Horst and Meara (1999) and Cobb (2005), using a matrix model to estimate incremental vocabulary growth, offer a valuable research approach to the issue of vocabulary learning through reading.

7. The 'lemma' is one of three levels of representation in Levelt's production model. It includes the semantic and syntactic specifications of a lexical entry and, in language use, mediates between the conceptual level and the 'lexeme', its morphophonological form. The semantic specification of the lemma includes the conceptual conditions for its activation and its syntactic specifications, such as category, tense, person, number, case and constraints on occurrence. It also includes a link to the corresponding lexeme. The mental lexicon may also store additional properties, such as stylistic features and relations to other words (Levelt, 1989: 187; after Kempen & Huijbers, 1983).
8. As Gass (1999: 331) points out, citing Swain (1985, 1995) and Swain and Lapkin (1995, 1998), 'This is somewhat simplified because output is also claimed to have a role in the actual learning process'.
9. To allow comparison with other contexts, we note that the grade 10 informants are 16–17 years old, drawn from sixth-form colleges and have had six years of formal English instruction.
10. This construct is a further elaboration of what Haastrup in her earlier study (Haastrup, 1991a) referred to as *flexibility* of processing.
11. This refers to whether target words do or do not offer linguistic cues that are transparent to advanced Danish students of English, determined through field testing.
12. In addition to quantitative analyses, it was possible to characterize group differences in terms of the processing profiles of the mature inferencer (university student), the immature inferencer (grade 7 student) and the intermediate inferencer (grade 10 student).

Chapter 2
Cross-linguistic Issues in Lexical Inferencing

with Kirsten Haastrup

This chapter serves two functions. It is first of all an extension of the research review in Chapter 1 that focuses in detail on a particular topic that has only recently begun to receive systematic study – cross-linguistic dimensions of lexical inferencing. It also provides the necessary background for Part 2 of this book, the trilingual study on this topic with a particular focus on how readers' (first language) L1 influences their (second language) L2 lexical inferencing.

Most research to date on L2 lexical inferencing has concentrated on L2 learners inferring the meanings of unfamiliar words embedded in written texts. Studies have convincingly chronicled such readers' high reliance on their proficiency in the text language for successful inferencing. However, despite a large body of research on lexical transfer[1] as it manifests in other contexts, few researchers have explored such influences in L2 lexical inferencing. What information there is on this topic has, with few exceptions, come from introspective reports of L2 learners or researchers' observations based on L2 data on lexical processing from mixed-L1 participants. Only recently have researchers begun to systematically compare L1 and L2 lexical inferencing by the same learners or L1 and L2 inferencing by groups of learners with different L1s and the same L2, as sources of specific insights into cross-linguistic influences in lexical processing.

Given the many gaps in research on these issues, the final section of this review will work from a broad to a narrow perspective, first considering our general understanding of such influences, then providing relevant examples from L2 reading and lexical processing studies, and wherever possible, from lexical inferencing.

First Language Influences in Second Language Lexical Inferencing

L1 influences on L2 performance, known as transfer effects, have been documented in all linguistic sub-systems, including pragmatics and rhetoric, semantics, syntax, the lexicon, morphology, phonology, phonetics and orthography (Odlin, 2003). Learners' L1 (or Ln) knowledge may affect formal linguistic aspects of L2 performance as well as semantic or pragmatic aspects (or meaning transfer). Whereas transfer of linguistic features has been studied intensively, relatively little is known about the way in which it may influence L2 processing. Odlin (1989: 73), however, referring to the weak relativist position, suggests that 'language may have an important – but not absolute – influence on cognition', citing preliminary evidence from transfer studies indicating that languages influence their speakers' cognitive capacities, for instance, to notice, categorize or recall content – even something as specific as the content of a picture. In a similar vein, Koda (2003, 2005) emphasizes that transfer may affect L2 processing skills as well as linguistic features, and that the effects of the former may be more enduring than those of L1 linguistic features. In her view, L1 linguistic conditioning 'channels subsequent language development and also molds the cognitive procedures accommodating its structural and functional peculiarities. ...[W]ord recognition, sentence parsing, and discourse processing systematically differ across languages' (Koda, 2003: 8–9).

The above quotation also underlines the fact that two or more languages and processing skills are involved in L2 reading. With respect to bilingual processing, Odlin likewise makes the point that there are fundamental differences in the knowledge base available to L1 and L2 learners. In his view, the knowledge base available in bilingual contexts is larger than that available in monolingual contexts, because bilinguals can draw on not one but two languages (Odlin, 1997: 154). Bilingual processing differs in certain ways from monolingual processing, so that while it may have a facilitative effect on, for instance, text processing, bilingual processing may also cause an additional burden. With reference to reading, Koda writes:

> In most instances, L2 learners are unfamiliar with word forms, both symbol and sound, but familiar with concepts through L1 words. Therefore, L2 word learning entails linking four, instead of three, lexical elements: symbol, sound, meaning, and L1 equivalent. (Koda, 2005: 63)

She adds that the majority of L2 readers get much less information from each word in an L2 text than they would in their L1 because few if any of the words are as well known as L1 words. All in all, this means that at every level there is more to be learned.

In the text below, we discuss the role played by transfer, highlighting the importance of the typological distance between the languages involved, i.e. if the learner's L1 and L2 are closely or distantly related languages.

The Importance of Typological Distance Between Languages

The concept of 'language distance' has a long history in linguistics. Weinreich (1953), Lado (1957) and other structuralists recognized its importance. More recently, typological analyses have contributed to the study of language transfer by providing a basis for estimating language distance, thus encouraging the study of transfer in terms of systemic influences, and allowing a clearer understanding of the relations between transfer and language development.

Viberg (1998a: 119) refers to the typological profile of a language as 'a crosslinguistically valid characterization of its structure, highlighting in particular what is universal and what is language specific', based on contrastive and general typological studies. Within such a profile is the 'lexical profile', most relevant to lexical inferencing, as a basis of comparison across languages. As an example of what such a profile would include, Viberg (1998b) provides a description of verb characteristics in Swedish for L2 learners, obtained through systematic mapping of such features as their semantic fields (e.g. concrete, mental, grammatical) and sub-fields (e.g. motion, possession; perception, desire; causal, modal), frequency or others. Evidently, such description of the languages of interest is needed for systematic comparison regarding transfer in L2 inferencing.

While similarity in semantic sub-features, as described above, of L1 and L2 words in closely related languages makes it easier for learners to acquire them, such similarity can facilitate acquisition even when the corresponding languages are typologically distant. A study by Yu (1996a, 1996b) demonstrated that Chinese L2 learners of English, whose L1 shares cross-linguistic similarities with English in the semantic components of motion verbs, performed better in using such verbs than Japanese-speaking learners of English whose native language does not have such similarities. This study is important because it suggests that the facilitating effects of typologically closely related languages may lie in the existence of cross-lingual similarities among particular sub-classes of features rather than in an abstract notion of language distance. Such an effect at the sub-feature level fits well with connectionist explanations.

The above case involving typologically distant languages (Chinese and Japanese versus English) must nonetheless be seen as an informative exception that supports, rather than negates, the importance of typological proximity in L2 processing and acquisition. Typologically close languages exhibit many different kinds of similarities in their sub-features that can serve as complementary sources of facilitation.

Also of importance is the learners' perception of the distance between their L1 and the L2 in question, at least with respect to purposeful appeal to L1 features. If learners intuitively conceive of L1 and L2 as closely related, they are more likely to be willing to attempt transfer of L1 linguistic knowledge, as demonstrated by Kellerman (1977, 1978) in the area of idiomatic expressions.

As to particular areas of language proficiency relevant to lexical inferencing, recent work on L2 reading by Koda (2005) and others is pertinent. Koda emphasizes the importance of L1/L2 typological differences with respect to aspects of L2 reading comprehension. Of interest here are her cases involving distantly related languages where the writing system of the L1 is different from that of the L2. The considerable impact this may have on L2 reading processes is discussed below.

In connection with lexis, important insights are found in the cumulative work of Ringbom and colleagues (Ringbom, 1987, 1992, 2007; Sjöholm, 1993, 1998) on the acquisition of English as an L2 in Finland.[2] Comparisons between groups of learners whose L1 is Finnish (a language distantly related to English) and groups of learners whose L1 is Swedish (a Germanic language closely related to English) have consistently supported the importance of L1 features in foreign language learning, and particularly, the facilitating effect of typological proximity between the L1 and L2.

In addition to language distance, learners' relative familiarity with the cultural concepts being expressed through each language may be expected to affect their performance. With respect to lexical inferencing, L1 readers faced with unfamiliar words are much more likely than L2 readers to have the language – and lexical – mastery as well as related cultural knowledge that will allow them to successfully infer an appropriate word meaning in context. English learning in Finland provides an excellent context for considering the balance between linguistic and cultural influences, as illustrated by Ringbom (1987). His study of culturally very similar Finnish-speaking and Swedish-speaking learners of English found different success rates favoring the Swedish speakers. Commenting on these findings, Odlin notes that '[w]hile cultural distance obviously matters, language distance matters even more' (Odlin, 2003: 443).

In this review, we acknowledge the importance of cultural knowledge, but also how difficult it frequently is to separate this from linguistic influences. Our focus here is on the literature involving linguistic features and language processing.

In the following sections, we make a major distinction between closely and distantly related languages in order to highlight the importance of typological distance in transfer.

Closely related languages

As discussed above, it is generally agreed that L2 acquisition is facilitated for learners whose native language (L1) is typologically similar to the target language (L2) due to the far greater possibility for positive transfer, which in turn frees up cognitive resources for other language learning tasks (cf. Ringbom, 1992; cited in Odlin, 2003: 440–441). As Koda (2005: 43) notes, transfer effects tend to be more positive than negative because one is adding a further system rather than replacing one.

A key feature in relation to lexis is the role played by cognates. Sjöholm (1976), in a comparison of Finnish and Swedish students on an English as a foreign language (EFL) test, interpreted the Swedes' better performance as probably due to shared cognates. Ard and Holmburg (1983) reported similar findings in their American study comparing the performance of Spanish and Arabic English as a second language (ESL) learners at the same proficiency level on an English vocabulary test:

> There is little question that lexical similarities in two languages can greatly influence comprehension and production in a second language. Cognates provide not only semantic but also morphological and syntactic information, and while some of the information may be misleading, some can facilitate acquisition. (Ard & Holmburg, 1983: 83)

They also observed that besides the benefits of recognizing cognates, another likely advantage for learners will be having additional time to concentrate on the unfamiliar words. It must, nonetheless, be noted that the presence of cognates does not always facilitate lexical processing and acquisition. Lexical similarities across languages can also be misleading for learners, as attested by the phenomenon known as 'false friends'. Evidence of such negative effects of cognates in connection with lexical inferencing is reported, for instance, in Haastrup (1991a).

Positive transfer has been demonstrated not only at various linguistic levels, but also for language processing skills. Koda (2005: 43) notes that many reading skill components developed in the L1 can be applied in an L2. For example, shared orthographic knowledge apparently provides long-term facilitation in L2 reading development, as it promotes mastery of L2 visual-information sampling skills. It also facilitates information integration from multiple sources by lightening the memory load.

Several relatively early lexical inferencing studies from Europe, using English as the target language (as a large proportion of lexical inferencing studies still do) provide examples of insights obtained from empirical data. These studies include three different L1s, the Germanic languages of Swedish, Austrian German and Danish, all three typologically closely related to English (another Germanic language). Palmberg (1985, 1988) studied Swedish-speaking Finnish children, using cognate-rich oral and written texts. He found a high level of lexical inferencing success in L2 English, brought about primarily by the learners' use of positive transfer of familiar lexical elements from Swedish and supported by shared narrative schemata. Successful learners' assumption of translational equivalence between formally similar English and Swedish words was evident.

Nemser and colleagues from Austria, in a project on the lexical development of Austrian German-speaking learners of English, included tasks in which learners attempted to assign meanings to unfamiliar L2 words. Using his theory of approximate systems, he characterizes lexical transfer 'as a predevelopmental assumptive strategy like the carrying over of the semantic grid of the L1 lexicon' (Nemser, 1998: 116). This quotation emphasizes Nemser's view that lexical development in L2 is not necessarily accompanied by substantial semantic development. This point has been elaborated in recent work by Jiang (2000), which will be discussed below.

As a third example, the recent Danish project discussed previously, was one of the first to compare L1 and L2 lexical inferencing by the same learners (Albrechtsen *et al.*, 2008). This comprehensive study (introduced in Chapter 1) addressed whether there is a difference between the quality of lexical inferencing in L1 and L2 for the same learners. The informants in grade 7, grade 10 and in their first semester at university were given parallel tasks in the two languages, i.e. a Danish task for L1 inferencing and an English task for L2 inferencing (see Haastrup *et al.*, 2004 for design issues). It was expected that operating in an L2 context would be more demanding than functioning in a similar context in L1, so that results for L1 inferencing would be superior to those for L2. Given the use of parallel tasks in L1 and L2, it was possible to say with certainty that differences found between L1 and L2 inferencing for the same informant could not be due to factors pertaining to the informant's maturity level, including his or her general cognitive development. The obvious candidates that might explain any differences found were L2 proficiency factors, among them, declarative lexical knowledge and – in terms of procedural skills – L2 reading skills. Data were collected on these two proficiency components for both L1 and L2.

Findings for the population as a whole, i.e. the within-subjects' data for informants at all three educational levels, confirmed the predictions. A comparison of the quality of the informants' lexical inferencing (including both the process and outcome measures), demonstrated that identical types of processing skills were involved in L1 and L2 inferencing, although in different proportions. More precisely, the magnitude of the difference between informants' results in L1, which were clearly superior to those in L2, was large: the use of advanced processing in the L1 was three times its use in the L2. The between-subjects analyses from the three educational levels showed that the youngest school learners had serious problems with the advanced processing types in L2. It appears that, at this level, they need to get their processing right in the L1 before this ability can be transferred to the foreign language. The gap between L1 and L2 inferencing was much smaller for the post-secondary group, but was still there, with lack of L2 lexical knowledge (vocabulary size and lexical network knowledge) appearing to be a main factor behind their inferior L2 inferencing behavior.

Finally, based on the cross-sectional findings from the present study of L1 and L2 inferencing (Haastrup, 2008), it was proposed that the processing continuum could be envisaged as a developmental continuum. However, only through analysis of longitudinal data (which were collected approximately 18 months later from these same participants, but not yet analyzed), can this proposal be properly validated.

Although the research presented above and related studies provide insight into positive transfer in lexical inferencing between closely related languages, they do not allow overall conclusions to be drawn about the degree to which such transfer occurs and under what conditions. What can be said is that readers appear more likely to report using L1 knowledge in L2 inferencing if their L1 is closely related to the L2, English; for example, Danish (Haastrup, 1991a, 2008) or French (Paribakht & Tréville, 2007) in contrast to speakers of languages that are typologically more distant from English such as Persian (Paribakht, 2005). Relatively greater reported recourse to the L1 has also been found with low-proficiency learners of English in both closely related, e.g. Danish (Haastrup, 1991a) and distant languages, e.g. Arabic (Bengeleil & Paribakht, 2004). Overall, however, few studies report L1 influences on lexical inferencing behavior and success. One of these is a study of Spanish-English bilinguals by Nagy et al. (1997), who found that 'L1' (Spanish) effects appeared to persist in L2 use in the form of Spanish syntactic knowledge. In spite of apparent low L2 learner awareness of L1 effects on their L2 acquisition and use, research on transfer in L2 reading suggests omnipresent and long-lasting, if sometimes quite subtle influences (Koda, 2005).

Distantly related languages

The languages and language pairs mentioned in this section are all referred to as distantly related to English (the L2 in most such studies to date). We use 'distantly' as a very broad term, including languages such as L1 Persian (an Indo-European language), L1 Chinese and L1 Korean (both non-Indo-European languages) in relation to L2 English. Obviously, in relative typological terms, some of these languages are much closer to English than others; in the following examples, we shall emphasize the most outstanding features distinguishing certain of them from English.

The first study by Ghahremani-Ghajar and Masny (1999), who examined the role played by the different writing systems in Persian and English and their influence on informants' letter recognition strategies, provides some evidence for transfer of L1 processing skills. The authors report that right-left directionality in searching for Persian letters is responsible for the Persian-speakers' reading of Roman letters in the same way. It took longer for Persian readers to respond to the leftmost position in the Roman letters. Also, since several vowels are not written in Persian orthography, Persian readers need to determine appropriate vowels for each word before a combination of consonants becomes meaningful. Therefore, Persian readers seem to be more 'word bound' than English readers, and spend more time reading individual letters and words. They may also transfer this habit to reading English texts and spend more time than necessary processing individual letters in English, resulting in slower reading and text comprehension (Ghahremani-Ghajar & Masny, 1999). Successful identification of words in Persian appears to involve not only attention to internalized probabilities of letter combinations, but ongoing verification of the word guesses in the larger discourse meaning context; in this case a very helpful approach that might be transferable to English.

Koda (2005) similarly starts her discussion of cross-linguistic influences in reading with orthography, but goes further into symbol-to-sound relations. She notes that in 'transparent' orthographies (such as French), phonological information is assembled mainly through letter-by-letter, symbol-to-sound translation. In less transparent orthographies (such as Persian), phonological information is often obtained only after a word has been identified, based on the reader's stored knowledge of the word. English orthography is morphophonemic, lying somewhere in between; it frequently preserves morphological information alongside phonemic descriptions in its graphic representation (Koda, 2005: 84). Thus, its phonologically equivalent words are often differentiated orthographically (e.g. threw and through; right and write). From this, one might expect that differences in L1 versus L2 sound-symbol relationships would systematically complicate L2 reading and lexical inferencing.

With regard to research on the influence of L1 in relation to lexical competence, some studies have shown that learners tend to avoid lexical items that do not have counterparts in their L1. Blum and Levenston's (1979) early study of native speakers of Hebrew versus learners of Hebrew from various linguistic backgrounds found that the latter group tended not to fill in blanks in a cloze test requiring Hebrew words that had no equivalents in their respective L1s. On this topic, Sjöholm (1998) reports such a tendency on the part of both Finnish and Swedish learners of English, but also pointed out that differences between the two groups related to the greater distance of Finnish from English.

> Since phrasal verbs exist in Swedish and because they are rare or expressed differently in Finnish, one would expect that Finns [would avoid] phrasal verbs more often than Swedes. Our data give strong support for this hypothesis, but it is true only of the idiomatic (opaque) phrasal verbs in the early stages of learning. (Sjöholm, 1998: 227)

Recent empirical evidence on lexical processing supports the view that all known meanings of a word are at least briefly activated by its orthographic form, even when the context imposes strong constraints limiting possible meaning (Koda, 2005: 35). This parallel activation of different meanings for a given word form may, however, occur to different degrees (Singleton, 2006). Such parallel activation implies that readers are involved continuously in meaning selection, even for well-known words, many of which are polysemous or involve determination of which homonym is the intended one. In the case of L2 users, research suggests that each time a familiar L2 word with an L1 lexical equivalent is encountered, its L1 translation is likely to be activated along with any known L2 meanings (Jiang, 2000; Paribakht, 2005). This proposal is compatible with Poulisse's (1995) observation that in bilingual speech production L1 and L2 translation equivalents may be activated simultaneously, as evidenced in slip of the tongue phenomena when learners produce blends of L1 and L2 words in speech.

In 2000, Jiang proposed the L1 lemma mediation hypothesis to characterize the transfer of L1 lemma information to L2 words identified as having L1 equivalents. He found support for this hypothesis in two subsequent empirical studies of semantic transfer, using a discourse completion test in which learners had to complete sentences from pairs of English words provided. The first study (Jiang, 2002) was with Chinese learners of English and the second (Jiang, 2004) with Korean learners of English. In both cases, he found support for the presence of L1 semantic structure in L2 representations. For Jiang (2000), the implication of the above mediation process for acquisition is that while L1 words are learned as both semantic and formal entities, L2 words with L1 lexical equivalents tend to be learned mainly as formal entities. Existing L1 concepts and semantic specifications will tend to be associated with the new L2 lexeme, short-circuiting the lemma construction process that characterizes L1 word learning. In his view, the initial adoption of an L1 lemma for an L2 lexeme is likely to have a long-lasting influence on the learner's understanding of that word, in that L1 lemmas for L2 words will continue to be activated in L2 use and may become fossilized at this translation stage. Furthermore, assuming that L1 lemma information remains present over time and continues to mediate L2 word processing even as L2 semantic and syntactic learning proceed and strengthen L2 intra-lingual networks, L2 learners at advanced levels will still face the greater demands of bilingual (versus monolingual) processing. Jiang (2000) also postulates that while L2 words without L1 equivalents will generally be difficult to learn even to the point of recognition, once the process of meaning creation and learning has succeeded, these words will be used with much greater automaticity and accuracy than L2 words learned through their L1 equivalents. This point requires empirical verification.

Paribakht's (2005) Persian/English inferencing study has provided new insights into the effect of the L1 lexicalization status of unknown words on learners' lexical inferencing behavior for distantly related languages, i.e. the extent to which there are lexical equivalents – single or compound, including lexical phrases in the learner's L1 – for given words. Her lexicalization hypothesis stipulates that the extraction of semantic and syntactic components of an unfamiliar word through inferencing may activate at least some elements of an existing L1 lemma in the reader's mental lexicon, possibly leading to activation of the item's L1 equivalent/translation. Since no lemma equivalent is present in the mental lexicon for L2 words that are not lexicalized in the L1, the lemma features assembled through inferencing are not recognized as part of a known construct, making it less likely that even an approximate (e.g. L1) meaning of the target word will be determined. In her study, readers were far more successful in accurately guessing the meanings of lexicalized than non-lexicalized words. A further study by Paribakht and Tréville (2007) comparing the inferencing behaviors of learners from Persian and French-speaking backgrounds when dealing with lexicalized versus non-lexicalized words in English largely supported this finding.

Conclusion

The sorting out of L1 transfer effects on L2 lexical inferencing from those of learners' proficiency, cultural knowledge, bilingual processing and other factors will require a multiple research approach. This would include further studies comparing L1 and L2 inferencing by learners with a given L1 at different L2 proficiency and educational levels, such as the Danish study (Albrechtsen *et al.*, 2008), and others comparing L1 and L2 inferencing by learners from several different L1 backgrounds with similar L2 proficiency and educational levels. As well, comparisons of L1 and L2 lexical inferencing by speakers of different L1s learning the same L2 are needed, such as the research reported in the present volume. These new studies and related ongoing work have yielded new insights into cross-linguistic influences on L2 processing specific to the languages involved. They have also provided information on relevant aspects of L2 proficiency and other influences in L2 lexical inferencing. Together they constitute the beginning of a response to Nemser's call for lexical studies with English as the target language and learners with a variety of closely or more distantly related languages (Nemser, 1998: 107). Now that we have some information on these issues, new questions arise. Can results from L2 lexical inferencing studies be generalized across languages? At what point in the state of the art can we begin to talk about lexical inferencing processes being universal? What aspects of lexical inferencing are language-specific? How many different combinations of language pairs, such as L1 Korean versus L2 Spanish, or L1 Italian versus L2 Arabic are needed? The study presented in Part II, Chapters 3–6 of this book, carries the inquiry further.

Notes

1. We use the term 'transfer' here to refer to the influence on language processing and outcomes resulting from similarities and differences between the target language and any other language that has been previously acquired (after Odlin, 1989), based on similarities between learned features across the two languages or a language user's perception of them. L1 transfer in L2 lexical processing thus involves native language influence on some aspect of this process or its outcomes. While one can refer to positive or negative transfer in terms of how its outcomes compare with target language norms, transfer itself appears to be a unitary process (Faerch & Kasper, 1987). Given the varied uses of the term over the past four decades and in different theoretical contexts regarding L2 acquisition, it is not possible to use the word more precisely without complex definition. As Odlin (1989: 28) noted, 'A fully adequate definition of transfer seems unattainable without adequate definitions of many other terms, such as *strategy*, *process*, and *simplification*'.
2. Finland is a bilingual country where both Finnish and Swedish are official languages. Finnish-speaking and Swedish-speaking Finns are close to each other in terms of general culture and education, although they are linguistically quite different. Finnish is not an Indo-European language, whereas Swedish is not only Indo-European but, like English, is a Germanic language. It thus provides an ideal context for studying differences in foreign language (English) learning by culturally similar speakers whose L1s are typologically closely related and unrelated.

Part 2
Trilingual Study of Lexical Inferencing in a First and Second Language

Background to the Trilingual Study

Part 2, consisting of Chapters 3–6, presents a trilingual study of lexical inferencing in readers' native language and a second language (L2) (English) by young adult speakers of Persian and French, two Indo-European languages with distant and close typological relationships to English, the common L2. A first objective is to identify procedures that are shared across languages in both first language (L1) and L2 lexical inferencing, as well as overall differences between L1 and L2 lexical inferencing. The main focus, thereafter, is identification of L1 influences in L2 lexical inferencing. This is achieved through comparative analyses of L1-L2 conditions for the Persian and French speakers, across the three L1s, and across the English L1 and L2 conditions. Particular attention is given to the possible role of typological distance between readers' L1 and L2 as this interacts with their lexical knowledge in lexical inferencing procedures and outcomes.

The primary objective of the trilingual study was to seek a better understanding of the processes and outcomes of L2 (English) lexical inferencing from written texts as influenced by readers' native language knowledge. Our goal is to understand the conditions that promote successful word comprehension through lexical inferencing by L2 readers, and related to this, the conditions that lead to their retention of new knowledge of word meanings following inferencing. Learners' previous L2 lexical knowledge is known to be a major factor in inferencing success and retention (Chapter 1). Another factor that has received little attention to date is what learners bring to the task in terms of relevant L1 linguistic knowledge. In this study, we have posed this issue in terms of a comparison between a group of Persian L2 readers, whose L1 is relatively distant typologically from English, in contrast with a group of French L2 readers whose L1 and English are typologically close. Given the evidence of L1 transfer to L2 performance in all aspects of language, our expectation was that L1 knowledge would influence resources they would bring to L2 inferencing, including lexical resources. In the study that follows (also see Paribakht, 2005; Paribakht & Tréville, 2007; Paribakht & Wesche, 2006), we pursue these issues in a presentation of findings from our cross-linguistic study of both L1 and L2 lexical inferencing involving young adult speakers of English, Persian and French, the latter two groups also learners of English.

The inferencing process is examined in terms of the kinds and patterns of knowledge sources (KSs) – including both textual cues and world knowledge – that these three groups used in L1 and L2 (English) lexical inferencing. Its outcomes are studied in terms of these learners' success in inferring appropriate word meanings in context, and in L2, their immediate post-inferencing retention of new word knowledge. Related objectives included determining cross-lingual commonalities in lexical inferencing that hold across L1 and L2 conditions, overall differences between L1 and L2 conditions, and the effect of the lexicalization status of target words in readers' L1 on their lexical inferencing procedures and outcomes. Finally, the role of L2 readers' receptive vocabulary knowledge in their lexical inferencing success and post-inferencing retention of new target word forms and meanings was examined as it might relate to the issue of the typological distance between the L1 and L2.

Overview

Chapter 3 presents the conceptual and methodological basis for the trilingual study. This is followed in the remaining chapters by presentation of empirical results and a concluding discussion.

Participants' use of different types of KSs in L1 and L2 lexical inferencing is examined in Chapter 4. A trilingual taxonomy representing all KS types used by speakers of the three languages in L1 and L2 conditions, along with examples from all conditions, is presented first. Shared cross-linguistic KS use patterns in L1 and L2 as well as proficiency-related general differences between L1 and L2 KS use are described in terms of this taxonomy. The core issue of Persian or French L1 influences on English L2 KS use is explored through within-subject comparisons of L1 and L2 KS use in both groups and comparisons across the groups. Influence of the L2 text language on L2 lexical inferencing is also explored through comparison of L1 English KS use with that of the two L2 groups.

Lexical inferencing success and, for L2 users, learning outcomes are examined in Chapter 5. The success of all three language groups in L1 and the Persian and French speakers in L2 is described and compared. Particular attention is given to differences that characterize overall L1 versus L2 inferencing, and within L2 inferencing, effects attributable to Persian and French group differences and to the lexicalization status of target words in the respective L1. L2 learning outcomes are reported in terms of overall gains as well as L2 readers' post-inferencing familiarity with previously unknown word forms and their retention of new word meanings. The role of L2 readers' previous lexical knowledge is also examined as this relates to both their lexical inferencing success and retention of new word meanings, and as it reflects the relative typological distance of their L1 from English.

Chapter 6 presents a synthesis of the main empirical findings of the research and their interpretations, as well as a discussion of their theoretical and pedagogical implications. Directions for future research are also discussed.

Chapter 3
Conceptualization and Methodology

Conceptualization

Lexical inferencing

Lexical inferencing is a cognitive strategy whereby a reader draws on contextual cues and background/world knowledge and combines them to arrive at a meaning for an unfamiliar word. Our previous research and related studies by others have revealed the complex nature of this process, which involves both declarative knowledge (linguistic and non-linguistic) and procedural knowledge (e.g. search for and identification of relevant cues in the text; combining information to arrive at a plausible meaning for the target word). Lexical inferencing has also been characterized as a process of lemma construction (de Bot *et al.*, 1997), which links the knowledge structures (KSs) used by the readers in the second language (L2) lexical inferencing process to the lexical knowledge components of Levelt's (1989) speech processing model, as adapted for receptive language processing. Paribakht's (2005) *Lexicalization Hypothesis* has advanced this argument, stipulating that the assemblage of the contextual cues in the process of lexical inferencing may activate an existing lemma in the readers' first language (L1 or Ln) mental lexicon, leading to word meaning comprehension. However, if there is no L1 lemma (or L1 lexical equivalent) for the target word in the reader's mental lexicon, there is no shortcut to word meaning comprehension and the process becomes one of a new lemma/word meaning construction, often leading to failure in comprehending the word's meaning (Chapter 1).

While some studies of lexical inferencing have focused mainly on identifying the knowledge sources (KSs) and contextual cues that readers draw on in the process (e.g. Haastrup, 1991; Paribakht & Wesche, 1999; Bengeleil & Paribakht, 2004), others have also examined the procedural abilities that learners bring to the task (e.g. Haastrup, 1991, 2008). A number of studies have also focused on the factors that affect this process and its outcomes (see Chapter 1).

Relatively little is known, however, about the influence of the learners' L1 on the L2 lexical inferencing process and its outcomes (success and word knowledge retention). Some anecdotal reporting of L1 influence on inferencing has appeared in the literature. For example, Nagy *et al.* (1997) reported an ongoing effect of L1 syntax on L2 English inferencing by fluent Spanish-English bilinguals, providing evidence of the long-lasting and specific nature of some L1 effects. Research has also indicated that learners' L1 may affect patterns and frequencies of use of particular KS types (e.g. Paribakht & Tréville, 2007; Paribakht & Wesche, 2006). The lexicalization status of the L2 target word in L1 has also been shown to affect the success of L2 lexical inferencing. In the studies by Paribakht (2005) and Paribakht and Tréville (2007), the lexicalization status of the target word in L1 showed a strong effect for success in lexical inferencing and word meaning comprehension (see Chapter 2 for a full discussion).

A better comprehension of L1 influences on L2 lexical inferencing, as distinct from other factors (e.g. L2 reading proficiency), requires a comparison of the L1 and L2 lexical inferencing of the same readers from different L1 backgrounds in the same L2. Several pairs of languages are needed in order to sort out language specific from L1 versus L2 issues. Such studies can also help us to understand what aspects of L1 and/or L2 lexical inferencing are shared across speakers of different languages versus aspects that are specific to given languages.

Aside from the research reported here, only the recent Danish project has, to our knowledge, reported comparisons of the same individuals inferencing in both L1 and L2 (Albrechtsen *et al.*, 2008). In that study, the researchers demonstrated a large gap between participants' lexical inferencing performance in L1 versus L2, even for those most proficient in English. Readers' L2 lexical proficiency (both vocabulary size and lexical network knowledge) was shown to be particularly important. While specific L1 influences were also identified, only Danish and English were involved in the study.

The present trilingual study addresses the above issues and brings the issue of relative typological distance between the readers' L1 and L2 into focus through its comparable data from speakers of Persian, an Indo-European language that is typologically distant from English, and French, a language that, like Danish, is typologically much closer to English. Thus, it is able to compare L1 influences on L2 lexical processing across several languages, and to distinguish them from other factors.

Language distance

As discussed in Chapter 2, one frequent explanation for observed influences of learners' native language knowledge on L2 lexical processing is the typological proximity of the two languages. This appears to relate to the presence of many shared or similar features or sub-features between the L1 and L2. Sub-feature similarities, when they exist, can also have a facilitating effect even between very different languages, but when two languages are typologically close, such correspondences will be found at many levels of the language system, so the effect is greatly compounded. Lexical examples include a facilitating effect of cognate recognition in L2 comprehension and production. On the other hand, cross-linguistic studies involving L2 speakers of English with typologically distant L1s such as Japanese and Persian, have demonstrated how L1 linguistic conditioning may constrain L2 processing, for example, with respect to letter and word recognition across differing orthographies. L1 processing experience has also been shown to influence both morphological and syntactic processing even at very high levels of L2 proficiency. What is apparent is that for learners of a given L2, each L1 may differentially influence the process and outcomes of L2 lexical inferencing. Comparative cross-linguistic studies involving different pairs of languages are needed on this issue. The current study is an attempt in this direction.

Research Design

This study involved an examination and comparisons of the L1 lexical inferencing behaviors of speakers of three languages (English, Persian and French), and L2 (English) lexical inferencing of the latter two groups. Introspective (think-aloud) methods of data collection were used. The analysis included comparisons of patterns of inferencing attempts, KS use, inferencing success, and in the case of L2 speakers, their success in inferring the meanings of lexicalized, non-lexicalized and total words as well as their retention of L2 word knowledge after inferencing. Correlational and item analysis of relationships among these variables and the role of previous lexical knowledge in success and retention of new lexical knowledge were also carried out, and the role of L1-L2 typological distance and L2 learning context in readers' lexical knowledge, KS use in lexical inferencing and inferencing outcomes were also investigated.

Choice of Persian, French and English

Persian[1] and French were chosen for this study as Indo-European languages accessible to the researchers, which represent different typological relationships with the target L2, English, as well as many differences from one another. While a precise understanding of what features of these languages are more universal versus more language-specific is still a distant objective, we can speak about relative typological distance (Persian being much farther from English than is French), speaker-perceived distance (Persian again being perceived by its speakers as being quite distant from English), and easily observed differences such as the higher incidence in Persian of words without lexical equivalents in English and the far larger number of cognates shared by English and French. The writing systems of Persian and English are also quite different; Persian uses the Perso-Arabic alphabet, a right to left direction of writing, and an orthography that does not represent all vowel sounds. In all these respects, French is relatively similar to English. Thus, Persian and French each provide its speakers with a different starting point and distance for the learner to progress with respect to English in terms of the relationship between its typological features and those of English. Because of this and also the typological distance between Persian and French, a cross-lingual study of speakers of two languages performing in English offers the possibility of sorting out L1 influences from other potential influences.

Research Questions

The study examined the following guiding research questions:

(1) Cross-linguistic patterns in L1 and L2 inferencing.
  - What are the shared characteristics of KS use in lexical inferencing across different languages? Across L1 and L2 conditions?
  - How do cross-linguistic L1 versus L2 lexical inferencing differ? How can differences be explained?
  - How does success in lexical inferencing compare within and across the L1 and L2 conditions?
(2) L1 influences on L2 lexical inferencing procedures and outcomes.
  - Does a reader's L1 influence his or her KS use in L2 lexical inferencing?
  - Does the L1 influence L2 inferencing success? L2 readers' retention of new word knowledge?

- Does the L1 play a role in L2 readers' ability to successfully infer meanings for lexicalized versus non-lexicalized target words? Their ability to retain their forms or meanings?
- What is the role of relative typological distance between the L1 and L2 in L2 lexical inferencing?

(3) How does L2 vocabulary knowledge relate to lexical inferencing success and retention of new word knowledge? Are these outcomes related to each other?
- How does readers' receptive L2 vocabulary knowledge relate to their success in lexical inferencing?
- How does receptive L2 vocabulary knowledge relate to their retention of new knowledge of L2 English target word forms and meanings after inferencing?
- What is the relationship of successful lexical inferencing to subsequent retention of new word knowledge?

Expectations and empirical approach

Our general expectations, based on known characteristics of the lexical inferencing process from previous studies, were that there would be some common patterns of KS use across all L1 sets and across both L2 data sets as well, indicating potential shared tendencies across these and other Indo-European languages. We also expected to find overall L1 versus L2 differences in both KS use and outcomes – among other things reflecting the considerable proficiency gap between native and non-native language users, and possibly also influenced by characteristics of English as a text language and learners' developing knowledge of it. English L1 and L2 comparisons also could provide an indication of what these (and other) young adult English learners may still need to know in order to become more efficient in lexical inferencing and as readers of English. Most crucial here, given the known influence of L1 in learning different aspects of L2, we expected to find evidence of L1 transfer to L2 inferencing in the cases of Persian and French speakers. This was expected to show itself through similar patterns of KS use between Persian L1 and L2 inferencing that were different from shared French L1 and L2 KS use, and possibly also be reflected in differential L2 lexical inferencing success and retention of new word knowledge by Persian and French speakers.

Methodology

Participants

Potential research participants, post-secondary students representing the three native languages (Persian, French and English), and in the first two cases also students of English, were located in Iran and Canada with the help of local colleagues involved in post-secondary English language education. Following administration of the *English Reading Comprehension Test* (see below) used for English as a second language (ESL) course placement at the University of Ottawa, participants were selected from among volunteers, based on their test performance. Three groups participated in the study:

- Twenty Persian-speaking undergraduate university students majoring in English at several universities in Tehran, Iran.
- Twenty French-speaking students at a post-grade 11 college (CEGEP) in Quebec (Outaouais/the Ottawa-Gatineau Region), Canada.
- Twenty English-speaking undergraduate university students in Ottawa, Ontario, who reported having only minimal, if any, knowledge of a second language. Some may have studied core high school French.

All three groups were similar in their status as post-secondary students, and both the Persian and French speakers had been studying English in school settings for many years and were continuing that study at the post-secondary level. The two L2 English groups also had similar scores on the English reading test (the selection criterion), reflecting high-intermediate reading proficiency. Their knowledge of receptive English vocabulary knowledge was measured using Nation's (1990) *Vocabulary Levels Test* (see Table 3.1 for scores on these tests). There were, however, several aspects of age, receptive L2 vocabulary knowledge, L2 proficiency, educational level and respective English learning contexts on which the two groups differed in ways that might have influenced some individuals' performance on the research tasks.

As shown in Table 3.1, the average performance scores of the two participant groups on the *Reading Comprehension Test*, a selection criterion, were fairly similar, with both groups representing a fairly wide range. On the *Vocabulary Levels Test* (Nation, 1990), the French speakers achieved numerically higher average scores, while the Persian speakers were distinguished by the large variability of their scores, with

Table 3.1 Average English reading proficiency and receptive English vocabulary scores for the Persian and French speakers

	Persian			French		
	Range	M	SD	Range	M	SD
Reading	27–39	32.1	3.8	23–39	34.1	4.5
Vocabulary	27–90	59.7	17.0	53–83	65.3	8.5

Note: The maximum possible score for reading is 60 and for vocabulary 90.

both higher and lower scores exceeding those of the French speakers. Differences in average group scores were not statistically significant, but these disparities suggested possible important differences between the two groups. With respect to other factors, the English- and Persian-speaking students, already in university, tended to be several years older than the French speakers and had already chosen their fields of study.

The French speakers, being somewhat younger[2] and still at the college level, in many cases had not yet chosen academic specializations, although many planned to transfer to university programs after the first CEGEP year. Reports during data collection by the two bilingual research assistants (one Persian-English, one French-English) suggested that, overall, the Persian speakers seemed more focused and motivated with respect to the tasks. The two groups also differed in their English learning context. In general, the younger French speakers had had less formal study of English at the post-secondary level than the Persian speakers. The Persian students, as English majors, were in most cases carrying out their university studies in English in Iran. They mainly heard and used English in the classroom context, so that their knowledge was based on formal study and mainly on reading and writing English and grammar study. For them, English was a foreign language, while for the French speakers, living in Gatineau (Quebec), contiguous to the bilingual national capital, Ottawa, English was a second language. Most had had much more informal exposure to English than the Persian speakers, over many years. In addition to studying English in school and at the CEGEP, most of the French speakers in the study were frequently exposed to oral and some written English through the media, music, in sports, with friends and in daily encounters. Furthermore, although both Persian and French mother tongue instruction continued to emphasize grammar even at elementary schools, and grammar was also emphasized at all levels of English L2 instruction in Iran, Quebec schools had over the preceding decade or more, increasingly emphasized communicative approaches to teaching English.

Instruments

English reading test

The *English Reading Comprehension Test*, developed at the University of Ottawa and used in placing students in intermediate and advanced ESL courses, was used to select the Persian- and French-speaking participants for the study. This test has three sub-tests, two of which present extended reading texts followed by comprehension questions, and the third, a multiple-choice cloze test. The readings on the version used were on the topics of 'Test Anxiety' and 'Sinister Statistics', with six and nine comprehension questions, respectively. The multiple-choice cloze on 'Culture Shock' had 30 items. The participants had 60 minutes to complete the test. Each comprehension question is worth 2 points and cloze items 1 point each, for a total possible score of 60.

Receptive English vocabulary knowledge

The *Vocabulary Levels Test* (Nation, 1990), used to measure the selected Persian- and French-speaking participants' receptive English vocabulary knowledge, consists of 90 items from five word-frequency levels (2000, 3000, 5000, the University Word List and 10,000 words). Each frequency level comprises six sections, each of which presents six words at that frequency level and three possible definitions. The testees are asked to match the target words with their corresponding definitions. The test has 90 items (18 in each level), and the maximum possible score is 90. The test estimates learners' receptive English vocabulary at different word frequency levels, and can be used to determine if they have enough vocabulary knowledge to read instructional texts that include words from those frequency levels.

Knowledge of target words

The *Vocabulary Knowledge Scale* (VKS) (Paribakht & Wesche, 1993, 1996, 1997; Wesche & Paribakht, 1996) was used to measure the Persian- and French-speaking participants' relative knowledge of each target word, both before and after the L2 lexical inferencing task, in order to capture immediate gains in knowledge of these words. In this measure, each word is presented individually to the test-taker, who responds to the appropriate elicitation category (Figure 3.1) and, if possible, provides either a synonym/translation or a sentence for categories 3–5. The result

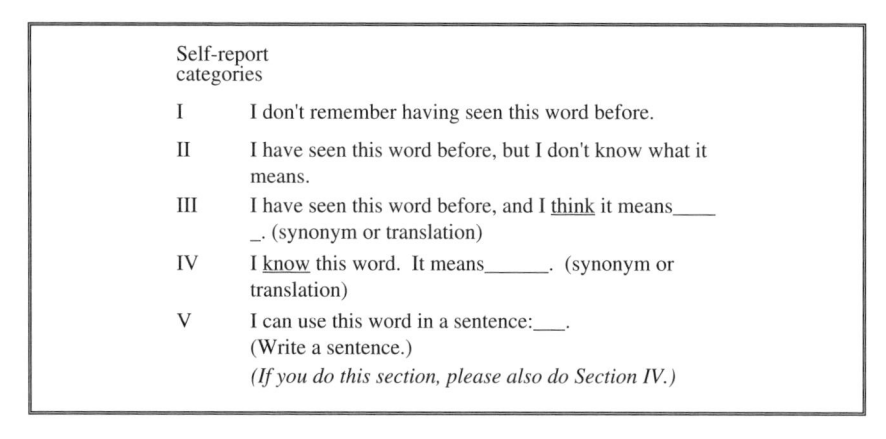

	Self-report categories	
	I	I don't remember having seen this word before.
	II	I have seen this word before, but I don't know what it means.
	III	I have seen this word before, and I <u>think</u> it means____ _. (synonym or translation)
	IV	I <u>know</u> this word. It means_____. (synonym or translation)
	V	I can use this word in a sentence:___. (Write a sentence.) *(If you do this section, please also do Section IV.)*

Figure 3.1 VKS elicitation scale: Self-report categories
Source: Paribakht and Wesche (1996: 178)

is then scored according to the scale in Figure 3.2. This combination of report and performance data leads to a scale ranking from 1 to 5 for each target word representing a range of knowledge from total unfamiliarity to the ability to use the word with semantic and syntactic accuracy in a sentence. The VKS has been shown to be sensitive enough to pick up incremental gains in the initial stages of learning particular words (Paribakht & Wesche, 1993, 1997)[3]; it also allows analysis of individual or grouped scoring categories for more specific information about what has been learned. In this study, information on new word-form recognition and word-meaning retention following the inferencing task were of particular interest. The first was reflected in movement from scoring level 1 to 2 from the first to the second VKS administration, and the second in movement from levels 1 or 2 to levels 3 to 5.

Target words and texts

Since one of the research questions in the study involved the effect on L2 inferencing of the 'lexicalization status' of the L2 target words (i.e. whether a given word has an equivalent word or phrase in the L1 of the given learner group, Persian and French),[4] the lists of target words for this part of the study comprised two word sets for each learner group. One set consisted of 25 words that are lexicalized (with single word or fixed phrase lexical equivalents) in the respective language, and the second set comprised 25 words that are not lexicalized, for a total of 50 target words for each learner group. It was not possible to have the

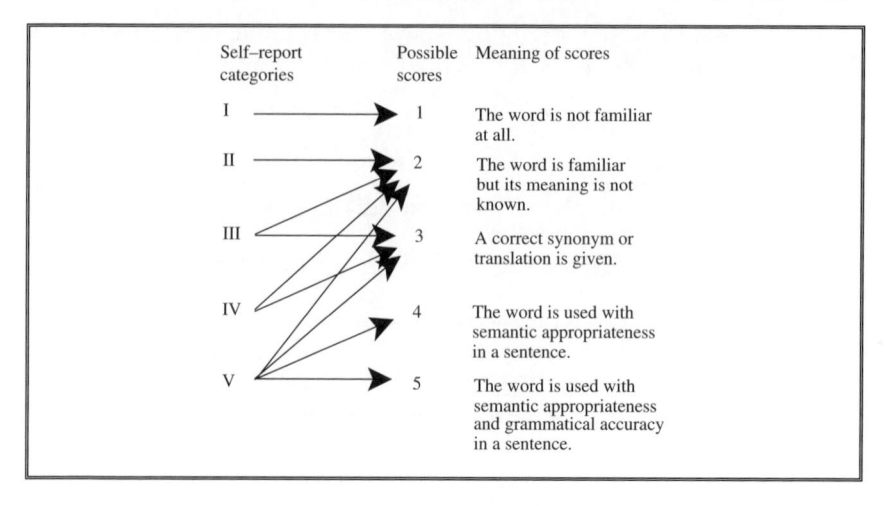

Self–report categories	Possible scores	Meaning of scores
I	1	The word is not familiar at all.
II	2	The word is familiar but its meaning is not known.
III	3	A correct synonym or translation is given.
IV	4	The word is used with semantic appropriateness in a sentence.
V	5	The word is used with semantic appropriateness and grammatical accuracy in a sentence.

Figure 3.2 VKS scoring categories: Meaning of scores
Source: Paribakht and Wesche (1996: 178)

same target words for both Persian and French speakers, since the English target words without lexical equivalents were different in each language. However, of the 50 words used for each L2 group, 15 were the same in the two sets (9 were lexicalized both in Persian and French, and 6 were not lexicalized in either Persian or French). See Appendix A for the list of these words and information on the common words.

In the selection of *non-lexicalized* words, two native speaker researchers, one from each language group, bilingual in English, compiled a list of words based on an extended, systematic search of written texts over a period of time, which they thought had no equivalents in their respective languages. These words were then checked against several English-Persian/French dictionaries, and other native speakers of each language were consulted. A list was then drawn up of words that represented concepts generally familiar to educated Persian or French speakers, but for which no lexical equivalents were found in the respective languages. Words that represent concepts unknown to unilingual participants (e.g. *snowshoes* for Persian speakers) were rejected, whereas concepts which could be paraphrased in L1, but for which single or compound lexical items do not exist in the respective language, were retained (e.g. *to elope, to indulge, proactive, prognosis, to stalk* for the Persian-speaking participants, and *to glimpse, to draft, bungling, spree* for the French speakers).[5]

Most words identified were nouns and verbs, while only a few were adverbs and adjectives. Thus, for each set of target words, lexicalized and non-lexicalized, a representation of each word type was sought, corresponding to the proportion in which these words were identified. Although adjectives and adverbs were limited in number, it was decided to retain them in the target word lists to provide a broader sample of word classes. The final list consisted of 10 nouns, 8 verbs, 4 adjectives and 3 adverbs in the lexicalized and non-lexicalized word lists, respectively.

The *lexicalized* target words were selected from established lists of words used in previous experimental research (Paribakht & Wesche, 1997). The lists consist of relatively infrequent words identified in English reading texts as being of medium to high difficulty for high-intermediate university ESL students. These words had been screened to remove French cognates, and the final selection had been made in consultation with experienced ESL instructors, and verified in a pilot study involving L2 learners whose reading proficiency was similar to that of the participants in the current study. The list of lexicalized words for each language group consisted of 25 words (e.g. *ambivalence, retroactively, deteriorating* and *to tackle* for the Persian speakers; *pawn, to thrive, giddy* and *warily* for the French speakers), representing the same four word classes (10 nouns, 8 verbs, 4 adjectives and 3 adverbs). The lexicalized and non-lexicalized target words were examined for their frequency in English (COBUILD Dictionary, 1995),[6] and the word lists were adapted as much as possible to represent similar frequencies. The 50 English target words were the same for Persian-speaking English as a foreign language (EFL) learners and English native speaker groups. Appendix B presents these target words and their relative frequency of occurrence in English.

The original target words were grouped thematically in mixed (lexicalized/non-lexicalized) sets and given to a native English-speaking writer to compose six short English general interest reading texts of approximately 200 words each, using 7 to 9 target words per text. Thus, target words represented 3% of the total words in each text. Our objective was to have texts where approximately 97% of the words were familiar to the participants, based on previous research indicating that a reader needs to know 95–98% of surrounding words to infer meanings for the others (Chapter 1). Table 3.2 provides a list of the topics of the texts used for eliciting lexical inferencing for each participant group.

The texts in which the target words were embedded provided semantically unambiguous and familiar contexts in which most or all

Table 3.2 Topics of English texts used for eliciting lexical inferencing

Groups	Topics
Persian speakers (L2)	1. Big City Dreams 2. Genetic Engineering 3. The Ice Age 4. Preserving the Environment 5. The World's Forgotten Poor 6. Marriage
English speakers (L1)	Same topics as above
French speakers (L2)	1. Human Clones 2. Human Rights 3. Global Warming 4. An Author's Life 5. Knowing the Future 6. Wedding and Marriage

other words were familiar to non-native speakers with high-intermediate reading proficiency. However, the presence of three to four non-lexicalized words in such short texts likely increased the difficulty of text comprehension beyond what it would have been with lexicalized unknown words. After editing by the researchers and other readers for clarity, difficulty level and appropriate target word context, the texts were formatted for the individual research sessions with the target words bolded, in large font, and printed one text to a page on plasticized sheets for data collection. See Appendix C for a sample text used with Persian-speaking participants with the target words in bold, and Appendix D for a sample text used with French-speaking participants.

L1 word sets

The same English texts were used for the English native speakers' L1 lexical inferencing task as for the Persian L2 readers, except that for the English speakers each target word was replaced by a pseudo word (since the original target words were already familiar to them).[7] Because they had the same texts and target words, this meant that the English speakers had a set of 50 target words. This matched and expanded data set allowed precise word-based comparisons of the L1 English and the L2 Persian data. For the Persian and French speakers' L1 inferencing tasks, a single, one-page, general interest L1 text aimed at educated adult readers was selected for each language group. The topic of the L1 Persian text

Conceptualization and Methodology

was 'The Meaning of the New Year's Celebration for Children', and of the L1 French text, 'Intuition'. Following selection of these texts, 25 target words (10 nouns, 8 verbs, 4 adjectives and 3 adverbs) were identified in each and replaced with pseudo words.

The pseudo target words were all possible words in the respective language, and were constructed to provide morphological and inflectional cues corresponding to those of the original L1 words, in order to give the native speakers access to the same range of KSs and cues at the *word* level as those available to the L2 readers from the original words. For example, the pseudo equivalent of *devastated*, *'beslocked'*, shares its past tense suffix. Appendix E presents one of the six English L1/Persian L2 texts, including the original target words (in bold) and their corresponding pseudo words (in parentheses). Appendix F provides the Persian L1 text with the original target words (in bold) and a list of their corresponding pseudo words (in parentheses). Appendix G presents the French L1 text and the respective original and pseudo target words.

Procedures

The data for the study were collected in four educational institutions in Canada and Iran over a period of approximately 10 months in 1999–2000. Introspective methods of data collection were used, involving individual research sessions for each participant with a researcher. Several days before the individual research sessions, the Persian and French participants attended group meetings to take Nation's (1990) *Vocabulary Levels Test*, and to fill out a questionnaire designed to elicit demographic information. Prior to the individual research sessions, small group orientation sessions were held to introduce the participants to the project and to provide training in think-aloud procedures. During the training session, the participants were first provided with a picture of a scene in a daily life situation and were asked to say whatever came to their mind by looking at the picture. This was followed by a task similar to the one used in the study, in which the participants were provided with a short text with several target words in bold and were asked to first read the paragraph quickly, then to read it again and try to guess the meanings of the target words. They were asked to 'think aloud' (in L1/L2 or both) about what they were thinking and doing while inferring the meanings of the words.

At the beginning of the individual research sessions for L2 speakers, the VKS was administered to gauge participants' initial level of knowledge of each target English word, presented in isolation. The overall research procedures for the reading and lexical inferencing task that followed were essentially the same for the participants in both L1 and L2, except that the English native speakers only did the L1 lexical inferencing task, while the Persian and French groups first completed the L2 task, followed by the L1 task. Thus, while in one session the English L1 speakers carried out only an L1 inferencing task, lasting approximately one hour, the L2 speakers completed the pre-task VKS, the L2 inferencing task, the post-task VKS and an L1 inferencing task. The L2 research task – English reading, inferencing and think-aloud – required approximately two hours for the learner groups, and the L1 inferencing task and VKS task for these participants required about an additional hour. No absolute time limit was set for completing either the inferencing tasks or the pre- and post-task VKS measures. This longer period of intensive work for the Persian and French speakers, involving multiple tasks in English, was demanding and likely tiring, and may have depressed their performance somewhat on the L1 inferencing and post-task VKS administration.

For the L2 inferencing task, the English texts were presented to the participants, one at a time and in the same order. The participants were asked to first read the text quickly for general comprehension and then to read it again and try to guess the meanings of the unknown target words[8] (indicated in bold font). They were also instructed to verbalize what they were thinking and doing while carrying out the task, and in the case of Persian and French speakers, to do this in their L1, English or both languages, according to their preference.[9] Two bilingual research assistants (one for Persian/English and one for French/English) conducted all the interviews. During the inferencing tasks, they prompted the participants as needed (without commenting on their performance or answering questions regarding the target words), intervening only to ensure that the participant continued self-reporting. They did not respond to any questions about the text or the target words or to requests to pronounce the words. They also avoided using words such as 'good', 'that's right' or any gestures or body language such as nodding in confirmation or indicating negation, or otherwise commenting on students' inferencing behavior, since that would have served as observer-induced clues to the participants. The interviewers took notes during the sessions on participants' responses related to each target word, and recorded anything remarkable about participants' non-verbal behavior as well as their own general observations. These notes were helpful in later transcript verification and interpretation. Following participants' completion of the L2 inferencing task, they completed the

Conceptualization and Methodology

VKS a second time, as a measure of immediate gains in their knowledge of the target words.[10] All inferencing tasks, including think-aloud responses and the research assistants' interventions were audio tape recorded.

Data Analyses

The tape recordings were transcribed and verified for accuracy. Analyses were then carried out for each participant and each target word (L1/L2) to determine

- whether he or she had attempted to infer a meaning for a target word;
- the KSs or contextual cues called upon in the process;
- if multiple sources were used, their sequence and whether the inferred meaning was contextually appropriate.

In the qualitative analysis of the data, the goal was to identify all indicated kinds of knowledge and contextual cues that the participants had used in trying to arrive at a meaning for each target word. For each L2 data set (Persian and French), a bilingual researcher and a trained research assistant carried out the transcription analysis. This involved reading each transcript multiple times to extract the above information and other participant and researcher comments relevant to the inferencing process. The types of KSs/contextual cues used by the participants in the inferencing process were identified and color coded. For this process, we referred to earlier classification systems and developed a taxonomy for KS use by Persian speakers inferencing in English (Paribakht, 2005). As the analyses progressed, several new KS types were identified for other data sets (see Paribakht & Wesche, 2006 and Paribakht & Tréville, 2007 for versions of the taxonomy developed at subsequent stages of data analysis). The adapted trilingual study taxonomy presented in this volume includes all KS types used in L1 and L2 lexical inferencing by participants from all three language groups.

Following the KS identification process, tabulations were made of the relative frequency with which participants used different KS sub-types and of the sequence of KS use when more than one KS was reported.

Each participant's transcript was also analyzed to determine whether the participant attempted to infer the meaning of each target word, and whether that inference was fully successful (correct), partially successful (approximate or partially correct meaning was given) or completely unsuccessful. The scoring system for success was as follows:

- 'full success': 2 points were awarded if the response was both semantically and syntactically appropriate;
- 'partial success': 1 point was awarded if an approximate meaning was inferred, or if the inferred word was semantically accurate but not syntactically appropriate (e.g. a noun instead of a verb or adjective was given);
- 'failure': zero was given if the participant provided a wrong meaning or gave up.

Examples of 'partial success' from the Persian L2 data are presented below.

(1) Topic *'Marriage'*; Target word: *slam*
'To [**slam**] the door means (close the door). It says *the couples who walk out of the room and [slam] the door'*.
(2) Topic *'The Ice Age'*; Target word: *sleet*
'[**Sleet**] should be (hail) because it has given the examples of rain and snow and has separated them with commas; this must be from the same family'.

Success scores for each participant were calculated from the scores for each item attempted, including separate scores for fully successful and for partially successful responses, calculated for total target words as well as separately for lexicalized and non-lexicalized target words, and a total (weighted) success score (the sum of weighted full and partial success scores).

Detailed data sheets were prepared for all participants in each condition, including measures for each individual and for each word, and by inferencing condition (language group; L1 or L2). This allowed subsequent analysis and tracking in the transcripts of examples of individual words and of individual and within-group differences in inferencing behavior. Descriptions and comparisons were then generated for each research question using the pertinent measures.

Notes

1. Persian is an Iranian language within the Indo-Iranian branch of the Indo-European language family. It is spoken mainly in Iran, Afghanistan and Tajikistan. 'Farsi' is the local name for Persian in Iran, and is also found in some linguistic literature in English by both Iranian and foreign authors. However, 'Persian' is more widely used in English. The Academy of Persian

Language and Literature officially supports the use of 'Persian' as more appropriate, due to its longer tradition in western languages and as a mark of cultural and national continuity.

Iranian Persian is normally written using a modified variant of the Arabic alphabet (Perso-Arabic script) with different pronunciation and more letters. It has 23 consonants and 6 vowels, only 3 of which are represented in Persian orthography.

Persian makes extensive use of word building and derivational agglutination to form new words from nouns, adjectives and verbal stems and affixes. New words are extensively formed by compounding two existing words into a new one.

2. Persian-speaking participants had equal numbers of males and females, but were heterogeneous in their age (10: 18–25; 4: 26–34; 6: 35 and above). French speakers were mostly female (14 female and 6 male), and more homogenous in their age (4 were 17 and the remaining were between 18 and 25).
3. The VKS was first developed in 1993 to track L2 learners' vocabulary knowledge gains in a comprehension-based ESL program at the Second Language Institute (now Official Languages and Bilingualism Institute) of the University of Ottawa. The instrument was subsequently refined and used in several follow-up studies (Paribakht & Wesche, 1996, 1997; Wesche & Paribakht, 1996).
For a discussion of the reliability and validity of the VKS, see Wesche and Paribakht (1996).
4. Lexical phrases are stored and retrieved from memory as if they were single word lexical units, e.g. phrasal verbs such as 'to run into' or 'come across', discourse markers such as 'on the other hand', 'as a result' and 'in conclusion' (see Nattinger & DeCarrico, 1992; Wray & Perkins, 2000; Wray, 2002).
5. In the past few years, borrowings or equivalents for a few of these words have appeared, e.g. 'to clone' in Persian. However, at the time of the data gathering (even today), the coined equivalents were not commonly known or widely used by educated Persian speakers.
6. COBUILD's (1995) word frequency categorization system has five levels of which the target words represent the three lowest frequency bands.
* least frequent (approximately 8100 words)
(10 non-lexicalized and 8 lexicalized items)
** low frequency (approximately 3200 words)
(six non-lexicalized and nine lexicalized items)
*** intermediate frequency
(three non-lexicalized and five lexicalized items)
Not specified in COBUILD
(five non-lexicalized and three lexicalized items)
7. The alternative to using pseudo words is to use very infrequent or technical words, in which case the texts would be very technical. However, the use of the same texts with pseudo words allows providing the target words with the same surrounding and within word cues to both native-speaking and non-native-speaking participants.
8. The ratio of known to unknown words in each passage was different for each participant. This was not, however, a concern in the study, as the focus of the research was to compare the way the participants inferred the meanings of

unfamiliar lexicalized and non-lexicalized target words, and the ratio of known to unknown words in each passage was the same for each participant when inferring either a lexicalized or a non-lexicalized target word (i.e. the ratio of known to unknown words would have affected the inferencing process for the two word sets for each individual in the same way).
9. Think-aloud procedures, which elicit information about the conscious cognitive processes involved in lexical inferencing, can be linguistically demanding for L2 speakers if done in the L2. Permitting the participants to use the language(s) of their choice and to switch between them as needed, alleviates this burden and allows them to more accurately and fully report their thinking processes than would requiring them to use one language or the other. This would also allow them to compensate for memory lags in retrieving a word in either language or when a word does not exist in one of the languages.
10. To measure long-term retention of the features of the target words, including form familiarity only, the VKS should be administered after some elapsed time. Due to short-term access to the participants, delayed testing was unfortunately not feasible in the context of this study.

Chapter 4
First Language Influences on Knowledge Source Use in Second Language Lexical Inferencing

This chapter presents a comparative analysis of the use of different linguistic and non-linguistic knowledge sources (KSs) in first language (L1) and second language (L2) lexical inferencing from written texts, by the English, Persian and French speakers in our study. As an approach to exploring L1 influences on L2 lexical inferencing, we sought first to determine shared aspects of KS use in lexical inferencing by L1 speakers of these three Indo-European languages, as well whether these shared L1 patterns also held for L2 inferencing. We then identified KS use patterns that differentiated L2 inferencing in English from L1 inferencing by the Persian, French and English speakers. We also explored KS use in inferring meanings for L2 words with lexical equivalents in the respective readers' L1 versus those without equivalents. The core issue of L1 influence on readers' L2 lexical inferencing was approached through a detailed analysis of KS use by speakers of Persian and French in both their L1 and in English (L2). Within-group L1 and L2 similarities, as distinguished from the other language groups' patterns, were viewed as an indication of possible L1 transfer – whether from readers' L1 linguistic knowledge or accustomed processing patterns. Finally, an analysis of lexical inferencing by the three groups in English, i.e. English L1 readers as well as Persian and French L2 readers, identified shared patterns of KS use across all three groups that did not correspond to the previously identified more 'universal' patterns. Such patterns were interpreted as a probable English text language influence in L2 inferencing.

Of primary interest in this investigation were the nature and the importance of L1 linguistic influences on readers' use of textual cues and background knowledge in L2 lexical inferencing in English. Where relevant, language-related cultural – including instructional – influences were also identified. Our approach to the study of L1 transfer in L2 lexical inferencing with respect to KS use also provided information about shared cross-linguistic KS use patterns, as well as the role of readers' proficiency in the text language and that of text language characteristics. As a supplement to these main analyses, the influence of target word class on KS use was also explored.

Issues

Shared processing tendencies across languages

The null hypothesis in cross-linguistic studies of lexical inferencing would be that, given the shared characteristics of all human languages, all readers – whatever their language or the text language – would approach this process in the same way. However, it is known that differences across human languages and related experience in one's native language influence L2 acquisition and performance. Of interest here is the extent to which the processing tendencies and kinds of knowledge readers from different L1 backgrounds use in generating L2 lexical inferences while reading are shared across different Indo-European languages and to what extent they appear to be language specific.[1]

Sources of difference between first and second language lexical inferencing

Relatively little is known about differences between L1 and L2 lexical inferencing, either in terms of how L1 and L2 readers generally differ in their behavior and outcomes, or how a given L1 might influence the way a reader would go about inferring the meaning of an unfamiliar word in a given L2 (here, English) and the linguistic and other knowledge resources he/she would bring to it. In this study, we have dealt with both of these aspects of L1 and L2 inferencing, the first having to do with 'nativeness' versus 'non-nativeness' in terms of linguistic proficiency and cultural knowledge as these operate across languages, and the second, the central issue here, with the nature of inter-lingual transfer from two different L1s to English (L2) inferencing behavior. Comparisons of L1 inferencing across three languages and of L2 inferencing by speakers of two distantly related L1s help sort out the effects of reader proficiency in the text language from those involving the influence of their L1.

Why study knowledge sources in lexical inferencing?

The study of KS use tells us how readers use different kinds of textual cues and their previous knowledge interactively in lexical inferencing. KS use involves both their procedural and declarative knowledge of the text language – and to some extent of the L1 and other languages – as well as relevant conceptual knowledge. Together these different kinds of knowledge underlie readers' ability to access and successfully utilize available textual information in arriving at appropriate meanings for unfamiliar words encountered in written texts. The KSs that they use also reveal what kinds of knowledge and information are needed to arrive at the meaning of a given word in a text. In this sense, KSs are indicative of the nature and properties of lexical knowledge.

The role of readers' language proficiency in lexical inferencing success and knowledge source use

Readers' ability to infer appropriate meanings for unfamiliar words is demonstrably related to their proficiency in the text language. More versus less proficiency confers an advantage within groups of L2 users and even among native speakers; thus it should not be surprising that quite advanced L2 users still tend to be far less successful than native speakers at similar educational levels when inferencing in a given language.

Research with L2 learners indicates that measures of L2 lexical knowledge, themselves highly correlated with measures of overall language proficiency and reading proficiency, are the strongest predictors of successful L2 lexical inferencing. In addition to knowing word meanings, other kinds of word knowledge are important (see Chapter 1). These include different aspects of a user's knowledge of a word, such as its syntactic behavior, its core and other meanings, its likelihood of occurrence overall and in specific contexts or registers, its co-occurrence with certain other words, its inflected forms in different word classes and its relationship to words in other known languages. These other aspects of word knowledge have been variably referred to in the literature by several terms, including 'depth' (which has also been used as an indication of how well a word is known), 'network knowledge' and 'lexical organization' (see Chapter 1; Henriksen, 1999, 2008; Read, 1993, 1998; Wesche & Paribakht, 1996). These and other features indicate the multiple networks by which it is associated with other words in the mental lexicon. It is these multiple associations that come into play in the identification and use of helpful KSs during lexical inferencing, just as they do in other kinds of language processing. In language processing, readers use their knowledge of the target language and other languages as well as other linguistic and world knowledge, as associations at all levels of linguistic organization are triggered by cues in the L2 text. Most of this knowledge, however, is at best only partially or indirectly tapped by existing tests of lexical knowledge. Lexical networks in an L1 tend to be richer and more complex than in an L2. As Meara (1996: 49) has noted, 'in general, L2 words have a smaller number of shared associations than would be the case in an L1 lexicon'.

First language transfer effects in second language lexical inferencing

Evidence of L1 influences on L2 performance has been found at all levels of language organization and in different kinds of language processing, such as reading and lexical inferencing from written texts (see Chapter 2). However, little is known about the nature of what is transferred across specific pairs of languages in lexical inferencing. Studies of L2 reading suggest that procedural as well as knowledge aspects of inferencing are involved. 'Cross-linguistic studies on sentence processing, for example, consistently show that the cognitive procedures involved in sentence comprehension and production are heavily constrained by the particular syntactic properties inherent in each language' (Koda, 2005: 14).

The present study bears on transfer of both L1 procedural knowledge and L1 declarative linguistic as well as related general knowledge as these influence L2 inferencing behavior. Successful inferencing involves a reader's search for and identification of textual cues relevant to the word meaning sought and use of relevant prior knowledge in generating appropriate guesses, followed by evaluation of these guesses in context, which in turn may lead to revision and new meanings to be vetted. As with other complex, highly contextualized procedures, the ability to infer word meanings is developed over time through practice in relevant contexts of use. L2 speakers, who have a lifetime of accumulated experience inferencing in their L1 in both oral and written contexts, may tend to over-rely in the L2 on internalized procedures that work well in their L1. For example, researchers have identified Persian (L1) to English (L2) transfer effects in reading related to the different directionality of the two writing systems (Ghahremani-Gajar & Masny, 1999), concluding that eye movement differences likely slow down L2 reading, which may negatively affect text comprehension. Such an effect would, in turn, impact lexical inferencing success. It is also reasonable to expect L1 influence in terms of the types of cues (or KSs) that speakers of a given L1 are more likely to seek in L2 inferencing, some of which may prove less useful in the L2 text language than in the L1.

With respect to the processing and acquisition of L2 linguistic features, the typological distance of the L2 from the L1 has been shown to influence language transfer in many areas, and similar effects would be expected in L2 lexical inferencing. For example, the lesser typological distance between French and English than between Persian and English would lead one to expect greater L1 transfer among speakers of French. Haastrup (1991a), in her study of Danish learners of English, recorded evidence of their frequent recourse to L1 sources in L2 inferencing, relating this to the fact that native Danish speakers rightly perceive the two Germanic languages to be closely related. French and English likewise share the same alphabet and many aspects of their writing systems, multiple morphological correspondences and omnipresent cognates. Persian shares none of these features with English. Furthermore, Persian script is written from right to left, and while it is phonologically based, not all vowel sounds are represented in writing, so that many words must actually be identified before they can be pronounced with certainty. For these reasons, one might expect Persian L1 readers to refer less than French L1 readers to *word* level cues such as orthographic form or morphology. They would then need to depend more on cues available at the *sentence* and *discourse* levels. In this study, we are interested in knowing whether such differences are shown by Persian versus French readers not only in L1, but also when inferring word meanings in English (L2).

It is clear that L1-related cultural knowledge also influences L2 reading comprehension and text processing (Carrell, 1993); however, it is difficult to sort out cultural from linguistic influences on inferencing behavior because typological proximity tends, for historical reasons, to overlap with cultural congruence and typological distance with greater cultural differences. One line of evidence for the claim that readers' familiarity with specific, often culturally bound concepts supports successful lexical inferencing comes from lexicalization studies. Paribakht's (2005) analyses of lexicalization effects on inferencing by the Persian-speaking readers in the trilingual study showed a high facilitation effect for unfamiliar English words that had lexical equivalents (and thus presumably greater cultural relevance) in Persian versus those that did not. In her study, the relatively low success rate of Persian speakers even for lexicalized words was probably at least partially due to their relative lack of cultural/conceptual familiarity with topics and perspectives in the English texts as well as to linguistic differences. In their comparative analysis of the Persian and French speakers' inferencing while reading in English, Paribakht and Tréville (2007) explained the notably greater success of the French speakers, despite similar English reading proficiency test scores to those of Persian speakers, in terms of the multiple cognates and many shared linguistic features between French and English, as well as the more similar cultural traditions of their speakers. These cross-lingual similarities were seen as offering cumulative support to the L2 reader, facilitating overall text comprehension and providing more background for the task of inferring particular word meanings. We consider these issues in more detail in the analyses reported below.

Multiple knowledge source use

While readers' overall patterns of KS use may be indicative of L1, text language and other influences on lexical inferencing, we have also considered their use of single versus multiple KSs to arrive at an inferred meaning. A single KS may not provide sufficient information for readers to retrieve or construct a plausible meaning for an unfamiliar word in context, leading to the use of further cues and knowledge before formulation of a guess. Even if a single cue leads to a guess, other information may be needed to verify or to refine this guess. When KSs are used in combination, some may tend to be reported first and others later, illuminating how different kinds of knowledge are used in lexical inferencing. For example, patterns of *initial* use of certain kinds of cues may reflect where readers seek and expect to find useful information, while the tendency to use certain KSs *post-initially* may signal their role in confirmation or refinement of inferences, providing further insight into how different kinds of knowledge are used in lexical inferencing. Seldom used KSs – such as cues to register, the writer's style or discourse schemata – may be more difficult to access and use, as well as restricted in their usefulness to target words or text segments that have particular characteristics.

One would expect proficiency to play an important but complex role in multiple KS use. Since many interacting factors are involved, the number of KSs readers use are not likely to correlate per se with their proficiency. L2 readers may often have a greater need than L1 readers to use additional cues to help them generate a plausible guess, but, on the other hand, are less likely to be able to recognize and use them efficiently. L1 readers who are capable of accessing additional KSs may have already reached an adequate guess with the first one. While they may use additional cues to verify or refine a guess, especially when there are several obvious possibilities, they don't necessarily do so. Multiple cue use patterns may also differ across languages, depending on the linguistic characteristics of written texts; thus the use in L2 inferencing of single versus multiple KSs and their sequence may reflect transfer from L1 processing.

Haastrup (1991a, 2007, personal communication) relates the way multiple cues are combined to the 'quality' of readers' KS use. For example, in cases where different kinds of cues suggest different meanings, the reader decides which kind of information is most crucial to his or her final guess. She emphasizes that while lower-level linguistic cues from the text may offer precise hypotheses about meaning, the discourse context and general world knowledge must always be considered by the reader if inferences are to be contextually appropriate. In terms of gauging given readers' inferencing ability, the availability of useful cues in the text should be taken into account in judging the quality of a guess, as well as their flexibility in taking advantage of what is there (Albrechtsen *et al.*, 2008).

Target word features

The guessability of an unfamiliar word meaning also depends on features of the word itself, in addition to factors of readers' proficiency, their familiarity with relevant concepts and their transfer of L1 procedural and linguistic knowledge. These features include the word's frequency of occurrence, which conditions the likelihood that L2 readers will have been exposed to it previously and have some (even subliminal) familiarity with its phonological or written form or meaning associations. Some words will be inherently more difficult to infer meanings for than others, for example, function words such as prepositions and discourse connectors, which while frequent, often lack clear semantic referents (Paribakht & Wesche, 1993). Word class may play a role: the nature and number of cues available for inferring a word's meaning (e.g. inflections, information from the sentence or discourse context) are related to its class. Adverbs are likely to have fewer and less specific meaning-oriented textual cues than nouns; they also relate to verbs. For their part, verbs offer specific tense and number cues, and like nouns also tend to have multiple semantic and associational links to the text's larger context of meaning. We have therefore included an initial exploration of relationships between target word class and readers' KS use patterns in this study.

Methodology

As described in detail in Chapter 3, the inferencing behavior of three groups of post-secondary students representing different L1s was studied, including their KS use. All three groups – speakers of English, Persian and French, carried out inferencing tasks in their respective L1s and the Persian and French speakers also carried out inferencing tasks in English, their L2. During task completion in individual research sessions, participants described aloud what they were doing and thinking, with occasional prompts from the researcher. These introspective verbal reports were tape recorded and transcribed, as were retrospective interviews at the end of the research session. The study of KS use reported in this chapter was based on transcripts of both kinds of reports.

Relationships among the three languages

As discussed in Chapter 3, Persian and French were chosen for this study of cross-lingual influences on lexical inferencing as Indo-European languages accessible to the researchers that represent close versus distant typological relationships with English as well as many differences from one another. For these reasons, this cross-linguistic study of speakers of two languages performing in the L1 and in English (L2) offers the possibility of distinguishing L1 transfer from other potential influences on L2 lexical inferencing.

Participants

The participants were 20 English-speaking university undergraduates in Ontario, Canada, 20 Persian-speaking undergraduate university students majoring in English at several universities in Iran, and 20 French-speaking post-secondary students at a post-grade 11 college (CEGEP) in Quebec, Canada. The Persian and French speaking groups had similar high-intermediate scores on the *English Reading Comprehension Test* used for English as a second language (ESL) course placement at the University of Ottawa; however, the two groups differed with respect to several demographic criteria and their English learning contexts. Both groups of English learners might be described as functionally bilingual readers. In contrast, the English-speaking participants reported having only minimal if any knowledge of a second language.[2] (Further details are given in Chapter 3.)

Data

The primary data for describing readers' KS use were the written transcripts of think-aloud protocols recorded while participants carried out elicited lexical inferencing of target words embedded in written texts. The resulting five data sets, three for L1 inferencing (in English, Persian and French) and two for L2 inferencing (in English by the Persian and French speakers) are derived from parallel tasks involving selected target words in each language embedded in short general interest texts. The L1 words selected as target items were replaced with pseudo words. The Persian L1 and French L1 tasks each involved 25 target words, while the L2 tasks involved 50 target words, 15 of which were the same, including 25 with lexical equivalents in the readers' L1 and 25 without such equivalents. The English L1 participants read the same texts as the Persian speakers, with pseudo equivalents for the 50 target words. Participants carried out the inferencing and think-aloud tasks in individual research sessions. Subsequently, each participant's think-aloud transcript for each target word was analyzed to determine which KSs he or she had reported using, as well as the sequences of multiple KSs. The KSs were initially classified based on an earlier taxonomy (Paribakht, 2005). This was then adapted to include all KS types used by participants from the three groups in either L1 or L2, thus providing a framework for comparing them. (See Chapter 3 for details on tasks and data collection.)

Expectations and empirical approach

Our general expectations in the study were that there would be some common patterns of KS use across all L1 sets and possibly across both L2 data sets as well, indicating shared cross-linguistic processing tendencies in lexical inferencing from written texts that might extend to many other languages. We also anticipated that general L1 versus L2 differences would apply to both Persian and French speakers' L2 inferencing due to their lower proficiency in English. Finally, we expected to find evidence of L1 transfer in L2 inferencing by the Persian and French speakers in shared patterns of KS use in Persian L1 and L2 inferencing, as distinguished from shared patterns in French L1 and L2 inferencing. At the same time, we expected that KS use by these two groups of speakers reading in their L2, English, would also to some extent correspond to characteristics of L1 KS use patterns of English L1 speakers, reflecting an influence of the text language on lexical inferencing. The English L1 and L2 comparisons might also provide an indication of what these (and other) young adult English learners may still need to know in order to become more efficient in lexical inferencing and as readers of English.

Findings

Taxonomies of knowledge source use in lexical inferencing

Overall, categorization systems and descriptions of the diverse types of KSs that readers use in lexical inferencing reveal the different kinds of textual information and knowledge that learners draw upon when trying to comprehend unfamiliar words. The categories themselves reflect the types of knowledge about words that these language users have, while actual cues and information that they use with given words reveal how declarative linguistic and world knowledge is used in lexical inferencing. Over the past decade, we and others have developed descriptive taxonomies of KSs used in lexical inferencing by L2 readers of English in our studies, including speakers from mixed L1 backgrounds (Paribakht & Wesche, 1999), Arabic speakers (Bengeleil & Paribakht, 2004), Persian speakers (Paribakht, 2005) and French speakers (Paribakht & Tréville, 2007). Paribakht and Tréville's taxonomy has been extended here to include findings regarding KS use by the L1 readers of Persian, French and English.

The trilingual study taxonomy presented in Figure 4.1 reflects all the KSs identified in the transcripts of think-aloud comments reported by L1 readers of English, Persian and French, and the same Persian and French speakers reading in English (L2) while carrying out lexical inferencing tasks based on written texts. It constitutes part of our findings in that it provides an overall report of the KSs used in L1 and L2 lexical inferencing by all three participant groups in this study. At the same time, it serves as a tool for exploring and presenting similarities and differences in KS use from the five data sets. The taxonomy is organized according to three major hierarchical categories of written language – *word*, *sentence* and *discourse* – depending upon whether the cues are found in the target word itself, within the same sentence as the word or beyond the sentence boundaries. A fourth main category is *non-linguistic (world) knowledge*.[3] Each of the main linguistic categories includes three or four sub-categories of cue types. Most of the linguistic KSs reported in this study were based on readers' text language knowledge, but in L2 inferencing, some were also from L1 associations, as found in other studies.

First Language Influences on Knowledge Source Use　　　　　　　　　　77

Linguistic Sources

L2-based sources
- **Word Knowledge**
  - *Word Association:* Association of the target word with another familiar word or a network of words.
  - *Word Collocation:* Knowledge of words that frequently occur with the target word.
  Word Morphology: Morphological analysis of the target word based on knowledge of grammatical inflections, stem and affixes.
  - *Word Form (written):* Knowledge of formal (orthographic or phonetic) similarity between the target word, or a part of it, and another word and mistaking the target word for another word resembling it.
- **Sentence Knowledge**
  - *Sentence Meaning:* The meaning of part or all of the sentence containing the target word.
  - *Sentence Grammar:* Knowledge of the syntactic properties of the target word, its speech part and word order constraints.
  - *Punctuation:* Knowledge of rules of punctuation and their significance.
- **Discourse Knowledge**
  - *Discourse Meaning:* The perceived general meaning of the text and sentences surrounding the target word (i.e. beyond the immediate sentence that contains the target word).
  - *Formal Schemata:* Knowledge of the macro structure of the text, text types and discourse patterns and organization.
  - *Text Style & Register:* Knowledge of stylistic and register variations in word choice.

L1-based sources
- **L1 Collocation**
  Knowledge of words in L1 that have collocational relationship with the L1 equivalent of the target word, assuming that the same relationship exists in the target language.
- **L1 Word Form**
  Knowledge of formal (orthographic or phonetic) similarity between the target word or a part of it and a L1 word.

Non-Linguistic Source
- **World Knowledge**
  Non-linguistic knowledge, including knowledge of the topic of the text and other related background knowledge.

Figure 4.1 Trilingual study taxonomy of KS use in L1 and L2 lexical inferencing

Knowledge source use in the trilingual study

All main taxonomic categories of *linguistic* KSs in the text language (i.e. *word, sentence* and *discourse* cues) as well as *non-linguistic* knowledge, were used by all participants from each language group in both L1 and L2 inferencing, as were most sub-categories within each *linguistic* category. Examples of each type of KS from representative student transcripts are provided in Figure 4.2. Persian and French speakers inferencing in their L2 (English) also reported using certain linguistic KSs from their L1 (see below), although L1 sources represented only a small proportion of KSs reported by either group and occurred only at the *word* level. With respect to KS sub-types, the only types not reported in one or more data sets were *word association*, never used by Persian L1 speakers, and *style/register*, never used by French L1 speakers nor by either Persian or French speakers reading in their L2 (English). These sub-types were also relatively infrequent in the other conditions.

This taxonomy provides a comprehensive categorization of the types of KSs used in lexical inferencing that is applicable to at least these three Indo-European languages for both native and high-intermediate L2 readers. Based on the taxonomy, this study has revealed a number of striking differences in the frequency of use of different KS types by L1 readers of the three languages, L2 readers with different native languages and L1 versus L2 speakers in general.

"Big City Dreams" (L1 English data)
Target word (pseudo): roshies (masterpieces)
word collocation, sentence meaning
P: (masterpieces) Obviously, everybody.... galleries where great (works) are displayed or attending concerts ... artists. Great (works) is just a standard phrase in English, so, that's why I assumed *roshies* are probably (works), pieces of art,
I: So then, previous words helped you guess?
P: Oh yes, the art galleries, when you are in the art galleries, museums, they say it is great (works), great pieces of art, something like that.

"Knowing the Future" (L2 French data)
Target word: craze
Sentence meaning
P: I didn't know what [**craze**] meant, but with the rest of the sentence, I think ... I'm just going to reread the phrase; ... it's (something that one believes deep down)

"How to make the New Year more memorable" (L1 Persian data)
Target word (pseudo): tashvir migardad (is provided)

Figure 4.2 Examples of KSs from transcripts of English, French and Persian speakers reading L1 and L2 texts

Sentence meaning
P: Wearing new, beautiful clothes that usually parents (provide) for them.
I: Why do you think it means 'provide'?
P: Considering the sentence that says someone else, their parents, (provide) it for them.

"Big City Dreams" (L2 Persian data)
Target word: indulge
Sentence meaning
P: I've read and heard the word [**indulge**] before but can't remember what it means…considering the sentence I guess it means (order). When guests or customers feel like having chocolate, they'll order it or they'll eat it. I am not sure.

"The Ice Age" (L1 English data)
Target word (pseudo): plish (sleet)
Word association, sentence grammar
P: (sleet) The next being *influenced* … *continually*. I just assumed by association with rain and snow, this would be (sleet), or (slush). It's another noun.

"How to make the New Year more memorable" (L1 Persian data)
Target word (pseudo): beshkalaanand (to offer)
Sentence grammar
P: It should read: *to* (show) *to their grandparents and grandmothers*. I guessed it from the verb.
I: From which one of the verbs?
P: Because there's a verb missing here, it's obvious that it must be a verb.

"Genetic Engineering" (L2 Persian data)
Target word: genocide
word morphology
P: [**genocide**] I think it means …. If we parsed it, it'd mean (to kill a generation).
I: How would you parse it?
P: *geno* means gene and generation, and *cide* means to kill. So [**genocide**] should probably mean (to kill a generation).

Figure 4.2 (*Continued*)

"Global Warming" (L2 French data)
Target word: decay
Word morphology
P: [**decay**] There's the word "dec"; it's an abbreviation, like oct" for eight....that would be ten years.

"The Ice Age" (L1 English data)
Target word (pseudo): filted (stalked)
word morphology
P: (stalked) *As the ice advanced ...larger animals* (hunted) *smaller ones...* (ate ...searched for, digested) ...it could be a number of things, but (hunted) because it's already past tense, "ed", just from that word's structure ...as opposed to (ate).

"Big City Dreams" (L1 English data)
Target word (pseudo): senclorated (sophisticated)
word form
P: (sophisticated) It was the ending of the word I guess, "ated".
I thought (decorated) right away. It's not used that often that way in English, but you are (decorated) if you are rich people wearing fur coats, that kind of thing.

"Knowing the Future" (L2 French data)
Target word: craze
L1 word form
P: [**craze**] That makes me think of the word "crise"... maybe because it means the rumours that were going around about the year 2000.

"The Ice Age" (L1 English data)
Target word (pseudo): vishel (layer)
sentence grammar, world knowledge
P: (layer) The next line would be *the melting ... soil*. I assumed that to be (layer), just by the structure of the sentence, *thick* being the adjective describing something. So I thought that would be (layer). And soil is formation of (layers).

Figure 4.2 (*Continued*)

First Language Influences on Knowledge Source Use 81

"Human Rights" (L2 French data)
Target word: plight
sentence grammar
P: [**plight**], It's as if it were a verb or something that I wouldn't understand. Well, it's not a verb because there's an article in front of it. (It's a name of something).

"The Ice Age" (L2 Persian data)
Target word: bleak
discourse meaning
P: [**bleak**] The only guess that I can make, for example, meaning (grim, pale .... desolate)
I: What helped you to make such a guess?
P: The sentence just before it reads *the millions of people who .... the continent were absent*, the words *were absent* .... and *have appeared rather bleak*, it seems as if it must be (desolate).

"Big City Dreams" (L1 English data)
Target word (pseudo): senclorated (sophisticated)
discourse meaning
P: (sophisticated) *senclorated people walking down busy streets;* (glamourous) people probably, just by the context of cities and celebrities, and the rich people.

"How to make the New Year more memorable" (L1 Persian data)
Target word (pseudo): raatekh (trivial/unimportant)
discourse meaning
P: (simple) points; I think 'these simple points' is correct because in several other places in the text the author referred to 'simple actions' such as changing the furniture, etc.

"Preserving our Environment" (L2 Persian data)
Target word: proactive
L1 word collocation
P: I think [**proactive**] means (exact); exact measurements. With measurements often such adjectives are used.

Figure 4.2 (*Continued*)

I: Why did you make this guess? P: With the word [measurement] they often use (exact, exact) measurements. I've often heard it this way. In Persian, and in English texts, too. ...This is the adjective that can be used.
"Human Clones" (L2 French data) Target word: withstand **formal schemata** P: [**withstand**]. The sentence is long; it takes up three lines. Two... in all, two propositions, plus you have a discourse connective, *however*, and another after that: *even if*.
"How to make the New Year more memorable" (L1 Persian data) Target word (pseudo): zhang (effort) **formal schemata** P: I'd take the word to be (therefore) or (then) because it wants to make a conclusion in its argument made about the points. Here we use the words (therefore) or (then), saying, *Therefore, to brighten up family members...*
"Weddings and Marriage" (L2 French data) Target word: giddy **punctuation** P: [**giddy**] It's between commas... that means that one can remove it ....the part between commas, it's (for describing the situation a little bit)
"Human Rights" (L2 French data) Target word: retaliation **world knowledge** P: [**retaliation**], I've already seen the word elsewhere because I play video games and I have a video with that name.
"Marriage" (L1 English data) Target word (pseudo): slatilance (annoyance) **world knowledge**

Figure 4.2 (*Continued*)

First Language Influences on Knowledge Source Use 83

P: (annoyance). *To the* (resentment) *of many couples their parents may insist upon running every detail of the wedding.* I just thought how it would be like if my parents decided to step in and run every step of my wedding, I would...(resent) the fact that they were trying to control me.
"L'intuition" (L1 French data)   Target word (pseudo): *dépenaissent (reconnaissent = famous)*   **world knowledge**   P: **dépenaissent** (admit, say, declare) possibly because I know that intuition helps a lot in making discoveries.
"How to make the New Year more memorable" (L1 Persian data)   Target word (pseudo): *miparaashad (teaches)*   **style and register**   P: *and* (teaches) *them.*   I: What made you think of this word?   P: It's really a matter of personal taste which word is best here; (teaches) *them that giving is better than receiving.* Of course, we could put other words here too: *to* (make them understand) *that...*   I: Why do you think we could also put 'to make them understand' here?   P: In fact, it shouldn't be (teaches) them, because this word has already been used in this sentence just before this word. It should be: (it makes them understand).

Transcription conventions P = participant, I = interviewer Normal font = translation of utterances from Persian or French to English or English L1 utterances [**Bold face**] = target words (actual and pseudo) *Italics* = words/phrases read from the text	[ ] = words spoken in English by Persian or French speakers ( ) = the inferred meaning(s) .... = pause ... = missing text ***Bold face italics***: knowledge source

Figure 4.2 (*Continued*)

Findings from the analyses of KS use by speakers of the three languages inferencing in L1 and L2 are organized around four issues:

(1) Cross-linguistic KS use patterns that may reflect widely shared processing tendencies across L1 lexical inferencing as well as L2 lexical inferencing, including shared KS use patterns in L1 inferencing across all three languages (English, Persian and French speakers) and shared KS use patterns in L1 and L2 inferencing in English (Persian or French speakers).
(2) KS use patterns that distinguish L1 from L2 inferencing and hold for both Persian and French speakers' inferencing in English, which may reflect proficiency differences.
(3) L1-related KS use patterns in L2 (English), which may reflect L1 transfer effects in L2 inferencing, including
   Persian speakers' KS use patterns that characterize both L1 and L2 inferencing
   French speakers' KS use patterns that characterize both L1 and L2 inferencing.
(4) Differences in KS use in L2 lexical inferencing with lexicalized versus non-lexicalized target words, which will likely reflect lexicalization effects in L2 inferencing.
(5) Shared English L1, Persian L2 and French L2 KS use patterns in English, which will likely reflect text language (English) effects in L2 inferencing.

Detailed information about KS use is given in the following sections for all data sets. First, the relevant tables are presented, followed by descriptions of KS use within the main *linguistic (word, sentence, discourse)* and *non-linguistic (world) knowledge* categories. Separate tables and descriptions of readers' use of specific KS sub-types within each *linguistic* category then follow (e.g. *word morphology, sentence grammar*). Information is then presented on readers' use of *single* versus *multiple* KSs in arriving at inferences, as well as the kinds of KSs they tend to use *initially* or *post-initially*. Finally, the relationship between KS use and target word characteristics such as *word class* is explored.

Readers' use of main knowledge source types in lexical inferencing

Table 4.1 shows in which level of language organization readers seek cues to the meanings of unfamiliar words. Relative frequency data on English L1, Persian L1 and L2, and French L1 and L2 readers' KS use involving

First Language Influences on Knowledge Source Use

Table 4.1 Readers' use of main KS types: Percentages of overall use in each condition

	Linguistic KSs in text language			L1 KS use by L2 readers: L1 word knowledge (L1W)	Total linguistic KSs	Total non-linguistic KSs: world knowledge (WK)	Frequency rankings of main KS types
	Word (W)	Sentence (S)	Discourse (D)				
English L1	16.8	48.5	16.1	n.a.	81.2	18.8	S > WK > W = D
Persian L1	3.8	64.6	21.9	n.a.	90.3	9.8	S > D > WK > W
Persian L2	8.4	73.4	14.2	0.3	96.3	3.7	S > D > W > WK > L1W
French L1	29.3	49.5	10.0	n.a.	88.8	11.2	S > W > WK > W
French L2	16.5	71.7	3.7	4.0	95.5	4.5	S > W > WK = L1W = D

the main linguistic and non-linguistic types in the taxonomy are given, in terms of the percentage of KS use accounted for by each major type and the order of importance of each, in the five lexical inferencing conditions.

Shared knowledge source use patterns in first language inferencing

As shown in Table 4.1, certain similarities hold across the three L1 conditions with respect to the use of main KS types in lexical inferencing. All three groups rely heavily on linguistic KSs in the text language for 81–90% of their KS use. All three language groups use KSs from all linguistic levels (*word*, *sentence* and *discourse*) as well as non-linguistic *world knowledge* in their L1 lexical inferencing, although the relative percentages for each main source vary dramatically. *Sentence* level KSs are by far the most important category for all groups, accounting for half to two-thirds of KS use in L1 inferencing. Next in importance for English L1 readers are *word*, *discourse* and *world knowledge* KSs, all of approximately equal frequency, while Persian L1 readers depend on *discourse* cues and French L1 readers depend on *word* cues as their second most important source.

Shared knowledge source use patterns in first and second language inferencing

The same shared tendencies that characterize L1 inferencing, i.e. the use of linguistic KSs in the text language at the *word*, *sentence* and *discourse* levels (*sentence* KSs being by far the most important), as well as non-linguistic *world knowledge*, are also found in both L2 data sets. Again, the relative percentages vary considerably between the Persian and French readers in L2 lexical inferencing.

Knowledge source use patterns that distinguish first language from second language inferencing

Certain use patterns for main KS types differentiate L1 from L2 data. While both L2 data sets show heavy reliance on L2 linguistic knowledge, each also reveals some use of L1 related *word* cues – although the specific cues used and their degree of use are different for speakers of Persian and French (see below). *Sentence* level KS use is higher for both groups of L2 (English) readers than for any L1 group, and accounts for a similar proportion of KS use for both (72–73%). Thus, in the L2, readers are largely limited to the immediate contexts of target words. On the other hand, non-linguistic (*world*) *knowledge* is used infrequently in both L2 conditions (the remaining approximately 4%), less than half the percentages found in any L1 condition. Again, these figures are similar for Persian and French speakers.

First Language Influences on Knowledge Source Use 87

First language transfer effects in second language inferencing
As may be seen in Table 4.1, certain patterns in the use of main KS types differentiate Persian from French speakers in both their L1 and L2 inferencing, suggesting L1 influences on KS use in L2 inferencing. In L1, Persian readers report a strikingly low use of *word* level cues overall (3.8%); it is the least important main category for them, while French L1 readers use *word* level cues most frequently (19.3%) and English L1 readers' use of *word* cues is intermediate between the two. *Sentence* level cues are most important for all three groups, but are most frequently used by Persian L1 readers, accounting for 64.6% of their KS use, while French L1 and English L1 readers use them less frequently and similarly (49.5 and 48.5%, respectively). L1 readers from all three languages use *discourse* cues substantially, although to varying degrees: Persian L1 readers use them most (21.9%), French L1 readers use them least (10%) and English L1 readers are again in an intermediate position (16.1%). Persian and French L1 readers use *world knowledge* to a similar degree (9.8 and 11.2%), both notably less than English L1 readers (18.8%).

When these same speakers of Persian and French infer word meanings in their L2, English, their respective patterns of KS use from *word* and *discourse* sources is strikingly different from one another, but somewhat similar to their L1 patterns. Persian L2 readers demonstrate a relatively low use of *word* KSs in English (8.4%) (plus 0.3% L1 *word* cues), although notably higher than in L1 and in the direction of English L1 patterns. By contrast, also relating to their L1 patterns, French L2 readers show high use of *word* KSs (16.5%), which, while not as high as in their L1 (29.3%), is almost identical to that of English L1 readers (16.8%). They also use L1 *word* cues 4% of the time, raising their total proportion of *word* level KSs to over 20%. This is quite high compared to Persian L2 readers. With respect to the use of *discourse* level KSs, Persian L2 readers, as in L1, attribute a relatively high percentage (14.2%) of their KS use to discourse cues, although lower than in L1. In contrast, French L2 readers use very few *discourse* KSs (3.7%), likewise an even lower percentage than in L1 (10%).

Text language (English) effects in second language inferencing
A comparison of Persian L2 and French L2 readers' KS use with that of English L1 readers (Table 4.1) suggests that English as a text language plays some role in KS use in inferencing by L2 readers. Persian L2 readers' increased use of *word* cues in comparison with L1 provides the strongest indication of this, followed by the reduced use of such cues by the French L2 readers from their L1 levels.

Lexicalization effects in second language inferencing

A further analysis of the Persian and French L2 readers' use of the main KS categories in lexical inferencing explores possible effects of the lexicalization status of target words in the respective L1s. In each case, readers were presented with 25 English target words with lexical equivalents in the L1 and 25 without such equivalents. Percentages of main KS types used with lexicalized versus non-lexicalized words are given in Table 4.2.

The most obvious point to be noted in Table 4.2 is that the patterns of use of main KS types by each L2 group for lexicalized versus non-lexicalized target words are very similar to one another. Given the fact that the target word sets differed from each other (due to different lexicalization patterns in the two languages), it is risky to claim that the slight differences that emerge for only one group of readers can be attributed to lexicalization effects.[4] Trends shared by the two language groups are potentially more important (e.g. slightly less use of *sentence* level cues and slightly more use of *discourse* level cues with non-lexicalized words). Overall, while the L1 lexicalization status of target words plays an important role in inferencing success (Paribakht, 2005; Paribakht & Tréville, 2007), this difference cannot be easily linked to differential KS use by readers. Rather, one is struck by the consistency of within-group KS use patterns with both word categories.[5]

Readers' use of knowledge source sub-types in lexical inferencing

This section presents a detailed analysis of readers' use of KS sub-types within each main linguistic category. Table 4.3 shows the relative frequencies of use of different *word* level KSs in the five conditions.

Shared knowledge source use patterns in first language inferencing

The three groups of L1 speakers each show unique patterns of *word* cue use; it is not possible to posit any shared L1 characteristics at this level beyond the fact that they all use some cues from each of three sub-types: *word form, word morphology* and *word collocation*, and both English and French speakers use some from the fourth, *word association*. The relative importance of each of these, however, is quite different for each language group. English L1 readers employ the four sub-types from 1.8 to 7.4% of their overall KS use, clearly favoring *word form* and *word morphology*. Persian L1 readers do not use *word association* cues at all, scarcely use *word morphology*, and report low use of the other two *word* KSs, the highest being *word collocation* (2.5%). *Word morphology* is the most

Table 4.2 L2 readers' use of main KS types in English with lexicalized and non-lexicalized target words

	English L2 linguistic KSs			L1 KSs	Total linguistic KSs (%)	Total non-linguistic KSs world knowledge (WK) (%)	Frequency rankings of main KS types
	Word (W) (%)	Sentence (S) (%)	Discourse (D) (%)	L1 word knowledge (L1W) (%)			
Persian L2 lexicalized words	8.2	75.0	13.0	0.3	96.3	3.6	S > D > W > WK > L1W
Persian L2 non-lexicalized words	8.6	72.0	15.3	0.3	96.0	3.8	S > D > W > WK > L1W
French L2 lexicalized words	16.2	72.7	2.6	3.1	94.6	5.5	S > W > WK > L1W = D
French L2 non-lexicalized words	17.6	70.8	3.8	4.9	96.6	3.5	S > W > L1W > D = WK

Table 4.3 L1 and L2 readers' use of *word* KSs in lexical inferencing

	Word total (%)	Word form (WF) L2 (%)	Word form (WF) L1 (%)	Word morphology (WM) (%)	Word collocation (WC) L2 (%)	Word collocation (WC) L1 (%)	Word association (WA) (%)	Frequency rankings of KS sub-types
English L1	16.8	7.4	n.a.	5.6	1.8	n.a.	2.0	WF > WM > WA = WC
Persian L1	3.8	1.2	n.a.	0.1	2.5	n.a.	–	WC > WF > WM
Persian L2	8.4	1.4	–	5.7	0.8	0.3	0.5	WM > WF > WC = WA
French L1	29.3	5.6	n.a.	13.1	7.2	n.a.	3.4	WM > WC > WF > WA

important *word* KS in French L1 (13.1%) and *word form* is the most important in English L1 (7.4%). All sub-types of *word* KSs are used frequently by the French L1 readers, all of them but *word form* somewhat more often than by English L1 readers and all strikingly more often than by Persian L1 readers.

Shared knowledge source use patterns in first and second language inferencing

With respect to Persian and French speakers' inferencing in English, it is likewise not possible to claim any overall 'shared' L1 and L2 patterns beyond the fact that all four sub-types are used somewhat.

Knowledge source use patterns that distinguish first language from second language inferencing

In L2, *word collocation* is used far less than in L1 by both groups of readers. The two most important *word* KS sub-types used by both groups in L2 are *word morphology* and *word form*. (These are also the two largest English L1 categories.) Both groups of speakers show some use of L1 *word* KSs. KSs reflecting L1 linguistic knowledge are rare in the Persian L2 lexical inferencing data; L1 *word collocation* is the only sub-type, accounting for 0.3% of KS use. The French L2 readers report more use of L1 linguistic knowledge; *L1 word form* is the only sub-type, but it accounts for 4% of their KS use. This use of L1 *word* KSs differentiates L2 from L1 inferencing. This and the notably lower incidence of *word collocation* in L2 than in any L1 condition would appear to be associated with these readers' lower proficiency in English.

First language transfer effects in second language inferencing

The L1 pattern of much lower use of each sub-type of *word* KSs by Persian than by French readers is very similar in L2; the Persian L2 readers again show lower use overall of L1 *word* cues and of three of the L2 *word* KS sub-types than do the French L2 readers (*word collocation* being the exception). Interestingly, however, the cross-lingual gaps are larger in L1 than in L2 KS use, suggesting that while there is L1 influence at work with respect to these three KS types, other factors, among them English as the text language, may play a role.

Text language (English) effects in second language inferencing

The most important *word* KS used in L2 by both groups is *word morphology*, an important English L1 *word* KS. Substantially greater use by Persian speakers in L2 than in L1 of *word morphology* cues (5.7 versus 0.1%) appears to be an effect of English as the text language, as may also be their somewhat reduced use in L2 by French speakers (10.1 versus 13.1%).

Table 4.4 L1 and L2 readers' use of *sentence* KSs in lexical inferencing

	Sentence total (%)	*Sentence meaning (SM) (%)*	*Sentence grammar (SG) (%)*	*Punctuation (P) (%)*	*Frequency rankings of KS sub-types*
English L1	48.5	43.9	4.5	0.1	SM > SG > P
Persian L1	64.6	52.6	11.1	0.9	SM > SG > P
Persian L2	73.4	59.0	13.5	0.9	SM > SG > P
French L1	49.5	36.1	11.2	2.2	SM > SG > P
French L2	71.7	58.3	12.9	0.5	SM > SG > P

Table 4.4 provides a detailed analysis of the use of *sentence* level KS sub-types.

Shared knowledge source use patterns in first language inferencing

All three *sentence* KS sub-types are used by all three L1 groups in the same order of importance, *sentence meaning* being in all cases and by far the largest sub-category for all – it accounts for 36.1–53.6% of *sentence level* KS use. This is followed by *sentence grammar* and *punctuation*, which are of minor importance compared to the others. The rankings are the same for all three L1 groups; nonetheless, their relative use of each sub-type varies considerably.

Shared knowledge source use patterns in first and second language inferencing

In L2 as in L1 inferencing, *sentence meaning* accounts for most KS use, followed by *sentence grammar*, then *punctuation*. L2 readers depend more on *sentence meaning* cues in L2 than in L1, however.

Knowledge source use patterns that distinguish first language from second language inferencing

The higher use of *sentence meaning* in L2 than in L1 (with a particularly large difference in French) is the clearest L1 versus L2 difference, as is a slightly greater use of *sentence grammar* in both L2 conditions. In fact, the relative use of each *sentence* KS sub-type by Persian and French speakers in L2 is more similar for the two L2 groups than to any L1 group. The relative importance of the two major *sentence* KSs in L2 appears to be related to these speakers' lower proficiency in their L2, limiting them more to the immediate context and the most familiar L1 KS type.

First Language Influences on Knowledge Source Use 93

First language transfer effects in second language inferencing
 Sentence grammar use is similar for Persian and French speakers in both L1 and L2 inferencing (and different from English L1 readers). In both cases, there may be a native language effect on L2 inferencing; since both L1 groups are similar in the use of *sentence grammar*, it is not possible to know for sure. Likewise, the influence of L2 instruction may be important in one or both cases; grammar is heavily emphasized in Persian and French mother tongue instruction and to some extent in English instruction for speakers of both languages.

Text language (English) effects in second language inferencing
 There is no apparent influence of English as a text language in terms of *sentence* KSs, given English L1 readers' relatively low use of all three KS sub-types in contrast to both L2 groups. Table 4.5 presents data on readers' use of different sub-types of *discourse* KSs.

Shared knowledge source use patterns in first language inferencing
 With respect to use of different types of *discourse* KSs, all three L1 groups use *discourse meaning* and *formal schemata*, while only the English and Persian L1 readers use text *style/register*. However, as with *word* KSs, the relative importance of each sub-type is quite variable. For Persian L1 and English L1 readers *discourse meaning* is primary, while French L1 readers use *discourse meaning* and *formal schemata* equally.

Shared knowledge source use patterns in first and second language inferencing
 Persian L2 and French L2 groups, as in L1, use both *discourse meaning* and *formal schemata* cues, although the latter very rarely. Neither report using *style/register* KSs.

Table 4.5 L1 and L2 readers' use of *discourse* KSs in lexical inferencing

	Discourse total (%)	*Discourse meaning (DM) (%)*	*Style/register (S/R) (%)*	*Formal schemata (FS) (%)*	*Frequency rankings of KS sub-types*
English L1	16.1	13.7	1.8	0.6	DM > S/R > FS
Persian L1	21.9	14.4	2.9	4.6	DM > FS > S/R
Persian L2	14.2	13.9	–	0.3	DM > FS
French L1	10.0	5.0	–	5.0	DM = FS
French L2	3.3	3.0	–	0.3	DM > FS

Knowledge source use patterns that distinguish first language from second language inferencing

The lack of use of *style/register* and the very low use of *formal schemata* cues in both L2 conditions is almost certainly related to the lower proficiency of these readers in the L2. However, as the relative importance of *formal schemata* by both groups is very close to its low use by English L1 readers, the text language may have some influence. *Style/register* is not used at all by French L1 readers, and only occasionally in English L1. Perhaps relatively few of the target English words lend themselves to stylistic analysis.

First language transfer effects in second language inferencing

As with *word* KS sub-types, Persian and French L1 readers differ strongly in their use of *discourse* KS sub-types in lexical inferencing, and these differences carry over to their L2 English KS use. *Discourse meaning* is far more important to Persian L1 readers (14.4%) than to French L1 readers (5.0%), and similar to English L1 readers (13.7%); both groups of L2 readers follow their L1 patterns in the use of *discourse meaning* cues (13.9 and 3.0%, respectively). Persian and French L1 readers are, however, similar in their use of *formal schemata* (4.6 and 5.0%, respectively), but use of such cues in L2 is rare for both. *Discourse meaning* is the main area of possible L1 influence.

Text language (English) effects in second language inferencing

There is no obvious English text language effect at work with respect to *discourse* KSs, except possibly the uniformly low use of *formal schemata* KSs in all three English conditions.

Synthesis of knowledge source use patterns in all five conditions

Table 4.6[6] ranks all KS sub-types in terms of the percentage of their reported use in each of the five conditions, showing the comparative overall importance of the various KSs that readers use in lexical inferencing. This table, unlike earlier ones, visually groups results into frequency bands. It also provides percentages (rounded to the nearest integer) in order to highlight main trends, and in the case of rare sources accounting for < 1% of reported KSs, provides details from 0.1 to 0.9%.

First Language Influences on Knowledge Source Use

Table 4.6 Synthesis of L1 and L2 readers' use of KS sub-types: Rankings within relative frequency bands

KSs	Very frequent	Frequent	Occasional	Rare
Frequency bands	*50–59%* / *35–49%*	*10–20%*	*2–9%*	*1% or less*
English L1 (%)	sm > 44	wk > dm > 19 14	wf > wm > sg > wa = sr = wc > 7 6 5 2 2 2	fs > p 0.6 0.1
Persian L1 (%)	sm > 53	dm > sg > wk > 14 11 10	fs > sr = wc > 5 3 3	wf > p > wm 1 0.9 0.1
Persian L2 (%)	sm > 59	dm = sg > 14 14	wm > wk > 6 4	wf = p = wc > wa < fs > L1wc 1 0.9 0.8 0.5 0.3 0.3
French L1 (%)	sm > 36	wm > sg = wk > 13 11 11	wc > wf > dm = fs > wa > p 7 6 5 5 3 2	
French L2 (%)	sm > 59	sg > wm > 13 10	wf = wk > L1wf > dm > wa > 5 5 4 3 3 2	p > fs > wc 0.5 0.3 0.1

Note: Percentages are rounded to the nearest integer, or in "rare" cases, decimal place.
Key: wm, word morphology; sm, sentence meaning; fs, formal schemata; wf, word form; dm, discourse meaning; s/r, style/register; wc, word collocation; sg, sentence grammar; wk, world knowledge; wa, word association; p, punctuation.

Synthesis of knowledge source use patterns shared in first and second language lexical inferencing

For each of the five data sets, one KS sub-type, *sentence meaning*, is by far the most important KS that all groups use when inferring word meanings. This KS accounts for 36–53% of reported KS use in the three L1 data sets and for 59% in both L2 data sets. No other specific source is even half as important as *sentence meaning* for any of the conditions. A wide variety of KSs are used in all conditions; of 11 different KS sub-types, between 8 and 10 are reported as accounting for at least 1% of KS use under each condition. However, the relative importance of all KSs other than *sentence meaning* varies depending on readers' native language and whether they are reading in their L1 or L2. For example, four different specific KSs (*world knowledge, discourse meaning, word morphology* and *sentence grammar*) are second in relative frequency of use in at least one condition (*discourse meaning* in two), accounting for 13–19% of KS use. These four are important sources in all or most of the conditions.

Sentence meaning is likely so important because it is not only meaning related, but is also 'local'; *sentence* cues are found in the near vicinity of the target word. Both the meaning orientation and proximity of cues to the target word appear to contribute to their overall usefulness to readers, with group variation depending upon the specific L1, native versus L2 proficiency and the text language. Readers' heavy dependence on other meaning-related KSs is also evident from their use of *discourse meaning* and *world knowledge*. These KSs together with *sentence meaning* account for 52–77% of reported KSs in the three L1 conditions (French L1 being lowest), and for 66–77% in the two L2 conditions (French L2 being lowest). Readers' reliance on local cues is likewise demonstrated by summing *sentence* and *word* level cue use in each condition, which together account for between 65 and 88% of reported KSs.

After *sentence meaning*, the sources that are frequently or occasionally used by all the groups are *world knowledge*, much higher in L1 (3–19%) than in L2 (4–5%), *sentence grammar*, somewhat lower in L1 (5–11%) than in L2 (13–14%), and *discourse meaning*, with very similar ranges for L1 (5–14%) and L2 (3–14%). At the *word* level, only *word form* accounts in all conditions for at least 1% of KS use (in Persian L1 and L2) up to 9% (in French L2, including L1 sources). *Word morphology* accounts for only 0.1% in Persian L1, but from 6 to 13% of KS use in the other four conditions.

The remaining KSs tend to be used only occasionally or rarely, in no condition accounting for more than 7% of KS use and generally much less. Of these, *word collocation* accounts for 2–7% in the three L1 conditions and for <1% in the two L2 conditions. *Word association* is used in all conditions except Persian L1, accounting for 0.5% in Persian L2 and for 2–3% in the others. *Punctuation* only exceeds the 1% threshold in French L1, at 2%, but appears minimally in the other conditions. All three L1 groups use *formal schemata* (1–5%), but L2 readers' use of *formal schemata* is below 1%. Finally, *style/register* accounts for 2% of English L1 and 3% of Persian L1 KS use, but is not reported in any other condition.

Synthesis of knowledge source use patterns distinguishing first language from second language inferencing

From the previous sections, it may be seen that there are systematic L1/L2 differences in readers' use of both main types and sub-types of KSs when inferring word meanings. Both Persian and French L2 readers depend more on *sentence meaning* and *sentence grammar* cues in English L2 than in their L1. Higher reliance on *sentence meaning* by L2 readers goes with less use of other KSs, such as *world knowledge*, *formal schemata*, *word collocation*, *punctuation* and *style/register*. These trends that distinguish the L2 from the L1 data almost certainly reflect L2 readers' lower language proficiency and lesser cultural familiarity with text content and organization. For example, their lower use of *world knowledge* than in L1 may, to some extent, reflect more superficial understanding and retention of text meaning than in L1. Weaker word knowledge and relative unfamiliarity with the topics discussed may undermine text comprehension and retention of text meaning in the L2. Cumulative text understanding at given points in the text may then be inadequate to support L2 readers' effective exploitation of lower-level linguistic cues in lexical inferencing. The lesser use of *word collocation* in L2 than in any L1 condition likely reflects weaker vocabulary knowledge in general, and particularly, of collocational relations. Finally, L2 readers' relatively infrequent attention to *style/register* or *formal schemata* cues, both of which are important to understanding complex written texts, may reflect their limited experience with such texts.

Synthesis of first language transfer effects in second language lexical inferencing

The many KS use patterns that characterize Persian or French speakers in both L1 and L2 lexical inferencing provide convincing evidence of transfer of L1 procedural and declarative knowledge to L2 lexical inferencing. Such patterns are apparent throughout the data for both Persian and French speakers.

Notable for Persian L1 speakers at the *word* level is heavier dependence on *word collocation* than other *word* cues. The only *word* level KS used even occasionally by Persian L1 readers, *word collocation* (3%), carries over to L2 inferencing (0.8%) even though it is related to high vocabulary proficiency. A further factor that may help explain why Persians are more sensitive to written English collocations is that these Persian L2 readers almost certainly read more extended texts in English than their francophone counterparts as their medium for both language and academic content learning. For their part, the fact that the French speakers pay more attention to pronounced word forms may partially reflect their English learning context in the bilingual national capital region of Canada, where they experience frequent oral interactions and media exposure in addition to formal language instruction.

At the *sentence* level, the ubiquitous use of *sentence meaning* cues is even higher for Persian L1 readers than for the other L1 groups, and further exaggerated in L2. The strong L1 dependence of Persian L1 readers on this and on *sentence grammar* is also seen in L2 processing patterns. Likewise, at the discourse level, high dependence on *discourse meaning* is also seen in both L1 and L2. In sum, Persian L1 readers depend heavily on *sentence meaning*, followed by *discourse meaning*, *sentence grammar* and *world knowledge*. Lesser sources include occasional use of *formal schemata, style/register, word collocation*, and rare use of *word form* and *punctuation*. Of these, when reading in their L2, English, they depend even more on *sentence meaning*, again followed by *discourse meaning, sentence grammar* and rare but similar use of *word form* and *punctuation*. They demonstrate reduced use of *world knowledge, word collocation* and *formal schemata*, and no use of *style/register*. Overall, L1 influence on KS use in lexical inferencing can best be seen in the continuing prominence of *sentence meaning, discourse meaning* and *sentence grammar* cues.

In French L1 inferencing, what is most striking is the greater use of all kinds of *word* level cues than by either Persian or English L1 readers. These include *word morphology* as the second most important KS after *sentence meaning*, as well as substantial use of *word collocation, word form* and *word association*. The same tendencies are seen in L2 lexical inferencing, although to a lesser extent, and *word collocation* is quite rare. The reduced use of *word morphology* and *word association* by French speakers in L2 is in the direction of English L1 patterns. French readers' substantial use of *sentence grammar* in L1 lexical inferencing is also seen in their L2 KS use, while the use of *discourse meaning*, low in L1, is even less frequent in L2 inferencing. *Punctuation*, occasionally used in L1, is rarely used in L2. In sum, compared to Persian (and English) L1 readers, French L1 readers depend heavily on a variety of *word* cues, plus *sentence meaning*, *sentence grammar* and *world knowledge*, with relatively low dependence on *discourse meaning*. They share relatively high use of *formal schemata* with Persian L1 readers. In their L2 lexical inferencing, L1 influence may best be seen in the continued prominence of diverse *word* cues, *sentence meaning* and *sentence grammar*, while *world knowledge*, *discourse meaning* and *punctuation* continue to be used, although less than in L1.

Synthesis of English first language knowledge source use as a benchmark for English second language inferencing

Proficiency and text language effects

It is reasonable to assume that the high success generally seen in L1 lexical inferencing is, among other things, related to readers' efficient use of KSs and the low success of L2 readers to their relative inability to access comparable information in a language they know less well (see Chapter 5). Differences in KS use in English lexical inferencing between native speakers and L2 Persian and French readers offer some indications of what these respective L2 readers may need to particularly attend to in English lexical inferencing. At the same time, L2 KS use patterns that differ from the same readers' L1 KS use in the direction of English L1 patterns can be viewed as likely reflecting learners' increasing proficiency in English.

To be more like English L1 readers in *word* level KS use in English, Persian L2 readers would need to rely more on *word* cues and to use a variety of them. In their use of *word morphology* cues, these readers (in contrast to their L1 KS use) report the same percentage of use in L2 (6%) as English L1 readers, and also occasionally use *word association*, which they do not use in their L1. It is likely relevant that *word morphology* is emphasized in English instruction in Iran. *Word form*, a frequently used KS in English L1 and French L1 and L2 lexical inferencing but rare in Persian L1, is similarly rare in L2 (far below English L1 use), while *word collocation*, a high-proficiency KS related to knowledge of lexical networks, remains well below Persian L1 as well as English L1 levels. At the *sentence* level, the English L1 model would also suggest greater reliance on *world knowledge* by the Persian speakers as they progress in English (L2) and less on *sentence meaning* and *sentence grammar*. It seems likely that their even higher reliance on *sentence grammar* in English L2 than in Persian L1 lexical inferencing (14%, moving farther away from English

L1 norms) is related both to the importance of this KS in Persian L1 and to the instructional emphasis it receives in both languages in Iran.

The French L2 readers, to be more like English L1 readers, would need to rely even less on *word morphology*, which they in fact already use somewhat less in English than in L1. They would, like the Persian speakers, have to develop the deeper lexical knowledge in English needed to use *word collocation*, and, like the Persian speakers, rely more on *world knowledge* and less on both *sentence meaning* and *sentence grammar*. Where French L2 readers differ most uniquely from English L1 readers, however, is with respect to the use of *discourse meaning*, a KS category that is also quite low in French L1 lexical inferencing. Unlike word *morphology, sentence grammar* and *punctuation*, all of which respond to specific instruction, improvement in the ability to identify and retain *discourse meaning* cues largely defies direct instruction, and rather appears related to cumulative reading experience and proficiency.

Readers' use of single versus multiple knowledge sources

The following section takes up another aspect of KS use; the tendency to use a number of different KSs in reaching an inference. Readers in all five conditions reported using multiple KSs to arrive at some of their inferences, and single KSs for others; in fact, a mixture of both characterized the great majority of participants from all five data sets. However, there were language-related and more general L1 versus L2 differences, as well. Table 4.7 shows the relative use of single versus multiple KSs in inferences made in each condition.

No overall shared L1 patterns are seen in these data aside from the fact that each L1 group used single as well as multiple KSs for a substantial portion of their inferences. English L1 readers used single KSs only 36% of the time, employing multiple KSs for 64% of their inferences. By

Table 4.7 Number of different KSs used per inference in each condition

KS use	Single (%)	Multiple (%)	KSs per inference	Range
English L1	36	64	1.7	1–5
Persian L1	68	32	1.5	1–4
Persian L2	59	41	1.5	1–4
French L1	77	23	1.2	1–3
French L2	53	47	1.7	1–5

contrast, Persian L1 readers reported using a single KS for 68% of their inferences and multiple KSs for only 32%. French L1 readers followed a similar pattern with an even higher use of single KSs (for 77% of their inferences), using multiple KSs for only 23%. In related measures, the English L1 readers reported the highest average number of KSs per inference (1.7) of all the L1 groups as well as the highest maximum number used by a participant for a single inference. The French L1 readers were lowest on both counts with an average of 1.2 and a range of 1–3, and the Persian L1 speakers in between.

The L2 readers from both groups, as in L1, reported more *single* than *multiple* KSs per inference, but performed more similarly to one another and somewhat more like English L1 readers than to their own L1 performances. Persian speakers inferencing in English reported a single KS for the majority of their inferences (59%) and multiple KSs for the rest, with an average of 1.5 KSs per inference and a range of 1–4, while the French speakers reported a single KS for just over half their guesses and multiple KSs for the remainder (average 1.7, range 1.5). It is also to be noted that both Persian and French readers used considerably more multiple sequences in English than in their L1, probably related to their lower proficiency and perhaps to an inability to quickly identify the best cues, as well as to the possibly greater variety of available cues in English, some of which (*word morphology, sentence grammar*) they had studied. These figures thus suggest a mixture of L1, proficiency and text language influences on L2 readers' use of multiple KSs.

The number of KSs per inference in itself, while likely bearing some relationship to difficulty, has no direct correlation with overall success rates under the different conditions. The English L1 readers, the most successful inferencers of all three L1 groups, used the most KSs per inference; however, the Persian and French speakers used more multiple sequences in their L2. While using more sources is not a guarantee of effective use, it does indicate that the reader keeps trying. Multiple KS use is clearly a complex phenomenon, and it is necessary to look in more detail at the data to unravel when, why and how additional KSs are used in given contexts. Two examples of inferences incorporating multiple KSs are given below.

'The World's Forgotten Poor' (L1 English data)
Target word (pseudo): duprenchous (presumptuous)
Word form, sentence meaning, world knowledge
P: [**Duprenchous**]... *We tell ourselves that it would be* [**duprenchous**] *to offer help when it is not requested. The first word that came to mind was*

(duplicitous) because of the sound, but that doesn't seem to really fit there... *to offer help when it is not requested.* Then I wrote (presumptuous) or (patronizing). That's where it started... just trying to get the sense. ...This is a very familiar sentiment. Most of us who are honest know about the excuses we make ourselves.

'How to make the New Year more memorable' (L1 Persian data)
Target word (pseudo): velaahatan (easily)
Word form, sentence meaning, style and register
[velaahatan] makes me think of (talvihan = implicitly) (unwillingly). From the meaning of the sentence and the style of writing, *waves of happiness and inner excitement of children that* (implicitly) *gets transmitted to others.*

Initial versus post-initial knowledge source use

In multiple KS use, certain kinds of KSs tend to be used more initially, as a single KS or first in a series, while others tend to be used more post-initially. This section considers whether such patterns may represent L1 versus L2 differences, L1 transfer or effects of English as a text language. Table 4.8 shows the frequency ranking for readers' initial KS use, which may be viewed as indicating the sources they perceive as likely most useful, contrasted with their post-initial KS use, perhaps invoked due to failure of the first to generate an adequate guess, or to verify or refine a guess.

Shared first and second language patterns
Table 4.8 shows that initial rankings of KS types according to relative frequency of use within each data set are largely but not entirely similar to post-initial rankings, and their relative amount of use varies widely. *Sentence meaning* cues are most often used initially in all five data sets. *Sentence meaning* use, while much lower post-initially, remains the most important KS for all conditions (matched in post-initial importance for French L1 speakers by *world knowledge* and *sentence grammar*). Data inspection reveals that *sentence meaning* is likely to appear as the second source or later when it is not the first (and sometimes several *sentence meaning* cues will be used in a sequence). An example of non-initial use of *sentence meaning* in an inference follows.

'Marriage' (L1 English data)
Target word (pseudo): kritch (slam)
Sentence grammar, sentence meaning, discourse meaning
P: (slam) *The stress of the whole experience may be enough for the couple to*

First Language Influences on Knowledge Source Use

Table 4.8 Relative frequency of initial and post-initial KS use in lexical inferencing

	Initial KS use				Non-initial KS use		
	Very frequent	Frequent (10–20%)	Occasional (2–20%)	Rare (1%)	Very frequent (>35%)	Frequent (10–20%)	Occasional (2–9%)	Rare (<1%)
English L1	sm > 52	dm > wk > 14 12	wf > wm > sg 8 6 5		sm > 48	dm > wk > 17 12	wf > wm > sg > 8 7 6	wc = wa = fs 1 1 1
Persian L1	sm > 59	dm > sg > 15 10	wk > fs > 9 4	wc 1	sm > 38	dm > sg > wk > 15 14 11	s/r > fs > wc > wf > 8 5 5 2	p 1
Persian L2	sm > 67	sg > dm > 11 11	wm > 7	wk = wf = wk 1 1 1	sm > 42	dm > sg > 20 18	wk > wm > p = wf > 8 5 2 2	wc = wa = L1wc = fs 1 1 1 1
French L1	sm > 36	wm > wk = sg > 13 11 11	wc > wf > dm = fs > wa > p 7 6 5 5 3 2			sm > wk = sg > wm > 19 19 19 11	wc = p > wf > fs > dm = wa > 8 8 6 5 3 3	
French L2	sm > 61	wm = sg > 11 11	wf > l1wf > wk > wa > dm 6 5 3 2 2		sm > 55	sg > 16	wm > wk > dm > wf > L1wf > 9 7 5 3 2	wa = p = fs 1 1 1

Note: Percentages are rounded to the nearest integer; those less than 1 are not reported. When rounded numbers are the same, their order in the table reflects their actual ranking.

Key: wm, word morphology; sm, sentence meaning; fs, formal schemata; wf, word form; dm, discourse meaning; s/r, style/register; wc, word collocation; sg, sentence grammar; wk, world knowledge; wa, word association; p, punctuation.

want to walk out of the room and [*kritch*] *the door*. I knew it was a verb, and what do people do when they walk out of the room and 'blank' the door? So I just automatically thought (slam) the door because they'd be upset because of the whole experience.

There is also a tendency toward greater use of a larger set of less frequent sources post-initially. The diversity of later used KSs is evident in the increased number of different KSs that account for at least 1% of KS use post-initially, up from two to four KSs in all conditions except French L1 (in which 10 KSs account for at least 1% both initially and post-initially). It is notable that *world knowledge* and *sentence grammar* tend to be used more post-initially.

Style/register and *word form*, exemplified below, are KSs whose relative use in at least one condition differs considerably *initially* and *post-initially*. Persian L1 speakers, the main users of *style/register* cues, always use them last, almost always in *multiple sequences* where they account for 8% of *non-initial* KS use. They are used occasionally and by only some readers, with a subset of words perceived to offer appropriate cues. Generally, the purpose appears to be to refine or confirm a guess. An example of the use of *text style/register* follows.

'*How to make the New Year more memorable*' (L1 Persian data)
Target word (pseudo): misalaavad (prepares)
text style/register
P: For this word I'd put in (gives). *Though Paniz was only 4 years old, she asked me: Who gives gifts to these kids....?* Other fancy words could also be used here but because the kid asking her mother is only four years old, we should naturally use simpler verbs.

French L2 readers are the main users of *word form* cues, both from French (L1 word form) and from the text language, English. These are both mainly used initially, accounting for 6% (L1 *word form*) and 5% (L2 *word form*), respectively. Both are associated with failure to identify an appropriate inference (in 59% of cases for L2 *word form* and 80% for L1 *word form*), even when used in conjunction with a meaning-oriented cue (generally *sentence meaning*). All French L1 readers used at least one of these cues, up to a maximum of 25 by one reader. Some readers who used them much less and in conjunction with other cues were successful in some of the resulting guesses. It appears that overuse may be related to wild guessing when the reader fails to identify a good meaning-related cue. L1 *word form* may indicate the conclusion that a similar looking or sounding word in the L1 will have some relationship to the target word,

First Language Influences on Knowledge Source Use 105

based on the French readers' perception that French and English are closely related. An example of *word form* use follows.

'An Author's Life' (L2 French data)
Target word: *warily*
Word form
P: [**warily**] According to the pronunciation that I would give it, 'rarement'. Editors rarely (rarement) supervise authors.

Word class

The issue of how word class may influence readers' lexical inferencing behavior is addressed in this section through analyses of the frequency of use of different KSs in relation to word class. Table 4.9 shows the overall average number of KSs used with target words from the four different word classes studied: *nouns, verbs, adjectives* and *adverbs*, and Table 4.10 shows the frequency ranking of KS sub-types by word class.

In Table 4.9, variation by word class in the average number of KSs used per inference is seen within each data set, with some shared trends. In all five conditions, *adverbs* show the highest average number of KSs per guess, matched or followed by *adjectives*, with *verbs* or *nouns* the lowest. These differences likely reflect, to some extent, the relative difficulty of inferring meanings for different classes of words, which may be assumed to vary across languages. While these patterns also hold for L1 English readers, they show the most consistency in the number of KSs used in inferences for target words in each class (between 1.7 and 1.8).

Table 4.9 Average number of KSs per inference in each condition by word class

	Average number of KSs used by word class				
	Nouns	*Verbs*	*Adjectives*	*Adverbs*	*Overall*
English L1	1.7	1.7	1.8	1.8	1.7
Persian L1	1.3	1.4	1.4	1.5	1.5
Persian L2	1.4	1.4	1.6	1.7	1.5
French L1	1.2	1.1	1.3	1.4	1.2
French L2	1.6	1.5	1.8	1.8	1.7

Table 4.10 Frequency rankings of KS sub-type use by word class: English L1 and Persian L2 readers

	Nouns	Verbs	Adjectives	Adverbs
English L1	sm>wk>dm>wm=wf>wa=sg 46 22 10 6 6 2 2	sm>dm>wm>wf>sg=wk>sr=fs 39 17 11 10 9 9 1 1	sm>dm>wk>wf>sg=wm 35 30 16 10 4 4	sm>dm>wm>wf>sg=wk>sr=fs 39 17 11 10 9 9 1 1
Persian L2	sm>dm>sg>wm>wk 60 15 10 8 4	sm>dm>sg>wk>wc=wm 68 12 11 5 2 2	sm>dm>sg>wm>wk 47 20 16 13 4	sm>sg>dm>wm 51 29 10 9

Note: Percentages are rounded to the nearest integer. Those less than 1 are not reported. When rounded numbers are the same, their order in the table reflects their actual ranking.

First Language Influences on Knowledge Source Use 107

The actual kinds of KSs used for each word class to some extent reflect the particular kinds of information afforded a reader who recognizes what a target word's class is, as well as formal characteristics related to that word class in the text language. This may be seen in Table 4.10, in the KSs used by English L1 and Persian L2 readers, the two groups who read the same English texts with corresponding (pseudo or actual) target words.

From Table 4.10, it is apparent that certain English L1 versus Persian L2 differences noted in the overall KS frequencies hold, such as higher use of *sentence meaning* and *sentence grammar* in all cases by Persian speakers and of *world knowledge* and *word* cues (other than *word morphology*) by English speakers. Beyond that, certain shared patterns in the rankings and relative frequencies of KS use by the two groups appear related to given word classes. Thus, both groups show high use of meaning-oriented KSs for *nouns*, with *sentence meaning, world knowledge* and *discourse meaning* totaling 78% of English L1 KS use, while for the Persian L2 readers, 75% of KS use involves *sentence meaning* and *discourse meaning*. Discourse meaning is particularly high for both groups with adjectives, which, while they modify specific nouns, may lack clear referents so that cumulative information is necessary to infer their meanings. *Word morphology* and *sentence grammar* are particularly important with adverbs, which are often marked by affixes such as /-ly/ and for which it is necessary to identify the verb qualified. Other patterns work with only the English L1 group – which should be able to access and use the best cues for successful inferencing; for example, higher use of *word morphology* and *sentence grammar* with verbs (which carry a lot of information in their endings and are an essential sentence component).

Summary and Discussion

From the taxonomy and the above analyses, it may be seen that readers in all five conditions used a wide variety of KSs when inferencing, drawing on cues from all levels of language organization and including both formal and meaning-oriented information. Sources included *linguistic* cues located within words, clauses, sentences or paragraphs as well as cumulative cues from earlier parts of a text, and readers' general and topic related *non-linguistic* knowledge.

Processing tendencies shared across languages

A number of shared KS patterns across the five data sets suggest cross-linguistic and L1/L2 commonalities in lexical inferencing processes. First of all, all groups showed a heavy reliance on linguistic KSs from the text language with relatively little reported use of explicit L1 linguistic knowledge. An important characteristic of KS use across all data sets was readers' primary dependence on meaning-related KSs, especially as the initial KS for an inferred meaning. Likewise, they tended to use 'local' cues, or those found in the word itself or within the immediate sentence context. *Sentence meaning* was the most important KS in all conditions, particularly for Persian speakers and even more in L2 than in L1, and it tended for all groups to be the first or only KS tried. If not used initially, it was also likely to appear later in a multiple sequence of KSs. Another meaning-oriented KS, *world knowledge*, was used in all five conditions but particularly in English and more in L1 than in L2. It tended to be used more post-initially (after either *sentence meaning* or another initial cue had been tried) by both Persian and French speakers. *Discourse meaning*, the third major meaning-oriented KS, was used particularly by Persian and English speakers, about equally initially or later in L1 or L2. *Sentence grammar* was particularly important in Persian and French L1 and L2, and *word morphology* in all groups but Persian L1. While most other KSs were reported about equally first or later in KS sequences, two rather infrequent ones, *formal schemata* and, in particular, *text style/register*, mainly used by L1 readers, tended to be found later in multiple sequences for refining guesses.

Participants in all five conditions reported using only a single KS for a large proportion of their inferences and more than one KS for others, up to a maximum of five (in the case of English L1 and French L2 readers). *Word* cues were prominent for both these groups, reflecting their availability in English and transfer of processing tendencies from French L1. Greater multiple KS use characterized lexical inferencing in L2 and in English as the text language. Thus, while multiple KS use may have partially reflected lower proficiency, it may have also been a consequence of L2 users' developing ability to use the diverse *word* cues offered in English texts. A further shared tendency across groups – that appeared related to the difficulty of inferring given word meanings – was the greater use of multiple KSs with adjectives and adverbs than with nouns and verbs, likely reflecting the often more precise or abstract cues needed to infer meanings of words in the former two classes.

A shared finding for Persian and French speakers inferring word meanings in English (L2) provided another indication of the stability of L1 processing tendencies. This was that the L1 lexicalization status of L2 target words did not appear to affect KS choice. L2 readers in each group tended to use the same KSs both for words with lexical equivalents in their L1 and for those without such equivalents.

These general trends appear to be applicable to L1 lexical inferencing across these three languages and to both L1 and L2 (English) inferencing by the Persian and French speakers. It is thus plausible that they may extend to literate speakers of other Indo-European languages. At the same time, the analyses revealed KS use patterns that distinguish between L1 and L2 readers, others that characterize L1 speakers of each of the three languages – some of which may carry over to L2 inferencing, and still others that characterize readers of English texts, whether they are L1 or L2 speakers.

Proficiency in the text language

An important distinguishing feature between L1 versus L2 KS use is L1 readers' greater use of *world knowledge*. This would seem to reflect the declarative knowledge encoded in the lexicons of these highly proficient L1 users, which allows them to more easily access and retain content relationships within texts, using their general knowledge base as well as linguistic proficiency. In addition to greater mastery of the linguistic code and discourse conventions, native or native-like proficiency would almost certainly subsume a deeper understanding of certain in-group cultural and societal issues inherent in texts originating in a given language.

As an alternative to the use of 'top down' cues that ensure the contextual relevance of guesses, frequent in L1, both Persian- and French-speaking L2 readers depended more on *sentence meaning* cues in English, seeking KSs in the immediate vicinity of the target word, and reverting especially to this most familiar KS type. They also used more *sentence grammar* cues in English L2 than in their L1s. With respect to *word morphology*, the Persian speakers used such cues much more in English than in their L1, while the French speakers, who used such cues in their L1 even more frequently than L1 English speakers, used them less in L2. Both cases involved adaptation toward English norms. *Sentence grammar* and *word morphology* were familiar to both Persian and French speakers from L1 structures, and both are amenable to instruction, two factors that likely influenced their importance in L2 inferencing.

First language influences on patterns of second language knowledge source use

The linguistic KSs reported by L2 readers, mainly based on the text language, showed a notable difference between the two L2 groups, reflecting the relative typological distance of each L1 from English. While the French speakers reported that 4% of their lexical inferences in English explicitly drew on L1 features, the Persian L2 readers only very rarely referred to L1 features – as would be expected considering both the actual greater typological distance of Persian from English as well as their likely perception of that distance. The Persian speakers' infrequent reference to L1 cues differs from Haastrup's participants in her 1991 study of English (L2) speakers of Danish, a Germanic language closely related to English. She found that lower proficiency L2 users reported guesses based on native language forms and associations more frequently than those with stronger English. In this study, the French speakers were more similar to Haastrup's participants in their use of L1 linguistic knowledge, tending to rely on one type of *word* level cue, L1 *word form* (pronouncing a similar L1 word out loud), for 4% of their reported KS use. This KS was readily available to them due to the large shared lexical base linking French with English. The fact that both Danish and French share the same alphabet with English as well as many word stems and cognates, no doubt also facilitates cross-linguistic associations of similar word forms. In a larger sense, the tendency to refer to L1 word forms is almost certainly related to L2 readers' perceptions of L1/L2 distance and to their experience with oral English. However, this particular L1 KS, used by the French speakers, was largely associated with failure to arrive at an accurate inference, and may have represented a lack of ability to access more fruitful KSs, especially meaning-based sources. It may also have represented overconfidence in apparently similar L1 word forms, related to perceptions of transferability of word features between French and English.

Aside from explicit reporting of L1 linguistic sources, indications of implicit L1 influences on L2 KS use were found throughout the data for both groups, in the unique patterns of KS use that characterized the Persian or French speakers in both L1 and L2 inferencing. Shared L1 and L2 KS use patterns for each group reflected preferred linguistic knowledge categories (e.g. *discourse meaning* for Persian speakers, *word morphology* for French speakers) and learned L1 processing tendencies in terms of where in the text readers looked for needed information (e.g. to the *discourse* level or *word* level, respectively).

While the Persian and French speakers shared a high reliance on *sentence meaning* and *sentence grammar* in both L1 and L2, the most notable difference between them involved Persian speakers' heavy use of *discourse* KSs (*discourse meaning* and *formal schemata*), which were seldom used by the French speakers. The Persian speakers' relative neglect of

First Language Influences on Knowledge Source Use 111

word KSs (except *word collocation*) may be partially explained by Persian orthography, which limits the value of *word* level cues as a reliable source of information for lexical inferencing in Persian. Several vowels are not represented in Persian orthography, so readers are accustomed to drawing on the meaning of the larger (*sentence* and *discourse*) context to identify the exact word they are reading and to be able to pronounce it accurately when reading aloud. These L1 Persian processing tendencies are carried over to L2 processing along with preferences for *sentence* and *discourse* KSs in lexical inferencing.

Given the nature of Persian orthography, L1 Persian speakers' relatively infrequent use of *word form* in comparison with English L1 and French L1 readers is not surprising. The fact that they seldom use *word form* in English may have to do both with their perception of typological distance between the two languages and with their relative lack of experience with oral English and with correspondences between written and oral English forms. Persian readers' substantial use of *word morphology* in English inferencing, a KS they did not use in the L1, on the other hand, is striking. As with *sentence grammar*, English language instructional emphasis in Iran on formal structures almost certainly plays a role, but the fact that Persian is also a highly inflected language gives them a conceptual basis for identifying and using morphological cues.

The relative lack of use of *discourse* level cues by French speakers in both L1 and L2 is also notable. It appears that they are able to get considerable information from *word* and *sentence* level cues in English as well as in French, so perhaps have a lesser need to refer to *discourse* cues. There is also the possibility that these French speakers, somewhat younger than the Persian speakers and as a group, less academically oriented, and who have learned oral English in a bilingual environment, are relatively less oriented toward reading extended texts either in their L1 or L2. More academically oriented French speakers might respond somewhat differently.

Overall patterns of KS use by these L2 readers of English from two rather different languages, considered in the context of other studies of L1 lexical inferencing, provide some explicit and considerable implicit evidence of L1 transfer effects on KS use in L2 lexical inferencing. A strong L1 influence is seen in Persian and French readers' emphases on using certain KSs in both L1 and L2 processing. Underlying L1 procedural competencies appear to play a role both in the types of KSs readers depend on in the L2 and in their ability to use them effectively. These cross-linguistic data illustrate well the frequently observed point that each L1 provides a different starting point with respect to features of a given L2, resulting in different transfer patterns. With respect to certain proficiency-related KSs, such as *word collocation* or *formal schemata*, the fact that they are used at all in L2 lexical inferencing may reflect the readers' ability to use them in the L1 and awareness that this information may be pertinent to certain words in the L2, whether or not they have the proficiency to use the KS successfully in the L2. L2 readers' use of the same KSs in inferring meanings of words without L1 lexical equivalents as they use with lexicalized target words, reflecting L1 KS use patterns although with far less success, is a further example of the stability of L1 KS use patterns.

Text language influences on second language knowledge source use

Finally, the L2 readers from both groups demonstrate integration of some processing strategies that are more typical of L1 English readers than of their own L1 use, particularly at the *word* and *sentence* level. The Persian readers' relatively high use of *word morphology* in English is an example, representing significant learning of something they seldom do in L1 inferencing. Likewise, the French speakers' reduced use of *word morphology* in L2 is much closer to English norms than that in their L1. But their task has been easier – i.e. learning *not* to do something in the L2. These French L2 readers, like English L1 readers, also use English *word form* cues, probably due partly to transfer, but also because they have considerable oral exposure to English through the media and in their bilingual environment in the Ottawa area; however, this does not serve them very well.

How one learns the language is also important. As noted previously, aspects of English that reflect categories that exist in L1 and are amenable to instruction seem to have been effectively learned by both groups (e.g. *word morphology* and *sentence grammar*). Others, such as greater sensitivity to *discourse* cues by the French learners, can probably only be mastered through intensive reading practice. In spite of their relatively advanced academic English proficiency, both groups of L2 learners still lack many aspects of L2 linguistic and related cultural knowledge that affect their lexical inferencing and limit its success. Continuing L2 development should bring with it greater convergence with English speakers' KS use patterns, and with it, greater success in arriving at accurate inferences.

Notes

1. Individual learner characteristics also play an important role in KS use, but with the exception of L2 receptive vocabulary knowledge, have not been systematically investigated here.
2. Some may have studied core high school French.
3. While the *word*, *sentence* and *discourse* levels of language organization provided a natural basis for sub-categorization of linguistic KSs, non-linguistic knowledge presented no obvious categorization. Initially, we attempted to distinguish knowledge of the immediate topic from more general knowledge, but found that in many cases it was impossible to make this distinction; furthermore, it was not crucial to do so for our purposes here. Therefore, *world knowledge* is an all-encompassing category for non-linguistic knowledge in this taxonomy.
4. Examples of this include French L2 readers' somewhat greater use of *world knowledge* for lexicalized words and of L1 *word* sources for non-lexicalized words.
5. The somewhat greater use by Persian L2 readers of *word association*, *word collocation* and *word form* KSs with lexicalized than with non-lexicalized target words may have had to do with the generally higher frequency of the former (see Paribakht, 2005: 725), and possibly wider range of use, both making probable greater previous exposure to them.
6. Table 4.6 re-displays some specific KS information that is also in Tables 4.1, 4.3, 4.4 and 4.5; however, percentages are rounded to the nearest integer.

Chapter 5
Inferencing Success and Initial Development of Word Knowledge

In this chapter, we describe and compare the success of the English-, Persian- and French-speaking participants in inferring contextually accurate meanings for unknown words in written texts in their respective first languages (L1s), and of the latter two groups in their second language (L2), English. We first consider overall L1 and L2 lexical inferencing success, seeking cross-linguistic similarities and L1 versus L2 differences. We then focus on L2 lexical inferencing and its outcomes in terms of both successful inferences and post-inferencing retention of new word knowledge in English by Persian and French L2 readers, for whom differential outcomes may potentially reflect L1 influence.

In addition to overall tendencies, the effects of L2 target word lexicalization status on inferencing procedures and outcomes are studied through separate analyses of successful lexical inferencing and meaning retention of target words that have Persian or French L1 lexical equivalents and those that do not. This analysis provides information on the importance of L2 readers' previous knowledge of approximately equivalent lemmas in the L1.

The role of Persian and French speakers' receptive English vocabulary knowledge in lexical inferencing outcomes is then examined through correlation analyses of a measure of their receptive English vocabulary knowledge with L2 lexical inferencing success and new knowledge of word meanings. These analyses add to our understanding of how L2 lexical knowledge may develop through reading and lexical inferencing. Linguistic features of Persian and French as these reflect their typological relationships with English, as well as participants' different English learning contexts, are then considered as possible explanations of both the differential L2 lexical knowledge and the L2 lexical inferencing outcomes of the two groups.

Issues

Several background issues are of particular relevance to this chapter. These include the role of readers' previous vocabulary knowledge in their successful inferring of word meanings for text comprehension, as well as in the relationship between lexical inferencing success and the subsequent retention of new word knowledge. The lexicalization status of unknown L2 words (whether there is an approximate L1 equivalent whose identification can shortcut the process of constructing a new meaning for a word) poses a special case of such previous knowledge. The importance of typological proximity between the readers' L1 and L2 as a source of potential support for lexical processing and learning is a related issue. Brief remarks on these points are given below, with references to more substantive discussions elsewhere in the book.

Previous vocabulary knowledge in lexical inferencing success and word learning

Research has established a relationship between measures of L2 readers' vocabulary knowledge in the text language and their success in inferring meanings for unknown words while reading (Chapter 1). Both vocabulary size and 'depth' measures have been shown to have predictive power for successful lexical inferencing from reading texts. A threshold effect has been demonstrated in different studies by which readers need to understand a very high proportion of the other words in a given text in order to be able to read the text unassisted and/or to be able to infer the meanings of unknown words; recent estimates place this at around 98%.

Research has also demonstrated gains in L2 vocabulary knowledge from extensive or thematic reading and from lexical inferencing tasks (Chapter 1). While gains in familiarity with new word forms is the most likely result of inferencing attempts, post-inferencing recall of word meanings has also been documented. Productive knowledge of new words is a less likely outcome. As with lexical inferencing success, L2 readers' post-inferencing retention of new word knowledge is related to their previous vocabulary knowledge. These issues will be pursued in this chapter with a focus on potential L1 influence on lexical inferencing outcomes.

Lexicalization

An earlier phase of this trilingual study examined the effect of the L1 lexicalization status of target L2 words in written texts on the lexical inferencing behavior of the Persian- and French-speaking participants (Paribakht, 2005; Paribakht & Tréville, 2007). The findings demonstrated that while the L1 lexicalization status of the target words had little effect on participants' use of different types of knowledge sources (KSs), it strongly affected their rate of success in inferring accurate meanings for unfamiliar L2 target words. Readers in both language groups were far more successful in guessing the meanings of lexicalized than non-lexicalized target words.

Beyond this shared finding, however, Persian speakers were less successful than French speakers in inferring accurate meanings for either lexicalized or non-lexicalized words and were more disadvantaged by non-lexicalized words. The authors concluded that non-lexicalized words may represent a notable hurdle for L2 readers in successful comprehension and interpretation of L2 texts, and that this effect may be stronger in a typologically distant language.

In this chapter, these data and issues are revisited within the broader frame of L1 versus L2 inferencing by the same speakers, English L1 inferencing, and consideration of the further issue of L2 readers' post-inferencing retention of new word forms and meanings. What is the role of readers' lexical proficiency in these outcomes? Is there evidence that French speakers are able to call on a richer repertoire of cues to target word meanings in English? Does a higher inferencing success rate go together with a higher rate of retention of new target word knowledge? Can the differential success of Persian and French speakers in English lexical inferencing for both lexicalized and non-lexicalized words be explained in terms of the role of language distance in language transfer?

Methodology

The methodology for the entire study is described in Chapter 3, including factors such as the English (L2) learning context that may have influenced performance under one or more conditions. Elements mentioned here are those particularly relevant to the study of lexical inferencing success and retention of new word knowledge.

Relationships among the three languages

French has typological proximity with English and, in addition, its speakers have a long history of cultural ties with English speakers. Together, these factors ensure many similarities across French and English lexicons, including patterns of lexicalization. Persian, on the other hand, is typologically distant from English and, historically, its

Inferencing Success and Initial Development of Word Knowledge 117

speakers have had relatively little cultural contact with English speakers. Educated young adult English users from these two language backgrounds thus present a useful case for the study of L1 transfer from languages with different typological distances from English on the process and outcomes of English lexical inferencing and the L2 vocabulary resources they bring to the inferencing task.

Participants

Three groups of post-secondary students from English, Persian and French L1 backgrounds were studied with respect to their success in inferring appropriate target word meanings in L1 and L2 and their retention of new L2 lexical knowledge following the L2 inferencing task. (See Chapter 3 for details.)

Data sources and procedures

As with the study of KSs in Chapter 4, our primary data sources for this chapter were transcripts of think-aloud protocols from individual research sessions in which readers inferred meanings for unfamiliar L1 pseudo[1] target words or L2 English words embedded in reading texts. Quantitative analyses are based on the number of words previously unknown to each participant for which they proposed inferred meanings. As noted in Chapter 3, most participants in all groups made a strong effort to infer target word meanings. In all three L1 conditions, participants proposed meanings for almost all of the pseudo target words. In L2, aside from the target words whose meanings they already knew (Persian speakers: 9%, French speakers: 4%), participants inferred meanings for most of them (Persian speakers: 79%, French speakers: 87%). The within-group percentages were similar regardless of whether the words had L1 lexical equivalents.

Participants' inferred meanings for the unfamiliar target words were scored as follows:

- A semantically and syntactically appropriate response (full success = 2 points).
- An approximate meaning or a semantically accurate but syntactically inappropriate response (partial success = 1 point).
- An incorrect meaning or respondent gives up (failure = 0 points).

Examples of partially and fully successful inferences are given in Figure 5.1.

English L1			
Topic	Target word	Full success	Partial success
"Big City Dreams"	indulge	(partake) (revel) (splurge)	(sample) (digging in)
"Genetic engineering"	inadvertently	(unknowingly) (unwittingly) (unexpectedly) (simultaneously)	(unstoppably) (catastrophically)
"The world's forgotten poor"	genocide	(mass homicide) (massacre)	(deaths)
Persian L2			
Topic	Target word	Partial success	
"Marriage"	monogamy	"I think it means (to stay loyal to each other). The next sentence says *will become romantically involved with another individual... prize* [**monogamy**]."	
"Preserving our Environment";	trickle	"[**Trickles**] means (to flow) because it is talking about [water] and uses the preposition [down] after [**trickles**]; so, *water* (flows down) *the mountain*."	
"The Ice Age";	glaciers	"I had not read or seen this word before. Here, because it's talking about an area covered with ice, I think it means (icebergs)."	

Figure 5.1 Examples of fully and partially successful inferences

Five *success* scores were calculated for each individual for both L1 and L2 inferencing tasks (as applicable), three for the main study involving total target word sets, and two for the sub-study of lexicalization effects in L2 inferencing that distinguished lexicalized and non-lexicalized words. They included (1) summed full success, (2) summed partial success, (3) total weighted success (summed total and partial success scores), (4) lexicalized full success, and (5) non-lexicalized full success.

Participants' immediate retention of new target word knowledge following the L2 inferencing tasks was determined through comparison of scores from pre- and post-task administrations of the *Vocabulary Knowledge Scale* (VKS) (Paribakht & Wesche, 1996; Wesche & Paribakht, 1996). The VKS (described in Chapter 3) involves both self-report and performance data on participants' knowledge of individual words. One of its important features for this study is that it can provide separate information on incremental changes in the learner's knowledge of both word forms and word meanings.

Following determination of overall patterns of lexical inferencing success in L1 and L2 conditions, the additional issues of target word knowledge retention by L2 learners and the effect of target word lexicalization on readers' inferencing success and knowledge retention were examined. Parallel to the study of lexicalization effects in KS use reported in Chapter 3, the latter analysis involved comparison of Persian and French speakers' success in inferring and retaining meanings for the 25 English target words that had L1 lexical equivalents and 25 that did not. Fifteen of the words were common to the Persian and French word lists. Nine of these were lexicalized both in Persian and French; six were not lexicalized in either language.

The research procedures (Chapter 3) were the same for the Persian and French speakers for both L1 and L2 tasks. These two groups, however, had multiple tasks and, therefore, longer research sessions than the English speakers, for whom inferring meanings for 50 L1 target words was the only task.

L2 readers' scores on the *Vocabulary Levels Test* (Nation, 1990), a measure of receptive English L2 vocabulary knowledge, were used to gauge the effect of previous English knowledge on L2 lexical inferencing outcomes.

Findings

Lexical inferencing success

Participants' full success, partial success or failure in inferring appropriate meanings for unknown target words in L1 and L2 are given for the three language groups in Table 5.1 in terms of the percentage of inferences of unknown words with each outcome.

L1 inferencing

As Table 5.1 indicates, readers in all three language groups were highly successful in inferring appropriate meanings for the pseudo target words in their respective L1 texts, with fully appropriate meanings for 89.3% of English L1 words, 79% of Persian L1 words and 62.8% of French L1 words. Partially appropriate inferences were also recorded in each case, so that the total percentages of L1 words for which some success was achieved were English L1: 93.6%, Persian L1: 83% and French L1: 74.3%.

These high levels of success are hardly surprising, given these educated native speakers' language proficiency and relevant cultural

Table 5.1 L1 and L2 lexical inferencing success of English, Persian and French speakers

	Full success (%)	Partial success (%)	Failure (%)
English L1	89.3	4.3	6.4
Persian L1	79.0	4.0	17.0
Persian L2	11.0	11.0	78.0
French L1	62.8	11.5	25.7
French L2	31.1	20.5	48.4

Note: Percentages were calculated with reference to the summed number of unknown words reported by participants.

knowledge for reading texts originating in their first languages, and the relatively low difficulty of the texts surrounding the pseudo target words. The lower success rates for the Persian and French groups relative to the English L1 speakers may, to some extent, be attributable to the fact that L1 inferencing was the final task in their lengthy research sessions. The differences between the Persian and French readers' inferencing success in their L1s, most striking with respect to the higher percentage of fully successful inferences for the Persian speakers, raises the issue of certain observed differences between the two samples; for instance, that the somewhat older Persian-speaking participants as a group seemed more academically oriented and were observed by the researchers as showing particularly high motivation to carry out the tasks as completely as possible.

L2 inferencing

Both the Persian- and French-speaking groups were far less successful at inferring appropriate word meanings for the target words in their L2 than in their L1. Persian speakers achieved fully successful inferences in only 11% of cases in L2 and French speakers in 31.1%. When partially appropriate inferences were added, the total percentages of L2 words for which some success was achieved were Persian L2: 22% and French L2: 51.6%.

Comparison of the overall success rates in L2 versus those in L1 suggests that quite apart from the specific languages involved, the very large L2/L1 gap must be mainly attributable to the difference between these post-secondary readers' high-intermediate L2 proficiency and their L1 proficiency. What is less clear is why the Persian speakers were

Inferencing Success and Initial Development of Word Knowledge   121

dramatically less successful than the French speakers in L2 lexical inferencing. Differences in procedural abilities were an unlikely explanation of this difference, since the two groups had comparable L2 reading proficiency test scores, and in L1 lexical inferencing, the Persian speakers were more successful than the French speakers.[2] Group differences in participants' English lexical knowledge were, however, likely to have played a role (see below).

Lexicalized versus non-lexicalized second language target words

A more detailed analysis of the two L2 groups' inferencing behavior when dealing with lexicalized versus non-lexicalized English words was carried out. Figures 5.2 and 5.3 show the relative success of the two participant groups in inferring unfamiliar lexicalized and non-lexicalized target words in terms of full and partial success, and failure. Table 5.2 presents *t*-test results comparing each group's inferencing success for the two types of words, using weighted success scores.

Across-group comparisons of full, partial and weighted success scores, shown in Figures 5.2 and 5.3 and Table 5.2, indicate that by all measures target word lexicalization status had a strong effect on inferencing success; both groups were more successful in inferring the

	Lexicalized	Non Lexicalized
■ Full success %	17.0	6.0
▨ Partial success %	11.0	11.0
☐ Failure %	72.0	83.0

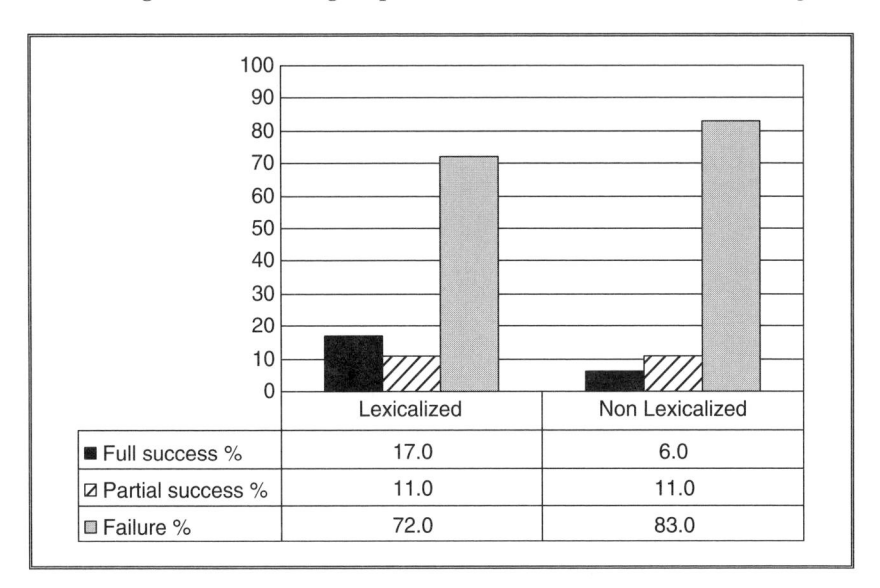

Figure 5.2 Success of Persian speakers in inferring meanings for lexicalized versus non-lexicalized L2 words

Table 5.2 Success in inferring meanings for lexicalized versus non-lexicalized words by Persian and French speakers

	Persian				French			
	Mean	SD	t-value	P	Mean	SD	t-value	P
Lexicalized	0.47	0.30	3.96	0.001**	0.89	0.28	3.06	0.006*
Non-lexicalized	0.24	0.14			0.76	0.29		

Note: Weighted total success scores were used. The maximum possible mean success score was 2. Individuals' scores for each inference (2, 1 or 0) were summed and then divided by the number of words inferred to calculate group means.
*P < 0.001; **P < 0.05.

Inferencing Success and Initial Development of Word Knowledge 123

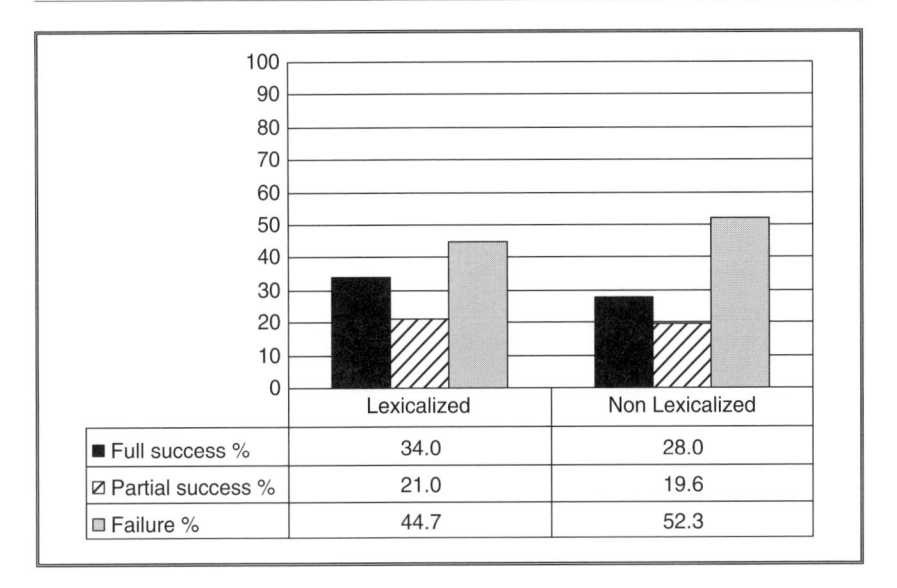

	Lexicalized	Non Lexicalized
■ Full success %	34.0	28.0
⊠ Partial success %	21.0	19.6
☐ Failure %	44.7	52.3

Figure 5.3 Success of French speakers in inferring meanings for lexicalized versus non-lexicalized L2 words

meanings of lexicalized than non-lexicalized words. Beyond this shared result, the Persian speakers were far less successful than the French speakers in inferring either lexicalized or non-lexicalized target English words. They also showed a greater disadvantage when inferring meanings for non-lexicalized words, achieving full inferencing success almost three times more often with lexicalized than with non-lexicalized words (17 versus 6%), while for the French speakers the difference was significant but smaller (34 versus 28%).[3]

Since the Persian- and French-speaking groups dealt with somewhat different sets of target words in their L2 lexical inferencing tasks, separate analyses were conducted on the 15 shared English target words to ensure that findings were not due to the particular word sets.[4] In these analyses, the Persian speakers were, as for the full data sets, notably less successful than the French speakers in inferring the meanings of both lexicalized (18.9 versus 35.8%, respectively) and non-lexicalized words (7.4 versus 23.4%, respectively). These success rates were quite similar to those for the complete target word sets, supporting the validity of those findings for the two groups.

Retention of new second language word knowledge through lexical inferencing

Both the Persian and French groups showed significant – if small – immediate gains in new English target word knowledge as a result of the L2 inferencing tasks, measured by summed VKS scores that reflect changes in both word-form familiarity and word-meaning recall. (See Chapter 3 for further explanation of the VKS.) Such gains reflect short-term retention; we were not able to administer a further VKS after a time delay, so we cannot know the extent to which this initial knowledge was retained over a longer term. Immediate gains are nonetheless important, because without retention at this point, any subsequent vocabulary knowledge development based on the inferencing task is unlikely. These results also provide evidence of the conditions in which vocabulary learning may occur through reading and inferencing.

Average gains for the Persian and French speakers for the full L2 word sets are shown in Figure 5.4, which presents pre-task and post-task VKS scores for each language group, followed by a t-test. Tables 5.3 and 5.4 present t-tests comparing pre- and post-task VKS scores for lexicalized and non-lexicalized words.

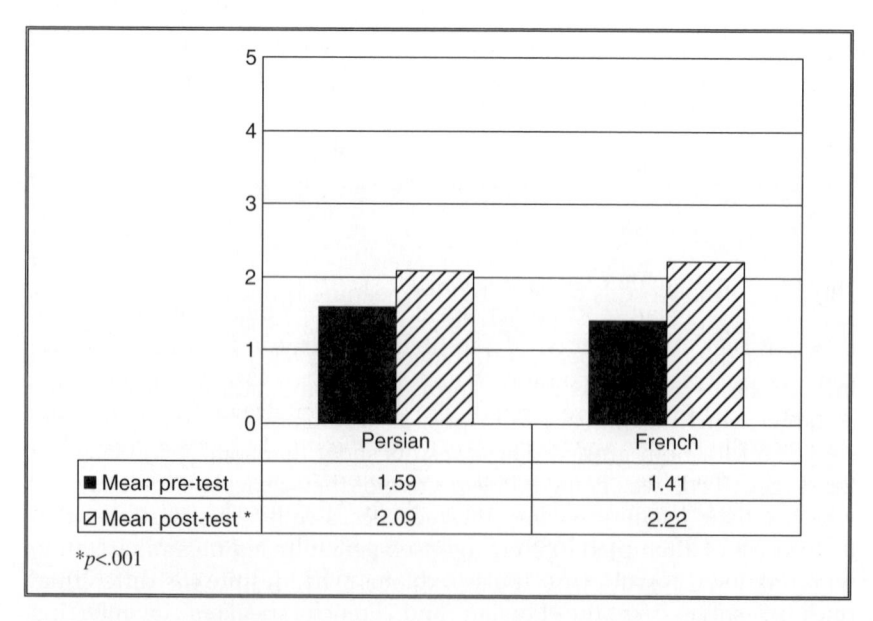

	Persian	French
■ Mean pre-test	1.59	1.41
▨ Mean post-test *	2.09	2.22

*$p<.001$

Figure 5.4 Pre-task to post-task gains in average VKS scores for all L2 target words by Persian and French speakers

Table 5.3 Pre-task to post-task gains in average VKS scores for lexicalized L2 words by Persian and French speakers

	Before inferencing VKS scores		After inferencing VKS scores			
	Mean	SD	Mean	SD	t-value	P
Persian	1.64	0.21	2.16	0.23	−7.98	0.000**
French	1.34	0.14	2.22	0.42	−9.94	0.000**

Note: The maximum possible VKS score for an item is 5.
 **P < 0.001

Table 5.4 Pre-task to post-task gains in average VKS scores for non-lexicalized L2 words by Persian and French speakers

	Before inferencing VKS scores		After inferencing VKS scores			
	Mean	SD	Mean	SD	t-value	P
Persian	1.54	0.19	2.03	0.12	−10.65	0.000**
French	1.47	0.13	2.21	0.27	−13.26	0.000**

Note: The maximum possible VKS score for an item is 5.
 **P < 0.001

As shown in Figure 5.4, average pre-task VKS scores for both groups on the total word sets and in Tables 5.3 and 5.4 for both lexicalized and non-lexicalized words were between levels 1 ('the word is not familiar at all') and 2 ('the word is familiar but its meaning is not known'), whereas post-task averages were around 2 for the Persian speakers and slightly higher for the French speakers. On average, the VKS levels corresponding to these results represent form familiarity, but not knowledge of target word meanings. Pre to post-task gains on this measure were significant for both groups. These results show that some knowledge of the target words was gained, irrespective of their lexicalization status or whether their meanings were inferred successfully. This indicates that the process of attempted inferencing itself generally led to familiarization with unknown word forms. It also explains why, despite the differential rates of success of the Persian and French speakers in inferring lexicalized and non-lexicalized words, their average post-task VKS scores were similar.

To better understand what lay behind these average VKS gain scores, the actual VKS levels reported for each word by participants for both pre- and post-task VKS administrations were examined in detail and compared across groups. Particular attention was given to score changes after inferencing that indicated either new knowledge of *word forms* (i.e. movement from initial VKS level 1 to post-task level 2), or new knowledge of *word meanings* (i.e. movement from initial VKS levels 1 or 2 to post-task level 3) (i.e. 'a correct synonym or translation is given'), or beyond (indicating its use in a sentence with semantic appropriateness (level 4) or its use in a sentence with both semantic and grammatical accuracy (level 5)). These results are presented in Figure 5.5 for Persian speakers and Figure 5.6 for French speakers.

Initially, both groups had high pre-task percentages of level 1 VKS responses to target words (Persian speakers: 37.6%, French

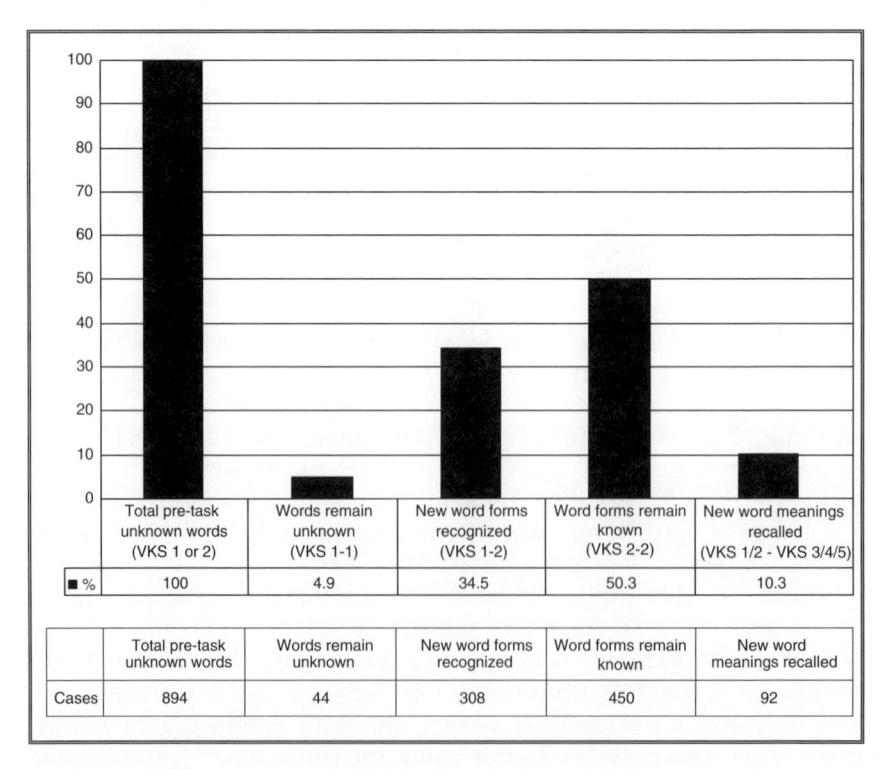

	Total pre-task unknown words (VKS 1 or 2)	Words remain unknown (VKS 1-1)	New word forms recognized (VKS 1-2)	Word forms remain known (VKS 2-2)	New word meanings recalled (VKS 1/2 - VKS 3/4/5)
%	100	4.9	34.5	50.3	10.3

	Total pre-task unknown words	Words remain unknown	New word forms recognized	Word forms remain known	New word meanings recalled
Cases	894	44	308	450	92

Figure 5.5 Pre-task to post-task changes in knowledge of L2 target words: Persian speakers

Inferencing Success and Initial Development of Word Knowledge 127

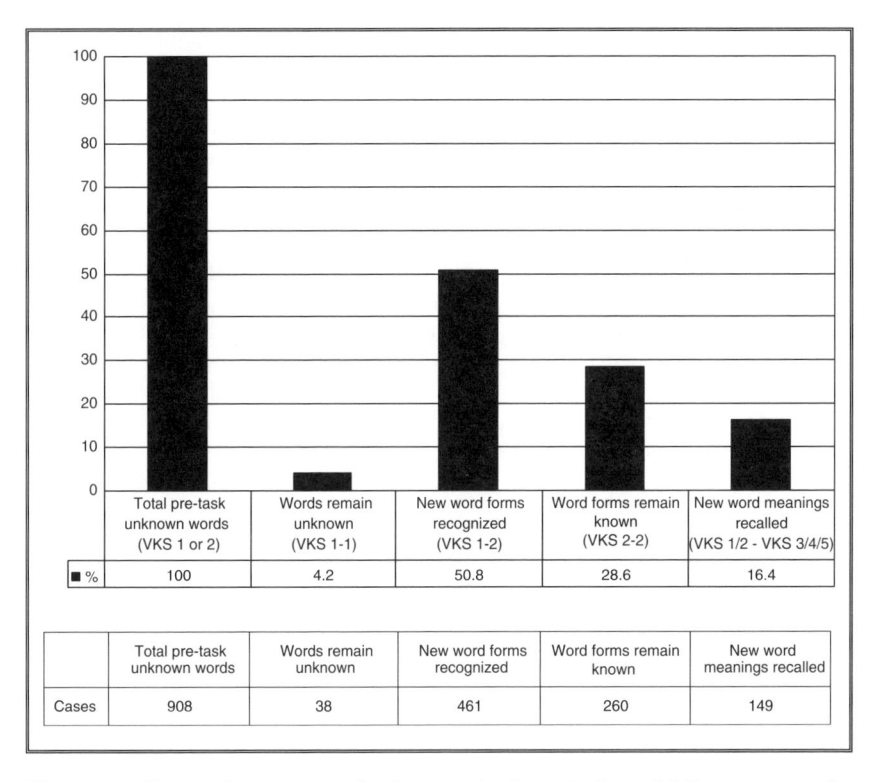

	Total pre-task unknown words (VKS 1 or 2)	Words remain unknown (VKS 1-1)	New word forms recognized (VKS 1-2)	Word forms remain known (VKS 2-2)	New word meanings recalled (VKS 1/2 - VKS 3/4/5)
%	100	4.2	50.8	28.6	16.4

	Total pre-task unknown words	Words remain unknown	New word forms recognized	Word forms remain known	New word meanings recalled
Cases	908	38	461	260	149

Figure 5.6 Pre-task to post-task changes in knowledge of L2 target words: French speakers

speakers: 56.6%) each represented as 100% in Column 1 of Figures 5.5 and 5.6. Column 2 shows that only small percentages of these words remained completely unknown following the L2 inferencing task (Persian speakers: 5.2%, French speakers: 4.2%). Column 3 indicates the percentage of formerly unknown words that participants recognized (VKS level 2) following the inferencing task (Persian speakers: 34.5%, French speakers: 50.8%). Column 4 reflects the percentages of words that participants reported having previously seen but did not know the meanings of, either before or after the inferencing task. The sum of columns 3 and 4, reflect all the cases of post-task word-form familiarity as the highest level reached, accounting for about three-quarters of all previously unknown words for each group (Persian speakers: 77.6%, French speakers: 73.6%).

From these figures, it may be seen that participants, through inferencing, gained word-form familiarity for most of the target words they had initially reported as never having seen. For most words for which they had already reported form-familiarity on the pre-task, the post-task response remained form-familiarity. This explains the post-task VKS scores reported above. However, some L2 readers in both groups did learn meanings for some of the target words during the inferencing task. As shown in column 5 of Figures 5.5 and 5.6, 10.2% of initial Persian responses at non-meaning levels (1 or 2) moved to at least level 3 at the second VKS administration, as did 16.4% of French responses. In these cases, initial learning of new target word meanings had occurred. These initial gains from the inferencing task in word-form familiarity, and more important, in recall of target word meanings that had previously been unknown, provide evidence pertinent to the role of lexical inferencing in the slow, incremental process of vocabulary acquisition from reading.

To further pursue the issue of how lexical inferencing may contribute to lexical development, the following section presents correlations between measures of previous English receptive vocabulary knowledge, inferencing success and post-inferencing recall of new L2 target word meanings and an examination of individual cases of successful L2 lexical inferencing as these relate to post-inferencing recall.

Relationship of vocabulary knowledge to lexical inferencing success and word-meaning retention

Table 5.5 and Table 5.6 present Pearson correlation analyses of Persian and French speakers' scores on the *Vocabulary Levels Test*, measures of inferencing success (full success and total (weighted) success) and VKS gain scores in word meaning knowledge, i.e. moving from pre-task non-meaning levels (VKS 1–2) to post-task meaning levels (VKS 3–5).

As may be seen in Tables 5.5 and 5.6, similar patterns of significant correlations among the measures of English vocabulary knowledge and lexical inferencing outcomes are found for both Persian and French speakers. In both analyses, scores on the *Vocabulary Levels Test* are significantly correlated with both lexical inferencing success and new post-inferencing knowledge of new target word meanings, in line with findings reported elsewhere. Furthermore, inferencing success scores are correlated with gains in word-meaning knowledge. This link is analyzed further through examination of each case of attempted inferencing

Table 5.5 Persian speakers' L2 receptive vocabulary knowledge, lexical inferencing success and gains in knowledge of target word meanings

	Vocabulary Levels Test	Full inferencing success	Total weighted success
Full inferencing success	0.63**		
Total (weighted) success	0.71***	0.94***	
Total non-meaning to meaning knowledge	0.76***	0.75***	0.73***

*$P < 0.05$; **$P < 0.01$; ***$P < 0.001$ (two-tailed)

Descriptive statistics ($N = 20$)

	Mean	SD
Vocabulary Levels Test	59.7	17
Full inferencing success	4.6	3.1
Total (weighted) success	13.4	6.9
Word-meaning retention	4.6	3.1

that resulted in either full or partial success in inferring an appropriate target word meaning as it related to retention of new word meanings. The results reflect a strong connection between these two positive outcomes of lexical inferencing. In 82% of the cases in which the Persian speakers successfully inferred the meanings of formerly unknown words (63% full plus 19% partial success), they were able to recall the new word meaning (and in some cases also able to use it in a sentence) on the post-task VKS. In 88% of the French speakers' cases of successful inferencing (58% full plus 30% partial success), they could do this.

In these data, then, successful inferencing appears to play an important role in initial learning of new L2 word meanings from reading texts, a very encouraging finding. At the same time, it must be emphasized that the high inferencing failure rates of these two groups of L2 readers (78.0% for the Persian speakers and 48.4% for the French speakers) reflect the uncertainty of reading and inferring unknown word meanings as a route to L2 vocabulary knowledge. Much more needs to be

Table 5.6 French speakers' L2 receptive vocabulary knowledge, inferencing success and gains in knowledge of target word meanings

	Vocabulary Levels Test	Full inferencing success	Total weighted success
Full inferencing success	0.79***		
Total (weighted) success	0.79***	0.98***	
Total non-meaning to meaning knowledge	0.68***	0.49*	0.53*

*$P < 0.05$; **$P < 0.01$; ***$P < 0.001$ (two-tailed)

Descriptive statistics ($N = 20$)

	Mean	SD
Vocabulary Levels Test	65.3	8.5
Full inferencing success	17.9	6.3
Total (weighted) success	45.5	14.3
Word-meaning retention	7.5	4.5

understood about how to ensure the conditions leading to inferencing success and retention before this relationship can be systematically employed to support vocabulary learning.

The correlation analyses show that greater receptive L2 vocabulary knowledge facilitates lexical inferencing and initial word learning. At the same time, the high inferencing failure rates indicate that a minimum threshold of L2 vocabulary knowledge may be needed for this relationship to be realized. Such a threshold would be expected, based on research showing that readers must know a very high percentage of the words in a text in order to understand that text unassisted or to successfully infer the meanings of words they don't know (Chapter 1).

To pursue this issue, we ranked L2 participants' scores for inferencing success and for post-inferencing gains in knowledge of target word meanings according to the ranking of their receptive vocabulary scores, and inspected these for evidence of a threshold of vocabulary knowledge above which successful inferencing and gains in word-meaning knowledge were more frequent and below which such gains were rare.

Inferencing Success and Initial Development of Word Knowledge 131

Differences in the vocabulary score distribution for both groups were evident; Persian speakers' scores covered a very wide range, from the lowest (27 of a possible 90 points) to two students who gained the maximum possible score (90). While five scores were above 70, five were below 50. (The French speakers were more homogeneous; their scores ranged from 53 to 83, with five above 70 and none below 50.)

In both groups, the students with the highest vocabulary scores consistently demonstrated gains in knowledge of word meanings (i.e. 3 or above on the VKS) for words whose meanings they had successfully inferred. The two Persian speakers with the highest vocabulary test scores demonstrated post-inferencing knowledge of 5 and 8 new target word meanings, all associated with successful inferencing, and the highest scoring French speaker, 16 new target word meanings. Most pre-task to post-task shifts from VKS levels 1 or 2 to meaning levels 4 and 5 – indicating successful use of the target words in sentences – were by French L2 readers. For both groups, vocabulary scores of 57[5] or more appeared to be the starting level for more frequent gains in new word meanings. The eight Persian speakers with the lowest vocabulary scores (from 27 to 54) gained from 0 to 2 new word meanings, averaging below 1, while the three French speakers with the lowest scores (from 53 to 55) gained from 1 to 3 new word meanings, averaging 2. Persian speakers with scores of 57 or more recalled (with one exception) from 3 to 10 new target word meanings after inferencing, averaging 5.7 new word meanings, while French speakers with scores of 57 or more recalled (with two exceptions) from 3 to 16 new word meanings, averaging 9.8.[6]

Given this apparent threshold, we carried out *t*-tests to compare word-meaning gains for participants with *Vocabulary Levels Test* scores above and below 57. Results for both groups were significant. While these numbers are small, the patterns are clear and the results for both language groups are similar. These findings lend support to the claim that there is a threshold of previous vocabulary knowledge below which successful inferencing and post-task gains in word meaning are unlikely, but above which such results can be demonstrated. Furthermore, they provide evidence that for readers whose level of L2 vocabulary knowledge is adequate for the texts and new words they are reading, successful lexical inferencing can indeed lead to initial retention of new word meanings as a potential step toward further lexical development.

These results also show a persistent difference in the relative success of the Persian and French speakers in this study, indicating that while the measure of receptive vocabulary knowledge used appears to largely explain the relative success of individuals, there is a group factor related to their L1 that is not captured by this measure. We believe that this factor has largely to do with previous lexical knowledge as it relates to the typological differences between readers' L1 and the L2.

In this study, many of the participants, particularly in the Persian-speaking group, were unable to successfully infer the meanings of the large majority of the target L2 words in English. These tended to be the same participants who showed little retention of new word meanings following the inferencing task. The English texts contained a high concentration of difficult words for most of these L2 readers, including almost all the target words, and our findings indicate that stronger L2 vocabulary knowledge would likely have facilitated greater lexical inferencing success for most if not all participants.

In particular, target words without lexical equivalents in readers' L1 were very difficult for these English learners to process and comprehend. Persian speakers, whose language is typologically more distant from English than French, were particularly challenged. Although non-lexicalized words were also more difficult than lexicalized words for the French speakers, Persian speakers' inferencing success was affected more strongly by the lexicalization status of the target words. Several examples from the transcripts are given in Figure 5.7, which illustrate not only the difficulty experienced by a Persian speaker in inferring the meaning of a non-lexicalized word, but also how the failure to comprehend the word interfered with his comprehension of the entire text.

While the two groups were roughly equivalent in reading proficiency, and their receptive English vocabulary test scores were not significantly different, more of the French speakers had relatively high vocabulary scores, which enabled them to infer more words successfully and retain a slightly higher percentage of the meanings they had inferred. It was not surprising that more of the French speakers had higher scores, in spite of the many years of study of the somewhat older Persian group, given the multiple linguistic relationships between French and English that would have provided them with a learning advantage throughout their studies and their naturalistic English learning context. Beyond their receptive English vocabulary knowledge, the French speakers' use of more varied *word* KSs in inferencing compared with the Persian speakers, suggested that they, in general, had richer L2 word knowledge to bring to the task. This went beyond recognition of word meanings and included varied associations with these words, for example, similar orthographical representations and derivational relatives of L1 words, and oral associations for L2 words.

Inferencing Success and Initial Development of Word Knowledge 133

> *In the following excerpts, the Persian L2 reader cannot infer the meaning of the non-lexicalized target word 'to clone' and as a result misunderstands the text and has problems guessing the meanings of other unfamiliar target words.*
>
> Topic *"Genetic engineering"*; Target word: *to clone*
>
> P: I can't guess [**clone**] because [**clone**]... We use [colony] in our language. [colony] means to live in groups but here I believe it wouldn't make sense .... I think the meaning of this [**clone**] must be important because it's been used many times in the text. I think the [point] of the story, that is, the theme, revolves around this word.
> I: Why do you think so?
> P: Because the example is about sheep and then here in fact the results of this experiment, this [**clone**], it becomes clear where they've got with their research.
>
> *Subsequently, when dealing with the target word [**to trigger**], the participant refers to 'clone' again and tries to make sense of the word.*
>
> Topic *"Genetic engineering"*; Target word: *to trigger* P: I think it must mean (doing something). In other words, it wants to say that in fact, who knows what the new technology might do? Some such meaning ....
> [**clones**] here means (groups) but it wouldn't make sense over there. Here I think it says scientists can (raise) some animals, creatures ... It has some such meaning. With this meaning for [**to clone**], the sentence there didn't make sense to me.
>
> *The participant continues to interpret the meaning of the target word 'to clone' in inferring "to snoop".*
>
> Topic *"Genetic engineering"*; Target word: *to trigger* P: It might mean (to investigate) because it says [file]. *Files, doctors' files*. The criminals might then have access to these files.... As I said [**cloning**] was important in the sentence. That is, if I'd known the meaning of [**to clone**], I might've better understood the text. In fact I know what the text is generally talking about, but I don't exactly understand it because of the word [**clone**].

Figure 5.7 Example of a Persian L2 reader's difficulties with a non-lexicalized word

From our findings, it appears that L2 lexical knowledge plays a major role in both inferencing success and immediate retention of new knowledge of word meanings as part of lexical acquisition, and that development of lexical knowledge is likely to be substantially facilitated when learners' L1 and L2 share many typological similarities – and in the case of French, historical and cultural links that have promoted similarities in the lexicons – including lexicalization patterns. In addition, naturalistic contexts for language learning and use are important in L2 lexical development, offering oral and written exposure to new words in varied contexts, and promoting motivation as well as practice in interactive and productive use of the second language.

Summary and Discussion

Lexical inferencing success

In their L1s, all participant groups were highly successful in inferring appropriate meanings for the pseudo target words, particularly the English speakers. The moderately lower L1 inferencing success of the Persian and French L1 readers may have been at least partially due to a fatigue factor, as noted previously. The even lower scores for French speakers in L1 may also reflect other group differences, such as academic experience and relative motivation.

Results were notably different for participants when inferencing in their L2, English. Persian speakers were fully or partially successful in only 22% of their L2 inferences, compared with a success rate of 83% in L1. The French L2 readers were also challenged, but not nearly as much as the Persian speakers, being fully or partially successful in about 52% of their L2 inferences as compared to 74% in L1. Since the L1 and L2 participants were the same individuals, eliminating extraneous research influences, much of the overall L1-L2 gap in inferencing success can be attributed to their non-native mastery of English. Beyond this gap, the differences found between the performance of the Persian and French participants in terms of L2 lexical inferencing success and subsequent gains in knowledge of new word meanings also appear to be largely related to their relative lexical proficiency in English, including but going beyond those aspects captured in the receptive English *Vocabulary Levels Test* and involving L1 transfer effects. In addition, the divergent performance of the two groups may also represent relevant differences not only in L2 linguistic and procedural knowledge, but also cultural familiarity with text features, such as concepts and points of view presented and schemata underlying the presentation of given topics in English texts.

The results of correlation analyses showed that for both groups, learners with a larger L2 receptive vocabulary size could more successfully infer the meanings of unfamiliar words, confirming that lexical knowledge is a critical aspect of the L2 proficiency needed as a basis for successful lexical inferencing. Furthermore, such success was linked to subsequent at least initial retention of new word knowledge. Subsequent examination of the data indicated a threshold of such knowledge needed to ensure reasonable inferencing success.

Inferencing Success and Initial Development of Word Knowledge 135

It is known that recognition vocabulary test scores do not fully capture the network aspects of lexical knowledge operant in L2 reading and inferencing. The data presented here suggest that important differences in lexical knowledge distinguish the Persian-speaking English learners from the French-speaking English learners. The most important of these differences – the relationship of the L1 to English, and to a lesser extent the learning context – advantaged the French speakers in English L2 inferencing and its outcomes.

The success of both Persian and French readers in inferring appropriate meanings for lexicalized and non-lexicalized target words showed a strong effect for lexicalization. Both groups were more successful in inferring appropriate meanings for lexicalized than non-lexicalized words, indicating the greater difficulty of the latter. The relatively dense embedding of non-lexicalized words in our reading texts likely added significantly to the challenge faced by all the L2 readers in their text comprehension and lexical inferencing.

At the same time, group comparisons showed that, in general, French speakers were more successful than Persian speakers in inferring the meanings of both lexicalized and non-lexicalized English target words.

Several important factors related to the relative typological distance of Persian and French from English probably contributed to the greater lexical inferencing success of the French speakers. Since English and French share many word derivations, lexicalization patterns and cognates, the French speakers were in an advantageous position to the extent that they could access that knowledge base in inferring unfamiliar English word meanings. In this study, even though no cognate target words were used, French-English lexical correspondences, including cognate relationships, in the texts surrounding the target words likely had some facilitating effect on the French speakers' cumulative text comprehension and thus aided their comprehension of unfamiliar word meanings. Further, as Ard and Holmburg (1983) observed, besides the benefits of recognizing cognates, another likely advantage for L2 learners from cognate languages may be that they have more time and mental energy to concentrate on unfamiliar vocabulary compared to speakers of more distant languages.

Although not systematically examined in the current study, differences between Persian and English orthography discussed in Chapters 2 and 3 may also help explain the Persian speakers' lower success rate in inferring (both lexicalized and non-lexicalized) English target words embedded in written texts. One difference is the lack of representation of several vowels in Persian, by which Persian readers may habitually focus more on processing individual letters in English, likely making it more difficult for them to recognize and store unfamiliar word forms as an anchor for new meanings. Another is the L1 to L2 shift in the directionality of written text (Persian is read from right to left), resulting in slower reading in English and subsequent poorer text comprehension (as noted by Ghahremani-Ghajar & Masny, 1999). Poorer comprehension would, in turn, almost certainly affect their L2 lexical inferencing success.

Furthermore, as discussed earlier, the historical cultural proximity of French to English – an ongoing lived reality in Canada – meant that cultural concepts in the English texts would be more familiar to the French speakers. Possibly even more important was their English as a second language (ESL) learning context in Canada's bilingual national capital region, an environment that provided considerable informal media and personal exposure to English alongside English instruction in the schools and colleges, which emphasizes oral and written communication for use in daily life. This more naturalistic language learning environment, in which oral, written and social language skills were being learned and used in informal as well as formal situations, compared with the largely written emphasis of the formal English instruction received by the Persian speakers, almost certainly meant that the French speakers brought richer and deeper English knowledge to the inferencing task. The English reading and receptive vocabulary test scores may have largely reflected the full English knowledge base of the Persian English as a foreign language (EFL) students, while the French speakers would have also had stronger speaking skills in English, and probably a richer store of associations for known words that could have facilitated their text comprehension and lexical inferencing.

Lexical development

Both Persian and French speakers demonstrated significant post-inferencing gains in target word knowledge following the L2 inferencing task. Nonetheless, these gains tended, in most cases, to involve learning to recognize new target word forms encountered during the L2 inferencing task, while post-task ability to recall new target word meanings was relatively infrequent overall.

This finding accorded with findings from other studies indicating that lexical development is known to be a lengthy, incremental process, normally requiring multiple exposures to new words in different contexts. As noted by other researchers, L2 lexical processing in inferencing when reading, while it leads to measurable development, is generally not in itself a rapid or a very efficient vocabulary learning procedure (Hulstijn, 1992; Kim, 2003; Paribakht & Wesche, 1997). Still, given the importance of reading in education and so many other aspects of modern life, the vocabulary learning that takes place through reading, perhaps much of it initiated through lexical inferencing, is over time no doubt considerable. Thus, it was encouraging to find that when inferencing was successful, in most cases it led to post-task retention of word-meaning knowledge for both Persian and French L2 readers. Furthermore, both lexical inferencing success and subsequent retention of new lexical knowledge were strongly linked to L2 readers' English vocabulary knowledge. It was also remarkable to find a consistent threshold level of vocabulary scores that held for both groups, above which successful lexical inferencing and subsequent retention of new word knowledge were increasingly likely with higher vocabulary scores, and below which L2 lexical inferencing was almost never successful.

These findings add to our understanding of the role of successful lexical inferencing in the development of lexical knowledge, and help explain earlier findings linking reading with lexical development in L1, as well as those that have shown that it is often not as strong a link for L2 users. The findings of this comparative study provide solid grounds for concluding that successful L2 lexical inferencing in reading and related lexical development are both mediated by readers' L2 lexical knowledge, which is itself strongly influenced by the typological proximity of the L1 and L2, particularly with respect to lexical features, including lexicalization patterns. L2 users' vocabulary knowledge also, to some extent, appears to reflect their context of target language learning and use. Finally, the findings provide insight into L1-related challenges that learners from various linguistic backgrounds may encounter in L2 reading and lexical inferencing.

Notes

1. Pseudo words with morphological cues relevant to the original target words should essentially require the same inferencing process as unknown lexicalized (as opposed to non-lexicalized) words. Because L1 readers expect to know the words, they may try a little harder than L2 users to figure them out.
2. In this study, no significant correlations were found for either group between L1 inferencing success and either of the L2 inferencing success variables. Given the procedural abilities involved in reading and inferencing and evidence from elsewhere of the transfer of L1 to L2 procedural skills (Koda, 2005), such a relationship would be expected. In this case, it seems likely that the large gap between L1 and L2 text language mastery and the difficulty of

the L2 tasks make it impossible to demonstrate such a relationship for these participants.
3. For both groups partial success rates, while differing from each other, remained essentially the same in both conditions: 11% for Persian speakers with both lexicalized and non-lexicalized words; 21 and 19% for French speakers, respectively.
4. See list of L2 target words, indicating shared words across the two data sets, in Appendix A.
5. There were no scores of 56 in either group.
6. Markedly atypical results were found for two French-speaking participants, who showed neither successful inferences nor gains in new word meanings. One of these participants also accounted for half the level 1 VKS scores ('never having before seen the word') on the post-task administration. These two cases were removed from this analysis.

Chapter 6
Trilingual Study Summary, Discussion and Implications

In this trilingual study, our primary goal was to gain a better understanding of how second language (L2) readers' native language knowledge (L1) influences their L2 lexical inferencing from written texts and its outcomes. In particular, we wished to examine L1 transfer in L2 inferencing in terms of the relative typological distance between the L1 and the L2. What kinds of help — if any — may come from the readers' L1? What might be the importance in L1 transfer of typological proximity between the L1 and L2, reflecting similarities of linguistic features in the two languages? How might the relative typological proximity of readers' L1 to the L2 appear to relate to readers' relative lexical proficiency in the L2? To their success in L2 lexical inferencing? To their subsequent retention of new word knowledge?

To answer these questions, we carried out a study of the processes and outcomes of L1 lexical inferencing from written texts by speakers of three Indo-European languages (English, Persian and French) and L2 lexical inferencing by the latter two groups in English, using introspective methods — as reported in Chapters 3 to 5. In this research, readers were asked to try to infer meanings for specific text-embedded target words they didn't know, so that both the incidence of inferencing and their attention to many of these words was probably greater than would have occurred in a natural reading situation. However, the nature of the process and outcomes of our inferencing tasks correspond to those of reading situations in which readers are motivated to understand L2 reading texts and to attempt inferring the meanings of unfamiliar words they encounter while reading, as often happens with university students studying through a second language and with L1 readers of technical texts in an unfamiliar field.

We first sought to determine shared — presumably more universal — aspects of L1 and L2 lexical inferencing across the three groups. Next, we looked at overall differences between L1 and L2 lexical inferencing that held across languages. We were then able to consider our main issue of L1 influences from Persian or French in English L2 lexical inferencing by the same readers. For each of these three issues, our analysis centered on the kinds of knowledge and contextual cues, or knowledge sources (KSs), that readers reported using when inferencing, as well as their success in arriving at contextually appropriate word meanings. We compared findings across L1 conditions, between L1 and L2 conditions in general and for the Persian and French speakers, and across the English (Persian and French L2 and English L1) conditions. We then examined L2 readers' retention of new word knowledge following the inferencing task, particularly as it related to their inferencing success, and as both related to their receptive English vocabulary knowledge. The results from these various analyses led us to then consider how transfer effects might relate to the relative typological distances between readers' L1 and L2, as manifested in their L2 lexical knowledge. In this chapter, we review and synthesize the most important findings from the trilingual study and discuss their implications for our understanding of L2 lexical inferencing, future research on this topic, and L2 reading and vocabulary instruction at advanced levels.

Shared Cross-linguistic Aspects of Knowledge Source Use in First and Second Language Lexical Inferencing

The issue of shared versus language-specific inferencing behavior in L1 and L2 lexical inferencing was examined through comparisons of readers' use of different KSs across the five conditions. KS use in lexical inferencing involves interaction of readers' own knowledge with cues from target words and textual features. In written texts, readers' search for clues from which to construct a word meaning begins with the target word form (or lexeme), which may provide information through its spelling, presumed sound associations or affixes. This search and the combined use of KSs in reaching an inference about the word meaning involve procedural knowledge (knowing 'how'), while the actual linguistic information and meaning content provided by the different KSs involve declarative knowledge (knowing 'that') (Chapter 1). This search for different aspects of a word meaning may be viewed as a process of lemma construction as the reader assembles and elaborates semantic, syntactic and functional elements of the meaning. This process may be short cut if the reader can identify an assumed lexical equivalent in L1 or another language, or a related L2 word, which may serve for immediate comprehension purposes. If no such equivalent is known, the construction process is far more demanding and less likely to succeed. In such a case, the reader may not comprehend the word meaning or at best may partially comprehend some aspects of it in context; meaning retention is then unlikely (Paribakht, 2005).

Characteristic patterns of KS use are viewed here as learned processing tendencies that indicate where in the text or target word readers tend to look for specific kinds of information on which to base their inferences. Among other influences on the L2 inferencing process, these patterns – while to some extent widely shared across languages – may also reflect characteristic processing tendencies in the speakers' L1.

A comprehensive taxonomy including all the KS types used in the five conditions was developed during the analysis and classification of participants' think-aloud protocols while inferencing (Chapter 4). It is both a study outcome and served as an important tool for comparisons of KS use across the L1-L2 and different native language conditions. The taxonomy is organized by main knowledge types (*linguistic* and *non-linguistic*), and in the case of linguistic KSs, by their location with respect to the target word; i.e. *word* KSs are part of or closely related to the target word; *sentence* KSs are within the same sentence as the target word; and *discourse* KSs are more distant, generally preceding the target word, and sometimes representing cumulative text understanding to that point. Each linguistic category has three or four sub-categories that indicate more precisely the type of knowledge involved. This trilingual taxonomy confirms the similarity of these participants' repertoires of KS use to findings from earlier studies of L2 inferencing by ourselves and others involving speakers of mixed or other L1s (e.g. Bengeleil & Paribakht, 2004). Differences are mainly related to the inclusion of L1 lexical inferencing data, which underlined the importance of KS sub-types related to very high language proficiency.

In this study, all participants from each language group used KSs from each major taxonomic category in both L1 and L2 inferencing, including many if not all the sub-types within each *linguistic* category. Readers in all five conditions used a wide variety of KSs, drawing on both meaning-oriented and form-oriented *linguistic* cues located within or near the target words, as well as on information from earlier (and occasionally later) parts of a text, and their own world knowledge. However, although the KS repertoire was essentially shared across all L1 conditions and most of it across the L2 conditions, the proportion of use of different KSs varied greatly, depending (among other things) on whether readers' L1 was Persian, French or English and whether they were reading in their L1 or L2.

All groups of readers primarily depended on cues that were meaning oriented (i.e. *sentence meaning, discourse meaning, world knowledge*).

Likewise, they tended to use 'local' cues, found in the word itself or close to it within the immediate sentence context (*word* or *sentence* cues). *Sentence meaning* was by far the most important KS type used in all conditions, tending to be the first or only KS tried, and also likely to appear as a second or later source in a multiple sequence of KSs. *Sentence meaning* cues are probably so important because they are both meaning related and local. In addition to *sentence meaning*, all data sets included a variety of other KSs; of 11 different KS sub-types, between 8 and 10 accounted for at least 1% of KS use reported in each of the five conditions.

Readers in all conditions sometimes reported using only one KS in arriving at their guesses and multiple KSs (ranging from two to five) for others.[1] Multiple KS use was related to English as a text language for both L1 and L2 inferencing; English L1 readers reported multiple KSs for most inferences, while the other two language groups tended to use mainly single KSs in their L1, but multiple sequences somewhat more frequently in English L2. This probably relates to English L1 readers' tendency to draw heavily on KSs from all three linguistic levels, unlike the Persian and French readers, and ultimately, on the ways that information relating to word meanings is distributed in the English language. The use of multiple KSs per inference was not directly related to successful inferencing; however, it often bore some relationship to word difficulty, coming into play when readers could not construct an appropriate word meaning with their first KS, or needed to confirm or refine a guess. Haastrup (2007, personal communication) emphasizes that while multiple cues are often needed for successful inferencing, what is important to success is the combination of different types of knowledge – as required for inferring a given word meaning in context. For example, lower-level linguistic (e.g. *word*) cues may offer precise hypotheses about a word's meaning, but consideration of the discourse context and one's general knowledge are also needed, to confirm that inferences are contextually appropriate (also see Chapter 1).

Sentence meaning was the major KS sub-type used, not only *initially* but also *post-initially* in multiple KS sequences. Additionally, readers often used less frequent KSs post-initially. Thus, KSs that might not serve for identifying a core word meaning could be useful in refining a guess, such as *formal schemata*, *style/register* or *punctuation*.

The general patterns of KS use and the KS repertoire described above were common across the Persian, French and English L1 lexical inferencing as well as in English L2 by both Persian and French speakers. They reflected both the shared procedures readers used in trying to construct word meanings and the actual declarative linguistic and conceptual knowledge they employed with specific target words. Given these cross-lingual commonalities and the similarities in the taxonomy to KS use in earlier studies, they can be considered to characterize shared aspects of lexical inferencing in at least these three Indo-European languages and might be expected to operate similarly in other Indo-European languages.

These findings regarding cross-lingual commonalities in lexical inferencing procedures may be interpreted as evidence that in coping with lexical gaps, educated adult readers share an underlying strategic competence through which they seek to access similar linguistic and non-linguistic KSs and whose implementation is affected by the availability of relevant knowledge and competencies. Related evidence for the existence of a common underlying strategic competence in dealing with lexical problems also exists in the literature on oral communication strategies. For example, Paribakht, in her 1985 comparative study of strategy use in oral communication of word meanings that were unknown to the interlocutors by Persian speakers at different English proficiency levels and English native speakers, likewise found shared patterns of use of KS types by all three groups. In both cases, adult L1 and L2 speakers share a well-developed strategic competence (as is evident for the same speakers inferencing in L1 and L2); however, they differ in implementing that competence simply because their strategic ability interacts with different levels of knowledge in L1 and L2 required for completing the language task at hand. An increase in L2 linguistic and other required declarative knowledge allows the speakers to better implement their strategic competence, but does not appear to affect the strategic ability itself. In implementing the lexical inferencing strategy (an aspect of their strategic competence), readers search the text for existing cues and also call upon their world knowledge. The effectiveness and success of their strategy use largely depends, however, on their recognition of appropriate textual cues (i.e. their receptive knowledge of linguistic cues embedded in the text), their general linguistic knowledge (including lexical knowledge) and their world knowledge. It must be pointed out, however, that while this may apply to highly educated adult informants, with whom most lexical inferencing studies have been carried out, developmental and educational factors play a role in other contexts, as has been demonstrated in several studies with young school learners (Haastrup, 1991a, 2008; Palmberg, 1985, 1988).

Overall First and Second Language Differences in Lexical Inferencing

First language versus second language use of knowledge sources

In this study, many individual difference factors that might influence L1 versus L2 inferencing behavior were controlled, because the same Persian and French speakers were involved in both. Therefore, the differences found between cross-linguistic L1 and L2 lexical inferencing must be largely attributed to participants' native versus non-native proficiency in the respective text languages and to any text language effects from English as an L2. Certain patterns of KS use shown by both the Persian and French participants when inferencing in English L2 were different from the KS patterns shared across the three L1 conditions. One L1/L2 difference, related to the bilingual knowledge stores of these L2 readers, was their explicit use of L1 linguistic KSs in formulating their inferences, reported in previous studies within languages as more characteristic of lower than higher proficiency students (Haastrup, 1991a; Bengeleil & Paribakht, 2004). Although recourse to L1 KSs occurred among both Persian and French speakers, it was relatively infrequent, particularly for the Persian speakers (see below), characterizing only a few students in each group. The vast majority of linguistic KS use in L2 was based on English language knowledge.

In L2, readers' use of *sentence meaning* cues was even higher for both groups than in their respective L1s or in English L1; L2 readers depended heavily on this most widely used KS. The L2 readers also used *sentence grammar* cues more frequently than in L1, and more than English speakers did. In this case, their frequent use was likely influenced both by their L1 (see below) and by the L2 instruction that both groups had received. These two important L2 KSs also represented local information. Many kinds of cues relevant to a given word in fact tend to be concentrated near the word or are part of it, and it is reasonable to assume that processing them together is easier than integrating information from more distant cues; thus less proficient language users could be expected to mainly use them. This has also been reported in other studies (e.g. Haynes, 1993).

Higher reliance on *sentence meaning* and *sentence grammar* by L2 readers was balanced with less use of other KSs in L2 inferencing. *World knowledge*, for example, was used much less overall in L2 than in L1 inferencing. This may have reflected readers' lesser facility in their L2 in understanding and remembering cumulative text meaning than in their L1, and possibly less familiarity with both the structure of and the ideas expressed in a text originating in their L2. In L1 inferencing, readers' rich and well-established lexical and other linguistic knowledge, including discourse conventions, facilitates their access to and retention of content relationships within texts and use of their general knowledge to support lexical inferencing. In addition, native proficiency tends to be accompanied by deeper understanding of in-group cultural issues inherent in texts composed by native users of that language. More specialized KSs related to high written language proficiency that were occasionally used in L1 but only rarely in L2, such as *formal schemata*, *punctuation* and *style/register*, could also be explained in terms of L2 users' lower reading and writing expertise in the text language. The far less frequent use of *word collocation* in either L2 condition than in any L1 condition was more specifically linked to weaker vocabulary knowledge in general, and particularly, less knowledge of collocational relations in written English.

Finally, it should be mentioned that the L1 lexicalization status of the L2 target words had almost no effect on L2 KS use patterns, even though it strongly affected success; participants essentially used the same kinds and proportions of KSs with both lexicalized and non-lexicalized words within each language group. This indicated considerable stability in KS use procedures regardless of target word difficulty.

First language versus second language lexical inferencing success

Differences between lexical inferencing success in L1 and L2 were notable. L1 readers from all three language backgrounds were highly successful in inferring appropriate meanings for the great majority of the target (pseudo) words embedded in native language reading texts. English L1 readers were most successful, followed by Persian L1, then French L1 readers. However, the same Persian and French speakers were far less successful at inferring appropriate meanings for target words in English (L2) (with only 22 and 51.6% success rates, respectively). Within this general picture, the lexicalization status of target words had a strong effect on inferencing success for both Persian and French speakers in English. Readers were far more able to infer appropriate meanings for L2 target words that were lexicalized in their L1 than they were for non-lexicalized words. As noted above, the low success in L2 inferencing of many of these readers undoubtably had to do with their inadequate English proficiency, experienced as high text difficulty. The English texts had been constructed so that all non-target words should have been familiar to these high-intermediate readers, with target words accounting for approximately 3% of the running text. Thus, even if readers didn't know meanings for any of the target words, they should have known approximately 97% of the surrounding words. In fact, readers in both the Persian and French groups demonstrated previous knowledge of the meanings for an average of about 9% of the target words (but as little as 2%) on the pre-task VKS, so that on average, the coverage of known words was close to research indicating that knowledge of some 98% of the different words in a text as being necessary for unassisted L2 text comprehension and higher than the 95% some earlier studies had indicated (Chapter 1). The apparent difficulty of the target words for most of these readers must, to a large extent, be attributable to the high concentration of non-lexicalized target words, which proved to be a major challenge, especially for Persian speakers, and may have impeded their cumulative as well as local text comprehension. The cultural content of several of the texts (e.g. *Marriage*) may also have contributed to text difficulty for them. Overall, the most obvious explanation for Persian and French speakers' much lower lexical inferencing success in L2 than in their respective L1s was their weaker lexical knowledge in L2, and relative English lexical knowledge was also probably the most important factor in both Persian/French and individual differences.

Persian and French First Language Influences on Second Language Lexical Inferencing Processes and Outcomes

To determine aspects of L2 inferencing that might be traced to L1 processing tendencies and knowledge, we examined the Persian and French speakers' KS use in both their native language (L1) and English (L2) in parallel, seeking similar L1 and L2 patterns that were unique to speakers of either language. Our findings confirmed the influence of L1 procedures and related linguistic knowledge to L2 lexical inferencing. Both Persian and French speakers demonstrated certain KS use patterns that characterized both their L1 and L2 English lexical inferencing and appeared to be related to L1 features. The two groups also differed in their L2 inferencing success and learning outcomes in ways that could be attributed to L1 factors.

First language transfer in second language knowledge source use

Explicit evidence of L1 influences on L2 lexical inferencing was seen in Persian and French readers' reports of using specific KSs from their native language; in the Persian case, this represented a very small proportion of their KS use, while for French speakers it was more prominent. Participants in each group used only one L1 source, and a different one. In both cases, these KSs were important in the respective L1s, suggesting L1 transfer of procedural knowledge, and in addition, explicit transfer of declarative knowledge. For Persian speakers it was *L1 word collocation* (guessing a target word meaning from an adjacent word whose L1 equivalent tended to co-occur with the L1 word having that meaning); such cues accounted for 0.3% of their KS use. French speakers reported using *L1 word form* (assuming relevance of a similar looking or sounding L1 word to the L2 target word), which accounted for 4% of their KS use.

It is not surprising that Persian speakers rarely referred to their L1 as a source of information in L2 inferencing, given the relative typological distance of Persian from English that would lead them not to expect L1/L2 similarities. French speakers could draw upon many French language similarities to English. Their use of *L1 word form* was facilitated by a shared alphabet and related sound-symbol correspondences in French and English orthographies, in addition to the large lexical base shared by the two languages, and probably also reflected their expectations that L1 knowledge might be relevant. Their readiness to use this KS in their L2 likely also reflected their experience with informal oral English in their learning context. While L1 transfer based on similarities between languages tends to facilitate L2 performance, positive effects are not guaranteed. *Word form* in general tends not to be a very useful KS, and in this study, the French speakers' use of it either with an L1 word or the L2 target word was almost always associated with unsuccessful inferences. Use of this KS often appears to reflect an inability or lack of adequate effort to identify more fruitful KSs, and in the case of *L1 word form*, perhaps unrealistic expectations as to the transferability of this kind of lexical information between French and English. Haastrup (personal communication, 2007) notes that she and her colleagues have frequently observed *L1 word form* use among younger and lower proficiency Danish English learners in their studies, and that it is likewise seldom related to successful inferencing. Other researchers have made similar observations, e.g. Ringbom (2007), who characterizes development in the learner's mental lexicon as proceeding from form to meaning. In Singleton's view (1994: 54),

> Formal processing does come prominently into play during the early acquisition of a given lexical item, but such processing predominates only where semantic processes find no avenue for the making of semantic connections.

More evident in our data than the transfer of L1 knowledge reported by L2 readers was the considerable evidence of implicit L1 influence on L2 procedures governing KS use. This was found throughout the data in the patterns that typified the Persian or French speakers' KS use in both L1 and L2 inferencing, which could not be otherwise explained. The tendency for speakers of a given L1 to emphasize use of certain KSs in L1 inferencing presumably is efficient for that language, given the high levels of L1 lexical inferencing success. The tendency to apply L1 procedures in L2 lexical inferencing, as in other cases of transfer, involves learners using what they already know in a new but similar situation. When added to shared cross-linguistic and similar L1-L2 KS repertoires and the apparent similarities of search procedures in inferencing, L2 learners may be reasonably well served by transferring what they do in L1 to L2 lexical inferencing. Evidently, though, this can be expected to work best between closely related languages.

Persian L1 influence on procedural aspects of KS use in English L2 lexical inferencing can best be seen in the shared L1-L2 prominence of *discourse meaning*, which most distinguished Persian from French KS use. The high importance of *discourse* cues in general for Persian speakers can be understood in that they are an alternative to *word* cues, which were seldom used in Persian L1 inferencing, in contrast to the other two L1 conditions – partly for reasons of orthography (see below). *Word* cues were likewise seldom used in L2 by Persian speakers, with the exception of *word morphology* (see below). Another instance of L1 influence was the importance of *sentence grammar* for Persian speakers in L1 and, in fact, moderately increased use in L2; this overall pattern was also found in French L1 and L2. A further Persian L1 influence can be seen in the occasional use in L2 of L1 *word collocation* – a KS associated with high proficiency and the most important L1 *word* KS for Persian L1 readers. *Word collocation* was very rarely used in French L2, although frequent in French L1.

In French L2 lexical inferencing, L1 influence may, in contrast, best be seen in the shared L1-L2 prominence of diverse *word* cues, which uniquely characterized the L1 KS use of French speakers. In L1, their use of all four types of *word KSs*, *word morphology*, *word collocation*, *word form* and *word association* was far higher than for Persian speakers, and with the exception of *word collocation*, this difference was also seen in L2 KS use. The shared L1 and L2 importance of *sentence grammar* for French L2 readers, parallel to the Persian pattern, likewise appeared linked to L1 use. It was over twice as frequent in all these cases as in English L1 inferencing. As noted earlier, L2 readers' shared use of *sentence grammar* probably also reflected English instructional emphases in both cases. The very low use of *discourse* cues and non-use of *style-register* seen in French L1 inferencing also characterized L2 KS use, and particularly distinguished them from Persian patterns.

Text language effects

L2 readers from both groups demonstrated integration of some KS use patterns that were more typical of the L1 English readers than of their own L1 patterns. The strongest examples are Persian readers' higher use of *word morphology* in English than in their L1, matching the proportion of English L1 use of this KS, and the French speakers' reduced use of *word morphology* in L2 in relation to their L1. *Word morphology* is familiar to Persian and French speakers from L1 structures and is amenable to L2 instruction, two factors which likely help account for these adaptations towards English L1 norms.

To be even more like English L1 readers in their KS use in English, these Persian L2 readers would need to rely more on a variety of *word* cues, less on *sentence meaning* and *sentence grammar*, and more on their *world knowledge*. For their part, the French L2 readers would need to rely even less on *word morphology*, develop the deeper lexical knowledge in written English that would allow them to occasionally use *word collocation*, rely less on *sentence meaning* and *sentence grammar*, and be able to make better use of *discourse meaning* cues and their *world knowledge*. As they become more proficient in English, both groups will presumably progress further towards English L1 norms. The extent to which Persian and French L1-like patterns would persist at higher proficiency levels and the possibility of effective instructional intervention for participants such as these, merit further study.

The above evidence of similarities between L1 and L2 KS use specific to speakers of a given L1 – while mitigated by L2 readers' relatively low proficiency as well as text language effects – demonstrates L1 transfer of both declarative and procedural lexical knowledge. (See below for further information about declarative lexical knowledge transfer.) From the preceding analysis, L1 lexical processing tendencies, while not always obvious, appear to have a long-lasting influence on L2 inferencing.

Differential second language lexical inferencing success of Persian and French speakers

The analysis of Persian L2 and French L2 readers' relative lexical inferencing success included both their success with full target word sets and separately for lexicalized and non-lexicalized target words. Persian speakers, who were notably more successful than French speakers in L1 lexical inferencing, were far less successful in L2 inferencing. When lexical inferencing success scores for lexicalized versus non-lexicalized L2 target words were compared, both groups showed a strong facilitation effect for lexicalized target words. Non-lexicalized words were very difficult for both groups. Of interest here is that they represented a much greater disadvantage for the Persian than the French speakers, who were likely helped by stronger L1-related lexical and textual knowledge that aided their overall text comprehension.

The differential success of the two groups of L2 users in inferring new L2 word meanings, particularly those of non-lexicalized words, appears to relate to their relative English lexical proficiency. L2 lexical knowledge has in recent years been recognized as a crucial proficiency component underlying lexical inferencing success. Research also supports the concept of a threshold level of vocabulary knowledge required for a given learner to comprehend given written texts and infer word meanings for those words that are not known (Chapter 1), a factor which operated within both groups in this study. Several studies have also shown that measures of vocabulary and network knowledge or 'depth' are even stronger predictors of lexical inferencing success than are measures of receptive vocabulary knowledge (Henriksen, 2008; Nassaji, 2004).

The data indicate that the French speakers brought stronger English lexical knowledge to the inferencing task. Some evidence for this may be found in the group averages and score distributions for the *Vocabulary Levels Test*. Average group scores were about six points lower for the Persian speakers. Although this difference is not statistically significant due to the very high variability of Persian speakers' scores, it was operant, given the evidence found for a vocabulary knowledge threshold needed for successful lexical inferencing that affected a much larger proportion of Persian students (below). Furthermore, it seems likely that these receptive English vocabulary test scores largely reflected the full

English knowledge base of the Persian English students, given their foreign language learning context, in which exposure to English was essentially confined to the classroom, unlike that of the French speakers who had learned English in a bilingual context. This context would have fostered better oral productive skills in English and almost certainly a richer store of real-life associations for known words that would not have been fully captured by the *Levels Test* and that could facilitate their text comprehension and L2 inferencing.

Relationships among second language vocabulary knowledge, lexical inferencing success and retention of new word forms and meanings

The role of L2 lexical knowledge in inferencing success and the relationships among vocabulary knowledge, lexical inferencing success and subsequent gains in word knowledge were further explored through correlation analyses for both groups on measures of (1) **receptive vocabulary** *knowledge* (*the Vocabulary Levels Test*), (2) *lexical inferencing success* and (3) post-inferencing **word-meaning retention** (tested by recall) for previously unknown word meanings. It was not feasible to measure delayed retention in this study; however, the post-task measure of immediate retention of new word knowledge indicated initial gains in target word knowledge as an index of potential longer-term word learning. Unfortunately, it was not possible to add a delayed retention measure to study longer-term learning effects.

Positive correlations were found for both groups linking the three measures. Thus, learners with higher English receptive vocabulary scores were more successful in inferring meanings of unknown words, and both initial vocabulary knowledge and lexical inferencing success were positively correlated with readers' post-task ability to recall the meanings of formerly unknown words. These relationships demonstrated the critical importance of previous vocabulary knowledge to lexical inferencing success as well as to initial learning of new word meanings.

The most important finding with respect to lexical development through inferencing, had to do with L2 readers' post-inferencing retention of new word meanings and the relationship of such retention both to their receptive vocabulary knowledge and to their inferencing success. Both successful inferencing and retention of new word meanings were relatively rare for the L2 readers, especially the Persian speakers, but the relationship between the two was strong and consistent. In over 80% of cases of full or partial inferencing success, in both groups, participants were able to recall the new word meanings when tested after completion of their other L2 tasks. Thus, when – rarely – lexical inferencing was successful, it generally led at least to initial retention of word meanings. The low percentages of retention reflected inadequate L2 vocabulary knowledge for the texts and words and unsuccessful inferencing rather than reflecting the inefficiency of inferencing itself as a path to word learning. Other studies of inferencing and word learning from reading with similar low success and retention rates show that this is not an uncommon situation. In fact, conditions for successful L2 inferencing are often not good, leading L2 educators to conclude that reading in L2 is not a very useful means of lexical development. As is clear in this study, the inferencing process has an important role in lexical development, but certain conditions are essential to its effectiveness. The strength of the relationship between inferencing success and subsequent initial retention of new word meanings by participants from both these different L1 backgrounds learning English, again supports the validity of this evidence for each group separately. Also noteworthy, in light of other findings, is that the French speakers retained the meanings of almost twice as many new words as the Persian speakers.

Gains in word-form familiarity were a frequent outcome of readers' attempts to infer word meanings regardless of their inferencing success. In fact, after the inferencing task, both groups reported approximately 75% of the target words as being familiar, although their meanings remained unknown. Only about 5% of the target words were reported as still completely unfamiliar, and these mainly by a small number of participants. Thus, a motivated process of lexical inferencing attempts appears likely to lead to post-task recognition of new word forms as familiar.

The above findings provide direct evidence that initial lexical knowledge may be gained through inferencing from written texts. Even when unsuccessful, the cognitive processing involved in reading and targeted lexical inferencing frequently leads to familiarity with new word forms. The recognition of a word form, even when its meaning remains unknown, is likely to make a word more prominent and noticed by the reader in a future encounter than an unfamiliar word form. It can then serve in a further encounter as a basis for subsequent association with a new word meaning (Hatch & Brown, 1995; Ringbom, 2007; Schmidt, 1990; Schmitt, 1998). However, far more important is that when lexical inferencing is successful, the new meaning is likely to be at least temporarily retained and can serve as a basis for further learning through subsequent encounters with the word. These findings support the long-debated proposal that successful lexical inferencing can be an important mechanism for L2 vocabulary learning through reading. Reframed, the issue should be about how to establish conditions that can promote these positive outcomes.

A vocabulary knowledge threshold for lexical inferencing success and word learning

Similar correlations for both L2 groups linking receptive vocabulary knowledge, inferencing success and post-task retention of new word meanings, together with the high variability of Persian speakers' receptive English vocabulary scores, permitted further examination of the data for evidence of a threshold vocabulary level below which inferencing success and meaning retention were very unlikely and above which they not only occurred, but tended to increasingly occur with higher scores. In both groups, participants with scores of 55 and below on the *Vocabulary Levels Test* (Nation, 1990) – eight Persian speakers and three French speakers – rarely retained new word meanings after inferencing, while readers with scores of 57^2 and above consistently did much better (Chapter 5). This existence of a threshold level was statistically confirmed for both Persian and French speakers through *t*-tests, which showed a significant difference in word-meaning retention between users in each group whose vocabulary scores were above or below 56 on the *Vocabulary Levels Test*. While the samples' sizes are small, the consistency of this finding across the two groups is reassuring. The threshold phenomenon indicated here also accords with findings of the previously mentioned studies of the percentage of words in a text that L2 learners must already know for unassisted comprehension of written texts. The structure of the *Vocabulary Levels Test* also supports such an interpretation, as the threshold score of 56 would appear to corresponds to relatively good knowledge of the first 3000 most common English words, but little knowledge at the 5000 level.[3]

The phenomenon of a threshold of vocabulary knowledge required for successful comprehension, lexical inferencing and retention of word meanings again underscores the crucial importance of lexical proficiency as the key condition for success in these reading-related activities. It also implies that the actual level of vocabulary knowledge required for reading varies with the difficulty of the text for given readers, the density of unknown words and the difficulty of those words. While this threshold was identified at the same level of measured receptive vocabulary knowledge for both groups, French L2 readers with vocabulary scores both below and above the threshold tended to have somewhat more success in inferencing and retention than Persian L2 readers with corresponding vocabulary scores, again suggesting that differences in lexical knowledge between the two groups go beyond receptive vocabulary knowledge.

Differential Receptive Second Language Vocabulary Knowledge and Lexical Inferencing Outcomes for Persian and French Speakers

What might explain the differential results of Persian and French speakers in overall English L2 inferencing and word-meaning retention, as well as with non-lexicalized target words, and individually when matched on vocabulary scores? These differences appear to largely reflect the two groups' relative lexical proficiency in English, including but likely going beyond those aspects measured in the receptive vocabulary tests to include other kinds of word knowledge described elsewhere as 'depth' (Read, 1993, 2000; Nassaji, 2004; Wesche & Paribakht, 1996), 'network knowledge' or 'organization' (Henriksen, 1999, 2008; Meara, 1996). Three possible reasons are proposed below, each relating to the nature of the L2 lexical resources the two groups brought to the L1 task, and all of which likely played a role. The first involves differential L1 to L2 transfer of procedural knowledge, and the second, declarative knowledge. Both are related to the relative typological distances of Persian and French from English as manifested in relative L1-L2 similarity in linguistic features. The third explanation has to do with the different English learning contexts of the Persian and French speakers. The explanations are followed by a discussion of relative L1-L2 typological distance in L2 readers' lexical proficiency.

First language transfer

The first explanation is that the Persian L2 readers' procedural knowledge related to L1 inferencing may place them at a disadvantage in English inferencing vis-à-vis the French speakers. That is, the Persian speakers' tendency to emphasize the use in L2 of certain KSs that correspond to their L1 KS use patterns, which themselves underlie effective lexical processing in Persian, may be less appropriate for English than French speakers' L1 KS use patterns. French L1 patterns may, on the other hand, be more applicable to English and require less adaptation to be effective. Thus, for example, the Persian speakers were not equipped to take advantage of English *word* cues to the extent that the French speakers could. At the same time, while they were efficient users of *discourse* cues and *world knowledge* in L1, which could have provided alternative information in L2, their English proficiency was not adequate for exploiting these more distant and dispersed cues. Effective application of procedural knowledge depends on having the necessary declarative knowledge.

The second explanation, in our view applicable alongside the first, has to do with Persian speakers' lesser declarative lexical knowledge in (or pertinent to) English. This includes their knowledge of word meanings, L1 lexical equivalents, and presumably also, their underlying knowledge of semantic, syntactic and other lexical associations for the L2 words they know. This knowledge appeared to generally be weaker than that of the French speakers, as seen in their receptive English vocabulary scores and in the number in each group who scored below the threshold level, as well as in the differential inferencing success of the two groups above and below the vocabulary knowledge threshold and with respect to non-lexicalized target words. In addition, the importance of overall depth of vocabulary knowledge or lexical network knowledge to text comprehension and inferencing found in recent studies (Henriksen, 2008; Nassaji, 2004), while not measured as a predictive variable in this study,[4] is suggested in our data by the diversity of *word* KSs used in lexical inferencing by all groups, but particularly in French and English L1 inferencing; i.e. spoken and written word forms, meanings of stems and affixes, and other kinds of network relationships such as word class, collocations and other meaning associations. Additionally, relevant conceptual knowledge underlying word meanings was available to the French speakers through their own language and culture from historical and ongoing linguistic and cultural relationships between English- and French-speaking societies. Thus, there would be a likelihood of much greater similarity across lexical 'equivalents' in the two languages. In the special case of cognates, which were not included among the target words, their appearance in the surrounding text together with derivations and other lexical correspondences presumably also aided the French speakers by providing a richer context of meaning for text comprehension and consequently for more successful lexical inferencing.

Second language learning context

Third, the different English learning contexts of the two groups provide a contrast that we believe also helps account for the findings. As described in Chapter 3, the Persian students were in a foreign language learning context in which they almost never encountered English users in informal environments; their exposure to English was essentially limited to classroom contexts or out of class reading, and their knowledge was largely based on formal study that emphasized the written language, particularly reading, and grammar. The French speakers, who were also continuing school English study at the post-secondary level, lived contiguous to the national capital of Canada in a French-majority city in which English is also a language of daily use. Even though their primary language was French, they were in frequent contact with oral and written English in the media and in a broad range of everyday situations. In addition, the French speakers were familiar with the culture of North American English speakers through a shared history and territory as well as their own life experiences. These aspects of the L2 learning context would have collectively supported French L2 readers' English text comprehension ability and facilitated lexical inferencing.

Transfer as related to the typological distance between the first and second language

In our view, the major factor underlying the French speakers' stronger lexical proficiency is that French is typologically much closer to English, so that these French speakers – both in previous English learning and during the research – were able to draw on a greater potential for positive L1 transfer of both procedural and declarative lexical – as well as other – linguistic knowledge. This factor can largely explain the richer L2 knowledge resources, especially lexical, that French speakers appeared to bring to the task, in spite of the Persian speakers' stronger L1 inferencing ability and academic background. Persian, although an Indo-European language, is typologically much more distant from English, differing from English in many of its features and sub-features. As discussed above, for Persian learners of English, orthographic differences represent an initial barrier in terms of the writing system, including opposite directionality, a different alphabet and the lack of written representation of several vowels; thus, its speakers must use a different approach to initial word identification than English speakers. By contrast, English and French share a similar writing system, including directionality, the alphabet and systematic relationships between sound-symbol correspondences in the two languages. Beyond this, shared aspects of the linguistic and cultural histories of English and French speakers have created a high proportion of shared word derivations, many cognates and similar overall lexicalization patterns in the two languages that enhance the transferability of declarative lexical knowledge between them. This may also contribute to more rapid L2 vocabulary development for these learners.[5] In our view, L1-L2 typological distance and related cultural phenomena are a major underlying explanation for the lexical proficiency differences observed between the Persian and French university readers of English in this study.

Finally, in addition to the contributions of typological L1-L2 proximity and cultural congruence to English performance by the French speakers, the different English learning contexts of the Persian and French speakers in this study also advantaged the latter in terms of their overall lexical proficiency. The greater success of the French speakers may be partially due to their learning of English in a context that provided frequent informal exposure to the language in daily life. In addition, their ability to take advantage of these English learning opportunities was almost certainly supported by the linguistic similarities of the two languages due to their typological proximity and to the long shared history of Francophone and Anglophone cultures over time and more recently in Canada.

What Have We Learned?

In conclusion, this trilingual study of L1 and L2 inferencing has added to our understanding of shared aspects of lexical inferencing across languages and both L1 and L2 conditions, as well as of differences between L1 and L2 inferencing. Beyond this, it has demonstrated the crucial importance of previous vocabulary knowledge in both lexical inferencing success and initial word learning, and most important, provided evidence of L1 influences on various aspects of L2 lexical inferencing and its outcomes.

Cross-linguistic commonalities

Across languages and in both L1 and L2 lexical inferencing, readers use common inferencing procedures and similar kinds of textual cues and both linguistic and world knowledge in their attempts to determine new word meanings. Overall inferencing procedures are similar across languages and in both L1 and L2 conditions in terms of general search procedures and the repertoires of knowledge types that readers employ, indicating a common underlying strategic competence. Speakers of different L1s also show distinct emphases in patterns of KS use related to features of their language, some of which carry over to their L2 KS use.

Differences between first and second language inferencing

L2 inferencing differs from L1 inferencing in certain ways, mainly related to readers' lesser proficiency in L2 and, to some extent, to L2 text language features. Procedural knowledge related to lexical inferencing, much of it shared across languages but some L1 specific, is developed in the L1 and tends to be transferred by the same readers to L2 inferencing where it may work reasonably well, particularly in a closely related language and if the learners' declarative lexical knowledge is adequate. Over time, some adaptation toward patterns shown by native speakers of the target language, influenced by instruction and the L2 learning context, is reflected in patterns of KS use. Still, L1 effects are persistent. Bilingual aspects of readers' lexical processing are also revealed in L2 lexical inferencing through readers' direct use of L1 linguistic information in their inferences. Readers' success in inferring appropriate word meanings is far greater in their L1 than in their L2, a finding that may be interpreted as mainly reflecting the large proficiency gap between their mastery of a native and a later language. Lexical inferencing procedures and the kinds of declarative knowledge involved are largely shared in L1 and L2 inferencing by the same learners, and the overall differences found in KS use, success and outcomes in L1 and L2 conditions appear to be mainly due to readers' proficiency differences in their two languages.

Role of second language lexical knowledge in lexical inferencing success and further lexical development

Our findings support the view that once the procedural skills underlying reading are assured, lexical knowledge is the most crucial element in lexical inferencing success and subsequent retention of new word meanings from written texts. In addition to the importance of such knowledge in distinguishing L1 from L2 inferencing procedures and success, the French speakers' stronger English lexical knowledge was similarly identified in this study as the major immediate factor explaining their greater lexical inferencing success in English (L2), including their relative advantage in inferring meanings of non-lexicalized target words. Perhaps most convincing were the strong individual differences within each condition with respect to inferencing success and for retention of new knowledge of word meanings as these correlated with previous vocabulary knowledge. All these findings accord with findings of previous L2 studies linking readers' existing vocabulary knowledge with successful inferencing or word learning while reading.

The process of attempting lexical inferencing while reading appears to promote familiarization with new word forms even when inferencing is unsuccessful. A close relationship was found between successful inferencing and subsequent recall by readers of the new word meaning when shown the word form, as measured following the inferencing task. While inferencing success was relatively infrequent in these data, particularly for Persian speakers, when it was successful, it tended to lead to initial retention of new word meanings, a vital step in carrying forward the word-learning process, illustrating how reading for meaning can lead to acquisition of new vocabulary. It thus appears that successful comprehension of a new word meaning in a written context as an outcome of lexical inferencing may be a highly facilitative antecedent for at least initial retention in memory of the form-meaning connection.

The level of lexical knowledge required for both success and retention varies with given texts and target words, in terms of the density of words unknown to the reader, their difficulty, and the quality of meaning cues accessible to the reader. Such a threshold level in terms of receptive vocabulary knowledge scores was identified for the texts and target words in this study, below which successful inferencing was extremely rare for either group, while above it, inferencing success increased. The threshold of 98% of known surrounding words to sustain unassisted text comprehension, identified in the most recent research (Nation, 2006), appears to have been too low for our texts and target words. We attribute this to the fact that half the target words were non-lexicalized in readers' L1, so that the considerable difficulty they presented for L2 readers, particularly the Persian speakers, likely interfered with both overall and target word related text comprehension. Also, while the surrounding text was relatively easy, the target words – especially the non-lexicalized ones – were likely more difficult, whereas in a 'natural' text the difficulty level might be more homogeneous. Thus, research words and texts such as ours might require a higher threshold.

Greater success in inferring meanings of lexicalized (than non-lexicalized) words and subsequent greater retention of their meanings by both learner groups in this study supports the view that lexicalized words are amenable to successful inferencing and thus to more rapid acquisition. This is likely due to a short-cutting of the lemma construction process when an approximate L1 or Ln equivalent is identified (Paribakht, 2005). Much more time and exposure to non-lexicalized words would be required for accurate understanding and elaboration of their meanings.

First language transfer in second language lexical inferencing

Our findings also support the claim that an L2 reader's L1 influences the process and outcomes of L2 lexical inferencing through transfer of both procedural and declarative knowledge. The potential for facilitative transfer is greater between more closely related languages than more distant ones, based on shared or similar linguistic features. The relative typological distance between the L1 and L2 appears to be an important underlying determinant of L2 learners' existing vocabulary knowledge, as well as of L2 readers' KS use in lexical inferencing, their success in inferring new word meanings, their initial retention of these meanings and their ongoing L2 lexical development. In this study, transfer of procedural knowledge was demonstrated in within-language group similarities in patterns of KS use by both Persian and French speakers as distinguished from each other and from English native speakers. Greater L2 lexical inferencing success and word-meaning retention by the French readers of English L2 as compared to the Persian group, in spite of other advantages of the Persian L2 readers, was in our view due to the French L2 readers' overall stronger lexical knowledge. This advantage – which would support better L2 text comprehension, more successful inferencing and better retention – can in our view be largely attributed to the relative typological proximity of French to English, expressed in similarities of linguistic features across the two languages, in contrast to the lack of such similarities between Persian and English. Following Ringbom (2007) and others, we can conclude that learners from different L1s start in different places in learning a given L2, use what they already know in L2 problem solving, and have a different distance to go with respect to mastering L2 sub-features. The more similar two languages are, the more useful one will be in learning the other. It must of course be mentioned that transfer of apparently relevant knowledge in the L2 may not always be positive. In addition, if it works reasonably well, the learner may not be adequately pushed to adapt further toward L2 norms. But these are minor inconveniences in light of the major facilitative transfer available to learners of L2s that are typologically close to their L1.

First language related cultural and social influences on second language lexical inferencing

The effect of cultural proximity cannot be directly measured, but our comparative results for Persian and French speakers and examples from the data indicate that it is operant. Sociocultural factors in the L2 learning context also support lexical development, particularly when the L1 and L2 are typologically close (as in the case of English and French) and when L2 learning occurs in a second language (versus a foreign language) context where the extended social context provides more opportunities for contact and exposure to L2 language and culture.

A Final Word

Our research findings reveal the complex nature of L1 influences on lexical inferencing and the related processes of text comprehension and vocabulary learning. Drawing on inferencing data from French- and Persian-speaking learners of English in both L1 and L2 and from English native speakers, they demonstrate the importance of previous L2 vocabulary knowledge in all three processes. They also provide insight into how all three processes are affected by the relative typological distance between learners' L1 and L2, as exemplified by two Indo-European languages with distant and close relationships to English. The findings contribute to our general understanding of lexical inferencing in terms of learners' use of different kinds of KSs and of the lexicalization status of target words in inferring new word meanings, and in turn, to the nature of lexical knowledge. They confirm the critical importance of readers' L2 lexical knowledge in successful lexical inferencing, and indicate clear links between such knowledge, successful inferencing and initial retention of new word meanings. The results thus add to our understanding of L2 lexical inferencing as an interface between processes of L2 reading comprehension and vocabulary acquisition. Finally, they offer implications for future research and for instruction that takes account of L1 influences in L2 reading and lexical development, and offer specific information relevant to Persian- and French-speaking learners of English.

Research Issues

The trilingual study research design involved several innovations that can inform other studies. First of all, we compared 'matched' Persian and French readers' performance in English with each other and with that of English native speakers. By comparing L1 with L2 inferencing by the same speakers, we could distinguish L1 transfer effects from other influences on L2 KS use or success, such as general proficiency or text language. Second, the use of pseudo target words with L1 readers, which provided morphological information to that of the original words, allowed us to use texts of the same difficulty level in L1 and L2, and identical texts (except for the target words) for English L1 and Persian L2. Finally, the *Vocabulary Knowledge Scale* (VKS) provided a measure of word-learning outcomes that allowed the sorting out of incremental gains in different aspects of initial word learning and their relationship to previous vocabulary knowledge and to inferencing success.

There were also several shortcomings and unforeseen outcomes in our research procedures. One was that our embedded study of the effects of target word lexicalization status resulted in a high concentration of target words, half of which were non-lexicalized, in our reading texts. This raised the level of text difficulty, likely depressing inferencing success somewhat and making it difficult to seek relationships between KS use patterns and successful inferencing. Another issue was the lengthy individual research sessions involving multiple tasks for L2 speakers (pre-, post-VKS, L2 inferencing and L1 inferencing), which may have resulted in some fatigue effects depressing L1 lexical inferencing performance for the Persian and French speakers. While the effects would have been similar for both L2 conditions, both may have been somewhat disadvantaged vis-à-vis the English L1 speakers. Third, it was not feasible for us to gather information on long-term retention of new word knowledge due to logistical challenges and our limited access to the participants. A third administration of the VKS might have allowed more definitive claims. Finally, our measure of previous English vocabulary was for receptive knowledge, not depth or overall network knowledge. The VKS, in fact, proved to be a consistent predictor of inferencing success and word-meaning retention for both groups in English L2. Furthermore, scores on this test allowed identification of a threshold of previous receptive vocabulary knowledge needed for lexical inferencing success in the L2 conditions. While it was very useful, recent research indicates that additional insights can be obtained through measures of vocabulary 'depth' or overall network knowledge, and such measures are to be highly encouraged in future research on lexical inferencing. As noted by Henriksen (2008), there is an ongoing need for development of appropriate measures and procedures to tap the various manifestations of vocabulary knowledge.

Directions for future research

Our experience carrying out this research leads us to suggest further research possibilities in the form of comparative studies of L1 influence on L2 inferencing using more pairs of languages with different typological distances from the target language. These could include

- studies of specific pairs of languages from typologically varied languages;
- studies in which the L2 pair is not English;
- studies involving more diverse and detailed investigation of the role of vocabulary depth/lexical networks in addition to receptive vocabulary knowledge in lexical inferencing success and retention of new word knowledge;
- longitudinal studies of the lexical inferencing process and its outcomes involving the same learners over time.

Implications for Second Language Reading and Vocabulary Instruction

Insights gained from this study can inform L2 instruction in several ways, as detailed below.

Inferencing training

Our findings showing a close relationship between successful inferencing and immediate post-task retention of new word-meaning knowledge are encouraging as to the potential of reading for meaning as a vehicle for vocabulary acquisition by advanced L2 learners, in that initial retention of new word meanings was found to be a likely result of successful inferencing. However, caution is also indicated, given the low overall rates of inferencing success for these English L2 users and the evidence supporting a threshold effect by which L2 readers must have a certain level of previous vocabulary knowledge relative to given texts and target words if they are to benefit from reading and inferencing activities. These findings demonstrate the complexity of applying these insights to advanced L2 instruction if they are to support word learning through inferencing.

It is clear that conditions that facilitate successful inferencing are a necessary part of any pedagogical strategy to promote inferencing and word learning through reading. These include using texts on familiar topics that are engaging for the given L2 readers and comprehensible to them without assistance; i.e. the texts must have a very low density of words that are unknown to the readers. The texts may also be manipulated to support inferencing, such as by providing glosses for difficult words or multiple choices for those targeted for inferencing.

Thematic reading can also be considered as a means of providing repeated exposure to targeted words in various contexts, thereby facilitating text comprehension and elaboration of previously acquired knowledge about the target words. However, as Cobb (2005) has cautioned, based on word frequency research in different kinds of texts, many useful but infrequent English words would not be encountered often enough through reading alone to ensure their eventual acquisition. When exposure is assured, texts must also provide adequate textual cues to support lexical inferencing that are accessible to the given readers. Furthermore, given the high levels of failure in L2 lexical inferencing, readers should be advised to verify their inferred meanings in context (Nation, 1990), and to consult a dictionary after inferencing for confirmation (Fraser, 1999). Haastrup (personal communication, 2008) suggests use of a monolingual dictionary, which itself promotes further inferencing as readers compare the various definitions offered as they are appropriate to the reading context. As Nation (1990) suggests, such an evaluative component is important for accurate text comprehension and interpretation, as well as for accurate initial word learning.

If these conditions can be met, training and practice in the use of the lexical inferencing strategy for enhancing text and word comprehension as well as receptive vocabulary development merit serious consideration by L2 programs.

What little research exists indicates that lexical inferencing is trainable and can enhance readers' confidence in dealing with unfamiliar words, their lexical processing skills and their strategic competence. Walters (2006), in a comparison of three training methods with ESL students, found all of them to have some potential, but the teaching of a general strategy for dealing with unknown words seemed to have the most promise. Fraser's (1999) study showed positive effects from such training by increasing the number of words attended to by L2 readers as well as the frequency and quality of inferencing. Such training may involve raising readers' awareness of the range of contextual cues and KSs available to them, and how they can use their conceptual knowledge (e.g. including topical and cultural knowledge) and linguistic skills (e.g. word analysis) in the process. The taxonomy of KSs developed in this study can be used as an inventory of knowledge and cue types, and the training can provide practice in locating diverse cues in reading texts (see also Paribakht & Wesche, 2006). As Albrechtsen *et al.* (2008) suggest, the quality of lexical inferencing procedures is dependent on interaction between declarative and procedural knowledge; so, both need to be developed for more effective lexical inferencing. Like other complex behaviors, lexical inferencing ability requires time to develop through frequent practice in relevant contexts.

Dealing with typological distance between readers' first language and the second language text language

Our data from learners from two languages (Persian and French) with different typological relationships to the target language (English) provided evidence of the long-lasting influence of the L1 in L2 lexical inferencing and also brought to light certain inferencing tendencies of the respective learner populations. The findings demonstrated the facilitative role of typological proximity between the L1 and L2 and the ways in which similarities in the linguistic features could positively impact the process and outcomes of L2 lexical inferencing. How can we take account of these findings in L2 pedagogy? In instructional contexts with homogeneous learner populations (often English as a foreign language (EFL) contexts), teachers could emphasize building on the strengths that the learners bring to the task, by, for example, drawing learners' attention to features shared by the two languages, such as cognates, as in the case of French speakers such as those in this study (also see Palmberg, 1985, 1988, for examples with young children). A common initial stock of words provides L2 readers with a richer overall lexical knowledge, putting them in an advantageous position for text comprehension, more accurate word-meaning comprehension and subsequent further vocabulary development. Enhancing these readers' cognate recognition should, however, be accompanied by caution about the misleading effects of false cognates and the need to confirm that assumed meanings make sense in context (cf. Tréville, 1990, 1996).

In the case of distant relationships between the L1 and L2, instructors could address L1 effects by filling in gaps where L1s are distant, providing information on the meanings of stems and the functions of affixes, with ample opportunities for practice in word analysis. They might also consider explicit teaching of relatively frequent and productive words that are not lexicalized in the readers' L1 – especially those related to learners' future needs in the L2, such as discipline-related terms for post-secondary students. The lower success rates in inferring the meanings of non-lexicalized words by both learner groups, especially Persian speakers, point to the more complex nature of these lexical items in immediate meaning comprehension and subsequent retention of meanings. These words are likely to lead to miscomprehension of text meaning, and thus if they are important to text understanding, they merit focused instruction (Paribakht, 2005).

Further evidence of L1 influence in L2 lexical inferencing was apparent in patterns of KS use by the learner groups in this study, likely due to these readers' L1 processing habits. Divergences from target language use patterns, such as Persian speakers' low attention to *word* level cues and French speakers' over-reliance on such cues relative to the English native speakers could be specifically addressed and balanced through instruction (see also Paribakht & Wesche, 2006).

Topic familiarity

The results of this study also point to the importance of relatively familiar topical information in text comprehension that can, in turn, facilitate lexical inferencing. Enhancing this dimension of L2 readers' knowledge through careful selection of texts focusing on a limited number of themes could benefit both reading comprehension and lexical inferencing.

Given the reciprocal relationship between reading and vocabulary development, Albrechtsen *et al.* (2008) are justified in suggesting that reading and word guessing strategies should be taught in combination. They further argue that the goal of reading a particular text is likely to affect the degree to which readers invest time and effort in processing a given unfamiliar word. In instructional contexts, it would seem wise to combine reading with explicit lexical inferencing tasks, aiming for task-induced involvement (see also Laufer & Hulstijn, 2001; Paribakht & Wesche, 1996; Wesche & Paribakht, 2000). Lexical inferencing tasks not only enhance readers' skill in the use of this strategy, they also make targeted words more salient and bring them to the readers' attention, a first step in acquisition (see Schmidt, 1990). Further development of vocabulary knowledge after inferencing can be promoted through repeated exposures to and use of targeted words in different contexts through thematic reading, instructional tasks and reading-based vocabulary exercises (cf. Paribakht & Wesche, 1996, 1997, 2006; Wesche & Paribakht, 1998, 2000).

Given the modest nature of the overall gains in vocabulary knowledge after brief exposure in reading and the lexical inferencing task in this study, it is clear that reading and successful lexical inferencing are not of themselves sufficient conditions for systematic L2 vocabulary development. We believe that they can make an important contribution, and that development of lexical inferencing ability should be a goal of L2 reading programs, given that it is often essential for text comprehension, and is a particularly important skill for advanced L2 users.

Notes

1. KS use may be somewhat under-reported in think-aloud data as learners may not be fully aware of all the information they draw upon.
2. There were no scores of 56.
3. The first 30 words are from the 1000–2000 level, 31–60 from the 3000 level, and 61–90 from the 5000 level (Nation, 1990; Schmitt *et al.*, 2001).
4. The VKS measures aspects of word knowledge 'depth' for particular words, but not associations with other words (other than synonyms). It is not a feasible approach to estimating overall vocabulary depth (Wesche & Paribakht, 1996). It was used in this study to compare pre- and post-task target word knowledge – the purpose for which it was designed (Paribakht & Wesche, 1993, 1997).
5. It must also be remembered that L1-L2 lexical equivalents are never exact; they will have somewhat different semantic boundaries. Thus, while they are quite helpful initially, native-like mastery of lemmas can only be achieved over time through further exposure and effort. In the long run, given the ongoing influence of L1 in L2 processing, it is possible that non-lexicalized words whose meanings have been constructed within the context of the L2, will eventually be mastered in a more native-like manner than those for which a largely similar L1 lemma was adopted (Jiang, 2000).

Appendices

Appendix A
Lists of target words

Target L2 words for the Persian speakers

English target words not lexicalized in Persian	English target words lexicalized in Persian
1. glacier	1. to trickle
2. breakthrough	2. intrusion
3. presumptuous	3. deteriorating
4. metropolitan	4. to tackle*
5. lounge	5. to flee*
6. catering business	6. devastated
7. genocide	7. desertification
8. to snoop	8. to slam
9. sophisticated	9. testimony*
10. to tow	10. decay*
11. prognosis	11. layer*
12. overwhelmingly*	12. lethal
13. intuitively	13. bleak*
14. chronologically	14. ambivalence
15. to trigger	15. to wipe out

Target L2 words for the French speakers

English target words not lexicalized in French	English target words lexicalized in French
1. to clone*	1. keenly
2. to implement	2. to thrive
3. mainstream	3. pawn
4. to backfire*	4. to withstand
5. plight	5. retaliation*
6. clout	6. testimony*
7. grimly	7. to flee*
8. overwhelmingly*	8. stowaway
9. to glimpse	9. tattered
10. smouldering	10. strife
11. to spark	11. layer*
12. to draft*	12. decay*
13. slouches	13. to spawn
14. bungling	14. to spray*
15. afterthoughts	15. bleak*

Appendices

Appendix A (*Continued*)

English target words not lexicalized in Persian	English target words lexicalized in Persian
16. to elope*	16. to blend
17. to stalk someone	17. to draft*
18. proactive	18. to spray*
19. monogamy	19. masterpiece
20. sleet*	20. retaliation*
21. to indulge	21. innuendo*
22. to clone*	22. inadvertently
23. to backfire*	23. retroactively
24. understatement*	24. frivolously
25. courtship	25. annoyance

Appendix A (*Continued*)

English target words not lexicalized in French	English target words lexicalized in French
16. cut off	16. to tackle*
17. understatement*	17. dolefully
18. to crave	18. warily
19. gaze	19. omens
20. poised	20. untimely
21. blandness	21. craze
22. arguably	22. to muster
23. spree	23. giddy
24. sleet*	24. innuendo*
25. to elope*	25. to strum

Note: Common words in the two lists are indicated by an asterisk

Appendix B

Lists of target words used for lexical inferencing with Persian speakers in English L2 and with English speakers in L1, with their frequency designation

Target English words not lexicalized in Persian	Target English words lexicalized in Persian
1. glacier*	1. to trickle*
2. breakthrough	2. intrusion*
3. presumptuous*	3. deteriorating**
4. metropolitan**	4. to tackle***
5. lounge**	5. to flee***
6. catering business**	6. devastated*
7. genocide*	7. desertification
8. to snoop	8. to slam**
9. sophisticated***	9. testimony**
10. to tow**	10. decay**
11. prognosis*	11. a layer***
12. overwhelmingly***	12. lethal**
13. intuitively*	13. bleak**
14. chronologically*	14. ambivalence*
15. to trigger***	15. to wipe out
16. to elope	16. to blend**
17. to stalk someone**	17. to draft***
18. proactive	18. to spray***
19. monogamy	19. masterpiece**
20. sleet	20. retaliation**

Appendix B (*Continued*)

Target English words not lexicalized in Persian	Target English words lexicalized in Persian
21. to indulge**	21. innuendo*
22. to clone*	22. inadvertently*
23. to backfire*	23. retroactively
24. understatement*	24. frivolously*
25. courtship*	25. annoyance*

* Infrequent
** More frequent than *
*** More frequent than **

Appendix C

Text used for lexical inferencing with Persian speakers in English L2 (target words are bolded)

Genetic Engineering

Have you ever wondered what it would be like to have an exact copy of yourself? It may not be as far off as you think. Researchers have long been interested in the idea, and scientific **breakthroughs** in this area have received a great deal of both positive and negative media coverage. The focus of much of the attention has been Dolly, a sheep that scientists in Scotland recently managed **to clone**. While she is hailed as a miracle by some, others worry that this first cloning may **inadvertently** set off a wave of unpredictable events. Who knows what the new technology might **trigger**? Scientists could breed clones of animals and human beings for use in scientific experiments or to act as organ donors. People could have themselves copied in a quest for eternal life. Religious cults might wish to create younger copies of their aging leaders. Obviously, most people would **intuitively** reject such uses of the new technology. However, once such technology is available, it is difficult to ensure that it is properly controlled. Most countries still have not developed policies to deal with cloning and similar activities. This lack of action may well **backfire** if nothing is done soon. Unless medical facilities are carefully controlled, for example, criminals could **snoop** through doctors' files to find the secret to cloning. Even more worrying is the potential for women to be forced to use their bodies to incubate cloned babies. Who knows what will happen? Only time will tell.

Appendix D

Text used for lexical inferencing with French speakers in English L2 (target words are bolded)

Human Rights

Article 1 of the Universal Declaration of Human Rights states: 'All human beings are born free and equal in dignity and rights'. However, even today, in many countries human rights are not fully recognized, and it requires considerable courage for citizens of these nations to speak out about the **plight** of those whose rights are abused. In many countries where human rights are routinely ignored, military governments are all-powerful and people fear **retaliation** if they draw attention to the problems of their fellow citizens. The **clout** of such governments is often so great that it is dangerous for human rights defenders to even work with those who suffer, let alone to speak publicly about their experiences. Faced with threats of torture, many would-be defenders remain **grimly** silent, fearing for their own lives and those of their associates. Advocates who are able to approach international bodies and give **testimony** about the violations of human rights which they have observed often face severe consequences from the military governments that they criticize. In many cases, human rights workers are forced to **flee** their homelands. Hostile governments may even try to block their paths out of the country. Sometimes they are forced to become **stowaways** on ships or trucks, traveling without identification and dressed in **tattered** clothing, as they try to reach the safety of a country far away. In the end, some fortunate defenders of human rights are able to escape the **strife** of their homelands and build new lives for themselves. Sadly, not everyone is so lucky, and many are forced to remain behind in countries where even the most basic principles outlined in the Universal Declaration of Human Rights are ignored.

Appendix E

Text used for lexical inferencing with Persian speakers in English L2 and with English speakers in L1 (target English words are bolded; pseudo target words are in parentheses)

Ice Age

If you could visit the North America of ten thousand years ago, you probably would not recognize it at all. No cities or freeways graced the landscape. The millions of people who now inhabit the continent were absent. In fact, the landscape would probably have appeared rather **bleak** *(tugid)*. Portions of what is now called the United States and much of what is now called Canada were covered by **glaciers** *(quallies)*. To say that the ice mass was very big would be a dramatic **understatement** *(lowartment)*. It would be more precise to describe it as **overwhelmingly** *(grushly)* vast, covering hundreds of thousands of square kilometers. The climate across North America was considerably colder than it is now. Influenced by the cold ice to the north, rain, **sleet** *(plish)*, and snow poured down continually. As the ice advanced southward, trees disappeared and wide valleys were carved from the plains. There was life on the continent, however. In the shadow of the great mass of ice, larger animals **stalked** *(filted)* smaller ones for food, and hardy grasses struggled to survive. Despite the harsh environment, a balance was reached. Eventually, the ice slowly retreated over many thousands of years, leaving behind a **devastated** *(beslocked)* landscape. However, it also left behind all the elements necessary for new life. The melting ice released sediment which formed a thick **layer** *(vishel)* of fertile soil. Trees grew again as the cold gradually released its grip on the land. Eventually people settled where once there had only been ice, and North America began to take the shape that we now know. When we consider these ancient events **chronologically** *(timically)*, we are reminded that the surroundings that are so familiar to us, and indeed, the history of nations, means little when considered in the perspective of geological time.

Appendices 175

Appendix F

Text used for lexical inferencing with Persian speakers in L1 with a list of the actual and pseudo target words in Persian and Roman alphabets (target Persian words are bolded; pseudo target words are in parentheses)

مفهوم عید برای کودکان

چگونه می توان سال نو به خصوص چند روز نخست آن را به روز هایی خاطره انگیز و مخصوص مبدل کرد؟ چرا شروع سال نو برای عده ای با شادی و زیبایی همراه است و برای عده ای دیگر تفاوتی با روز های قبل ندارد؟ آیا تا به حال به این **مساله** (ندوا) فکر کرده اید؟ آیا فکر کرده اید چگونه با ترسیم زیبایی مسایلی بسیار کوچک، می توان سال نو را خاطره انگیز و زیبایی را برای خود و خانواده به **ارمغان آورد** (مجدا نمود)؟

چند نمونه کوچک را که تجربیاتی جالب از خوانندگان است، با یکدیگر مرور می کنیم تا دریابیم که شادی های کوچک تا چه اندازه می توانند در زندگی تغییراتی **شگرف** (ملوج) به وجود آورند.

همیشه گفته اند که عید و آغاز سال نو، مخصوص بچه ها و جوانان است. شادی زایدالوصفی که در کودکان و نوجوانان از **شروع** (مران) سال نو به وجود می آید، قاعدتاً نمی تواند برای بزرگسالان توجیه پذیر باشد. کودکان این گلهای کوچک زندگی مشترک با هر کار تازه و کوچکی شاد و سرحال شده و این شادی را مستقیماً در کل خانواده تعمیم می دهند. مادری نوشته بود زمانی که خود کوچکی بیش نبودم از رسیدن کارت های تبریک که پیام سال نو را داشت بیش از اندازه خوشحال می شدم. ولی حالا با با داشتن یک فرزند ۳ ساله دیگر **حوصله** (مسلون) انجام این کار ها را نیز در خود نمی دیدم. می زمانی که با رسیدن کارتی از جانب دوستم، شادی دختر کوچولویم را دیدم **به فکر افتادم** (کلاویدم) که هر چند خودم نیز از رسیدن این کارت بیش از اندازه خوشحال شدم، اما تنبلی بیش از حد مانع از این است که بخواهم **پاسخی** (متالی) به این کارت بدهم. دخترم نیز کوچکتر از آن بود که بتواند چیزی بنویسد بنابراین **تصمیم گرفتم** (شوانیدم) به جای نوشتن، مدادهای رنگی و ورقهای نقاشی او را در اختیارش بگذارم تا به زعم خویش آنچه را که برایش زیباتر است بر روی کاغذ ترسیم کند. نتیجه کار بسیار عالی بود. شادی دخترم از این که توانسته بود در جشن عید به این طریق سهیم باشد **غیر قابل وصف** (مترون) بود.

تصاویر شادی که کودکان ترسیم می کنند، به منزله کارتهای شاد و زیبای نانوشته ای است که علاوه بر سرگرم کردن کودکان در آستانه سال نو ارسال موج شادی و نشاط درونی کودکان است که **به راحتی** (ولاهتاً) به دیگران انتقال می یابد. تغییر دکوراسیون منزل و چگونگی مبله کردن منزل یکی دیگر از **روشهایی** (مغاینی) است که می توان برای برای شما و خانواده تان جالب کند. به گفته روانشناسان تغییر دکوراسیون، و بوجود آوردن تحولی هر چند **غیرمحسوس** (ملتوک) در محیط خانه یکی از عل بروز شادی در میان خانواده ها است که از اهمیت آن نباید غافل بود. پس از یک سال که چشم به دیدن تمام **وسایل** (ژواک) و نوع چیدن آنها در منزل عادت می کند، با اندک تغییری می توان روحیه ای شاد را به اعضای خانواده بخشید و با این ترتیب آنها را واداشت تا در آغاز سال جدید، با سفره ای پر از لبخند های شیرین، خانواده و دوستان خویش را پذیرا باشند.

معمولاً (چلاوآ) برای کودکان بسیار سخت است که معنای عید و سال نو را دریابند. بخصوص در این برهه از زمان که کودکان در کل از زندگی نسبتاً بهتری برخوردارند و در طول سال نیز به عناوین مختلف هدیه دریافت می کنند، درک این مطلب که کادوی عید چه تفاوتی با دیگر هدایا دارد کمی سخت است. مادر پانیذ ۴ ساله می گوید، سال گذشته زمانی که برای هدیه عید برای دخترم، عروسکی را که دوست داشت خریدم، تصمیم گرفتم در کنار این شادی درسی از مهربانی و نشاط نیز به وی بدهم. پس همانروز او را به **بیمارستانی** (نرازینی) بردم که بچه های کوچک را که از دردهای مختلف به خصوص سرطان رنج می بردند از نزدیک ببیند. با این که پانیذ فقط ۴ سال داشت از این رسید که هدایای عید این بچه ها را چه کسی **تهیه می کند** (می سلاود)؟ و زمانی که از من پاسخ منفی شنید، به طرف یکی از دخترنچه های بیمار رفت و با دادن عروسک محبوب خود به او و نشاندن گل بوسه ای بر صورت تکیده اما زیبای آن دختر بیمار، عید را تبریک گفت. پانیذ با این کار خود ثابت کرد منظور از عید و سال نو را درک کرده و به دنبال آن است که با هم با هدایای مهربانی شروع سال جدید را به دیگران تبریک بگوید. این امر تا اندازه ای به کودکان یاد می دهد که روحیه و معنای عید و سال نو چیست و به آنها **می آموزد** (می پراشد) که بخشیدن بهتر و زیباتر از دریافت کردن است.

آغاز سال نو و عید معمولا به معنای شروعی مجدد است. در واقع این کلمات برای اکثر کودکان و نوجوانان، واژه های جادویی هستند. **تلاش** (ژنگ) برای به وجود آوردن روحیه ای شاد در اعضای خانواده، حتی با کمترین کارها که ممکن است **اصلا** (شکوا) به نظر هم نیایند، موجب می شود تا سال جدید برای اعضای خانواده، طلیعه بهترین ها باشد. سعی کنید با درست کردن شیرینی هایی که کودکان بسیار دوست دارند آنها را شاد کنید. بسیاری از بچه ها از اینکه ساخته و پرداخته دست خود را به پدربزرگ و مادربزرگ خود **تعارف کنند** (بشکلانند)، از شادی در پوست خود نمی گنجند.
یکی دیگر از **نکاتی** (پاژانی) که عید و سال نو را برای بچه ها و حتی جوانان جالب و جذاب می کند، در بر کردن لباس های نو و زیبایی است که معمولا از طرف والدین برای آنها **تهیه می شود** (تشویر می گردد). خانم شیرازی، مادر ۳ فرزند ۴ تا ۹ ساله می گوید: زمانی که بچه ها در نهایت خوشی و شادی رسیدن سال جدید هستند، دیگر اصلا متوجه این که لباس ها از طرف چه کسی تهیه شده نیستند و تنها آن را با کمال میل مورد استفاده قرار می دهند. به شرطی که به آنها بیاموزید هر چیزی حد و **مرزی** (ماکلی) دارد و مهربانی ها و بخشش ها هرگز در هیچ زمینه ای نباید **فراموش بشود** (خندیش گردد)، با خرید وسایل و حتی یک تکه لباس نو، شادی آنها را چند صد برابر می کنید.
تلاش کنید تا سال نو را با رعایت همین نکات به ظاهر **کم اهمیت** (راسخ) به سالی پر از شادی و نشاط مبدل کرده، درسهای مهربانی و ایثار را با همین کارهای کوچک و در همین سنین پایین به آنها بیاموزید. سال خوبی را در پیش رو داشته باشید.

List of the Persian actual and pseudo target words

No.	Actual words	Pseudo words	Actual words	Pseudo words
1.	مساله	ندوا	mas'ale	nadvaa
2.	به ارمغان آورد	مجدا نمود	be armaghaan aavard	majdaa namoud
3.	شگرف	ملوج	shegerf	malouj
4.	شروع	مران	shorou'	maraan
5.	حوصله	مسلون	hosele	masloun
6.	به فکر افتادم	کلاویدم	be fekr oftaadam	kalaavidam
7.	پاسخی	متالی	paasokhi	motaali
8.	تصمیم گرفتم	شوانیدم	tasmim gereftam	shavaanidam
9.	غیر قابل وصف	متروش	gheyre ghaabele vasf	matroush
10.	به راحتی	ولاهتاً	be raahati	velaahatan
11.	روشهایی	مغانینی	raveshhaaye	maghaanini
12.	غیرمحسوس	ملتوک	gheyre mahsous	maltouk

Appendices

Appendix F (*Continued*)

No.	Actual words	Pseudo words	Actual words	Pseudo words
13.	وسایل	ژواک	vasaa'el	zhavaak
14.	معمولاً	چلاواً	ma'moulan	chalaavan
15.	بیمارستانی	نرازینی	bimaarestani	naraazini
16.	تهیه می کند	می سلاود	tahiyye mikonad	misalaavad
17.	می آموزد	می پراشد	miaamouzad	miparaashad
18.	تلاش	ژنگ	talaash	zhang
19.	اصلاً	شکواً	aslan	shakvan
20.	تعارف کنند	بشکلانند	ta'aarof konand	beshkalaanand
21.	نکاتی	پاژانی	nokaati	paazhaani
22.	تهیه می شود	تشویر می گردد	tahiyye mishavad	tashvir migardad
23.	مرزی	ماکلی	marzi	maakeli
24.	فراموش بشود	خندیش گردد	faraamoush beshavad	khandish gardad
25.	کم اهمیت	راسخ	kam ahammiyat	raasekh

Appendix G

Text used for lexical inferencing in French L1 (target French words are bolded; pseudo target words are in parentheses)

L'intuition

Ce qui nous permet parfois d'entrevoir la solution d'un problème alors qu'il vient à peine de se poser, ce qui nous permet occasionnellement de deviner les pensées des autres, voire leurs antécédents et leur destin, c'est notre intuition. Mais, les individus rationnels que nous sommes se fient peu à leur intuition. Pendant longtemps, nous l'avons **considérée** (chatinée) comme une sorte de don un peu bizarre. Cependant, l'intuition est **récemment** (boutiment) devenue un véritable objet d'étude pour quelques éminents **chercheurs** (mireurs) (psychiatres et neurophysiologistes) qui s'accordent pour la situer dans l'hémisphère droit du **cerveau** (firton) et qui soutiennent qu'elle est, comme l'intelligence, une voie d'accès à la connaissance dont tout **individu** (quiranti) dispose à des degrés **divers** (inuts).

En fait, l'intuition serait une partie de l'intelligence humaine, une puissance ancestrale **solidement** (pracinement) ancrée dans le cerveau, émergée des profondeurs de l'instinct, grâce à laquelle **l'espéce** (l'ucane) humaine a su s'adapter, se protéger et se **maintenir** (blonnir) en vie. L'apparition du langage, catalyseur de la pensée logique consciente, **remonterait** (couponnerait) seulement à deux cent cinquante mille ans. Ce serait le point tournant à partir duquel l'être **humain** (gourin) a développé ses facultés de raisonnement aux dépens de ses facultés intuitives. Tout au long des millénaires que l'homme préhistorique a traversés, alors qu'il ne **possédait** (saponait) pas encore la parole, il a dû pourtant se protéger en défiant les **innombrables** (gerondables) dangers de la nature et en rusant avec des prédateurs aussi voraces qu'effroyables. Or, si notre ancêtre anthropopithèque, il y a quatre millions et demi d'années a **surmonté** (dirové) tant d'obstacles, c'est qu'il a été capable d'agir vite et bien et qu'il a eu recours à cette forme pré-verbale de l'intelligence qu'est **l'intuition** (l'ergofaction). Alors que la pensée rationnelle, analytique, séquentielle et linéaire, morcelle le problème posé, l'intuition permet de le **saisir** (mortir) globalement, dans son **ensemble** (imbe), et d'en voir la réponse instantanément avant d'y avoir réfléchi. C'est ainsi que les grands savants et les artistes **reconnaissent** (dépenaissent) souvent qu'ils ont eu l'intuition de leurs découvertes ou de leurs créations bien avant de les avoir réalisées.

aujourd'hui (Jonadeu), certains chercheurs s'occupent de réhabiliter l'intuition. Ils veulent montrer que ce qu'on appelle, à tort, 'le flair', 'le sixième **sens** (froin)' ou 'un éclair de génie' constitue une activité cérébrale essentielle, indissociable du succès et de la survie. Le **monde** (hacre) des affaires, au Japon en particulier, commence à devenir très réceptif à cette idée et à en tenir compte dans le recrutement de personnel. La principale difficulté est de mesurer la **capacit**é (seaupaté) intuitive d'un individu. À défaut d'un test d'intuition qui pourrait être le complément d'un **test** (crut) d'intelligence, le psychologue américain A. Garr a mis au point une série de questionnaires d'auto-évaluation dont on **retrouve** (viroute) fréquemment des extraits ou des adaptations, pas très **sérieuses** (fideuses), dans les magazines populaires.

References

Albrechtsen, D., Haastrup, K. and Henriksen, B. (2008) *Vocabulary and Writing in a First and Second Language – Processes and Development*. Houndsmill: Palgrave MacMillan.

Ard, H. and Holmburg, T. (1983) Verification of language transfer. In S. Gass and L. Selinker (eds) *Language Transfer in Second Language Learning* (pp. 157–176). Rowley, MA: Newbury House.

Bengeleil, N. and Paribakht, T.S. (2004) Reading proficiency and lexical inferencing by university EFL learners. *The Canadian Modern Language Review* 61 (2), 225–249.

Bensoussan, M. and Laufer, B. (1984) Lexical guessing in context in EFL reading comprehension. *Journal of Research in Reading* 7 (1), 15–32.

Bialystok, E. (1983) Inferencing: Testing the 'hypothesis testing' hypothesis. In H.W. Seliger and M.H. Long (eds) *Classroom Oriented Research in Second Language Acquisition* (pp. 104–123). Rowley, MA: Newbury House.

Blum, S. and Levenston, E. (1979) Lexical simplification in second language acquisition. *Studies in Second Language Acquisition* 2, 85–94.

Brown, C.M. (1993) Factors affecting the acquisition of vocabulary: Frequency and saliency of words. In T. Huckin, M. Haynes and J. Coady (eds) *Second Language Reading and Vocabulary Learning* (pp. 263–286). Norwood, NJ: Ablex.

Brown, C.M., Sagers, S. and LaPorte, C. (1999) Incidental vocabulary acquisition from oral and written dialogue journals. In M. Wesche and T.S. Paribakht (eds) *Incidental L2 Vocabulary Acquisition: Theory, Current Research and Instructional Implications. Special Issue: Studies in Second Language Acquisition* 21, 259–283.

Brown, G. (1998) Inferring word meaning: First and second language comprehension. In D. Albrechtsen, B. Henriksen, I. Mees and E. Poulsen (eds) *Perspectives on Second and Foreign Language Pedagogy* (pp. 29–39). Odensee: Odensee University Press.

Brown, G. and Yule, G. (1983) *Discourse Analysis*. Cambridge: Cambridge University Press.

Carrell, P. (1993) Some issues in studying the role of schemata, or background knowledge, in second language comprehension. *Reading in a Foreign Language* 1, 81–92.

Carton, A. (1971) Inferencing: A process in using and learning language. In P. Pimsleur and T. Quinn (eds) *The Psychology of Second Language Learning* (pp. 45–58). Cambridge: Cambridge University Press.

Chaudron, C. (1985a) Intake: On models and methods for discovering learners' processing of input. *Studies in Second Language Acquisition* 7, 1–14.

Chaudron, C. (1985b) A method for examining the input/intake distinction. In S. Gass and C. Madden (eds) *Input in Second Language Acquisition* (pp. 285–300). Rowley, MA: Newbury House.

Chern, C.I. (1993) Chinese students' word-solving strategies in reading in English. In T. Huckin, M. Haynes and J. Coady (eds) *Second Language Reading and Vocabulary Learning* (pp. 67–85). Norwood, NJ: Ablex.

Coady, J., Magoto, J., Hubbard, P., Graney, J. and Mokhtari, K. (1993) High frequency vocabulary and reading proficiency in ESL readers. In T. Huckin, M. Haynes and J. Coady (eds) *Second Language Reading and Vocabulary Learning* (pp. 217–226). Norwood, NJ: Ablex.

Cobb, T. (2005) The case for computer-assisted extensive reading. *Contact* 31, 55–83.

Cronbach, L.J. (1942) An analysis of techniques for diagnostic vocabulary testing. *Journal of Educational Research* 36, 206–217.

de Bot, K., Paribakht, T.S. and Wesche, M.B. (1997) Toward a lexical processing model for the study of second language vocabulary acquisition: Evidence from ESL reading. *Studies of Second Language Acquisition* 19, 309–329.

de Bot, K. and Schreuder, R. (1993) Word production and the bilingual lexicon. In R. Schreuder and B. Weltens (eds) *The Bilingual Lexicon* (pp. 191–214). Amsterdam: Benjamins.

Dupuy, B. and Krashen, S. (1993) Incidental vocabulary acquisition in French as a foreign language. *Applied Language Learning* 4, 55–63.

Dörnyei, Z. (1994) Motivation and motivating in the foreign language classroom. *Modern Language Journal* 78, 273–284.

Dubin, F. and Olshtain, E. (1993) Predicting word meanings from contextual clues: Evidence from L1 readers. In T. Huckin, M. Haynes and J. Coady (eds) *Second Language Reading and Vocabulary Learning* (pp. 181–202). Norwood, NJ: Ablex.

Elley, W. and Mangubhai, F. (1983) The impact of reading on second language learning. *Reading Research Quarterly* 19, 15–67.

Ellis, N.C. (1994) Implicit and explicit language learning – An overview. In N.C. Ellis (ed.) *Implicit and Explicit Learning of Languages* (pp. 1–32). London: Academic Press.

Ellis, N.C. (2002) Frequency effects in language processing: A review with implications for theories of implicit and explicit language acquisition. *Studies in Second Language Acquisition* 24, 143–188.

Ericsson, K.A. and Simon, H.A. (1984) *Protocol Analysis*. Cambridge, MA: MIT Press.

Ericsson, K.A. and Simon, H.A. (1987) Introspective methods. In C. Færch and G. Kasper (eds) *Introspection in Second Language Research*. Clevedon: Multilingual Matters.

Ericsson, K.A. and Simon, H.A. (1993) *Protocol Analysis: Verbal Report as Data* (rev. edn). Cambridge, MA: MIT Press.

Færch, C. (1984) Strategies in production and reception, the empirical evidence. In A. Davies, C. Criper and A.P.R. Howatt (eds) *Interlanguage* (pp. 49–70). Edinburgh: Edinburgh University Press.

Færch, C. and Kasper, G. (1983) Plans and strategies in foreign language learning and communication. In C. Færch and G. Kasper (eds) *Strategies in Interlanguage Communication* (pp. 20–60). Harlow: Longman.

Færch, C. and Kasper, G. (1985) Procedural knowledge as a component of foreign language learners' communicative competence. In H. Bolte and W. Herrlitz (eds) *Kommunikation in Sprachunterricht* (pp. 169–199). Utrecht: Institut 'Franzen', University of Utrecht.

Faerch, C. and Kasper, G. (1986) The role of comprehension in second language learning. *Applied Linguistics* 7, 257–274.

Faerch, C. and Kasper, G. (1987) From product to process – Introspective methods in second language research. In C. Faerch and G. Kasper (eds) *Introspection in Second Language Research* (pp. 5–23). Clevedon: Multilingual Matters.

Frantzen, D. (2003) Factors affecting how second language Spanish students derive meaning from context. *Modern Language Journal* 87, 168–199.

Fraser, C.A. (1999) Lexical processing strategy use and vocabulary leaning through reading. In M. Wesche and T.S. Paribakht (eds) *Incidental L2 Vocabulary Acquisition: Theory, Current Research and Instructional Implications. Special Issue: Studies in Second Language Acquisition* 21, 225–241.

Gass, S. (1988) Integrating research areas: A framework for second language studies. *Applied Linguistics* 9, 198–217.

Gass, S. (1997) *Input, Interaction, and the Second Language Learner*. Hillsdale, NJ: Erlbaum.

Gass, S. (1999) Discussion: Incidental vocabulary learning. *Studies in Second Language Acquisition* 21, 319–333.

Ghahremani-Ghajar, S. and Masny, D. (1999) Making sense in a second orthography. *International Review of Applied Linguistics* 125/126, 229–251.

Green, D.W. (1993) Toward a model of L2 comprehension and production. In R. Schreuder and B. Weltens (eds) *The Bilingual Lexicon* (pp. 249–277). Amsterdam: John Benjamins.

Haastrup, K. (1987) Using thinking aloud and retrospection to uncover learners' lexical inferencing procedures. In C. Faerch and G. Kasper (eds) *Introspection in Second Language Research* (pp. 197–212). Clevedon: Multilingual Matters.

Haastrup, K. (1991a) *Lexical Inferencing Procedures or Talking about Words: Receptive Procedures in Foreign Language Learning with Special Reference to English.* Tübingen: Gunter Narr.

Haastrup, K. (1991b) Developing learners' procedural knowledge in comprehension. In R. Phillipson, E. Kellerman, L. Selinker, M. Sharwood Smith and M. Swain (eds) *Foreign/Second Language Pedagogy Research* (pp. 120–133). Clevedon: Multilingual Matters.

Haastrup, K. (2008) Lexical inferencing procedures in two languages. In D. Albrechtsen, K. Haastrup and B. Henriksen *Vocabulary and Writing in a First and Second Language – Processes and Development* (pp. 67–111). Houndsmill: Palgrave MacMillan.

Haastrup, K. and Henriksen, B. (1998) Vocabulary acquisition: From partial to precise understanding. In K. Haastrup and Å. Viberg (eds) *Perspectives on Lexical Acquisition in a Second Language* (pp. 97–124). Lund: Lund University Press.

Haastrup, K. and Viberg, Å. (eds) (1998) *Perspectives on Lexical Acquisition in a Second Language*. Lund: Lund University Press.

Haastrup, K., Albrechtsen, D. and Henriksen, B. (2004) Lexical inferencing processes in L1 and L2: Same or different? Focus on issues in design and

method. *Angles on the English-speaking World* 4, 111–128. Copenhagen: Museum Tusculanum Press.
Harley, B. (1995) Introduction. The lexicon in second language research. In B. Harley (ed.) *Lexical Issues in Language Learning* (pp. 1–28). Ann Arbor, MI: John Benjamins.
Harley, B. and Hart, D. (2000) Vocabulary learning in the content-oriented second language classroom: Student perceptions and proficiency. *Language Awareness* 9, 78–96.
Hatch, E. and Brown, C. (1995) *Vocabulary, Semantics, and Language Education*. Cambridge: Cambridge University Press.
Haynes, M. (1993) Patterns and perils of guessing in second language reading. In T. Huckin, M. Haynes and J. Coady (eds) *Second Language Reading and Vocabulary Learning* (pp. 46–64). Norwood, NJ: Ablex.
Haynes, M. and Baker, I. (1993) American and Chinese readers learning from lexical familiarizations in English text. In T. Huckin, M. Haynes and J. Coady (eds) *Second Language Reading and Vocabulary Learning* (pp. 139–150). Norwood, NJ: Ablex.
Hazenberg, S. and Hulstijn, J. (1996) Defining a minimal receptive second-language vocabulary for non-native university students: An empirical investigation. *Applied Linguistics* 17 (2), 145–163.
Henriksen, B. (1999) Three dimensions of vocabulary development. In M. Wesche and T.S. Paribakht (eds) *Incidental L2 Vocabulary Acquisition: Theory, Current Research and Instructional Implications. Special Issue: Studies in Second Language Acquisition* 21, 303–317.
Henriksen, B. (2008) Declarative lexical knowledge. In D. Albrechtsen, K. Haastrup and B. Henriksen (eds) *Vocabulary and Writing in a First and Second Language – Processes and Development* (pp. 22–66). Houndsmill: Palgrave MacMillan.
Henriksen, B., Albrechtsen, D. and Haastrup, K. (2004) The relationship between vocabulary size and reading comprehension in the L2. *Angles on the English-speaking World* 4, 129–140.
Hirsh, D. and Nation, P. (1992) What vocabulary size is needed to read unsimplified texts for pleasure? *Reading in a Foreign Language* 8, 689–696.
Horst, M., Cobb, T. and Meara, P. (1998) Beyond a Clockwork Orange: Acquiring second language vocabulary through reading. *Reading in a Foreign Language* 11, 207–223.
Horst, M. and Meara, P. (1999) Test of a model for predicting second language lexical growth through reading. *The Canadian Modern Language Review* 56, 308–328.
Hu, M. and Nation, P. (2000) Unknown vocabulary density and reading comprehension. *Reading in a Foreign Language* 13, 403–430.
Huckin, T. and Bloch, J. (1993) Strategies for inferring word meaning from context: A cognitive model. In T. Huckin, M. Haynes and J. Coady (eds) *Second Language Reading and Vocabulary Learning* (pp. 153–178). Norwood, NJ: Ablex.
Huckin, T. and Coady, J. (1999) Incidental vocabulary acquisition in a second language: A review. In M. Wesche and T.S. Paribakht (eds) *Incidental L2 Vocabulary Acquisition: Theory, Current Research and Instructional Implications. Special Issue: Studies in Second Language Acquisition* 21, 181–193.

Hulstijn, J.H. (1992) Retention of inferred and given word meanings: Experiments in incidental vocabulary learning. In P.J. Arnaud and H. Bejoint (eds) *Vocabulary and Applied Linguistics* (pp. 113–125). London: Macmillan.

Hulstijn, J.H. (1993) When do foreign-language readers look up the meaning of unfamiliar words? The influence of task and learner variables. *Modern Language Journal* 77, 139–147.

Hulstijn, J.H. (2001) Intentional and incidental second-language vocabulary learning: A reappraisal of elaboration, rehearsal and automaticity. In P. Robinson (ed.) *Cognition and Second Language Instruction* (pp. 258–286). Cambridge: Cambridge University Press.

Hulstijn, J.H. (2002) Towards a unified account of the representation, processing and acquisition of L2 knowledge. *Second Language Research* 18 (3), 193–223.

Itzés, K. (1991) Lexical guessing in isolation and context. *Journal of Reading* 32 (5), 360–366.

Jiang, D. (2004) Semantic transfer and its implications for vocabulary teaching in a second language. *The Modern Language Journal* 88, 416–432.

Jiang, N. (2000) Lexical representation and development in a second language. *Applied Linguistics* 21, 47–77.

Jiang, N. (2002) Form-meaning mapping in vocabulary acquisition in a second language. *Studies in Second Language Acquisition* 24, 617–637.

Joe, A. (1995) *Text-based Tasks and Incidental Vocabulary Learning*. Wellington, New Zealand: English Language Institute.

Kellerman, E. (1977) Towards a characterization of the strategy of transfer in second language learning. *Interlanguage Studies Bulletin* 21, 58–145.

Kellerman, E. (1978) Giving learners a break: Native language intuitions about transferability. *Working Papers in Bilingualism* 15, 309–315.

Kempen, G. and Huijbers, P. (1983) The lexicalization process in sentence production and naming: Indirect selection of words. *Cognition* 14, 185–209.

Kim, H. (2003) Vocabulary comprehension of advanced ESL learners in academic reading: A collective case study. MA thesis, University of Ottawa.

Kintsch, W. (1998) *Comprehension: A Paradigm for Cognition*. New York: Cambridge University Press.

Koda, K. (2005) *Insights into Second Language Reading: A Cross-linguistic Approach*. New York: Cambridge University Press.

Krashen, S. (1989) We acquire vocabulary and spelling by reading: Additional evidence for the input hypothesis. *Modern Language Journal* 73, 440–463.

Krashen, S. (2003) *Explorations in Language Acquisition and Use: The Taipei Lectures*. Portsmouth, NH: Heinemann.

Lado, R. (1957) *Linguistics across Cultures*. Ann Arbor, MI: University of Michigan Press.

Laufer, B. (1988) What percentage of text-lexis is essential for comprehension? In C. Laurén and M. Nordmann (eds) *Special Language: From Humans to Thinking Machines* (pp. 316–323). Clevedon: Multilingual Matters.

Laufer, B. (1997) What's in a word that makes it hard or easy: Some intralexical factors that affect the learning of words. In N. Schmitt and M. McCarthy (eds) *Vocabulary: Description, Acquisition and Pedagogy* (pp. 140–180). Cambridge: Cambridge University Press.

References

Laufer, B. and Hulstijn, J. (2001) Incidental vocabulary acquisition in a second language: The construct of task-induced involvement. *Applied Linguistics* 22, 1–26.
Lessard-Clouston, M. (2005) Learning and use of specialized vocabulary among native and non-native English-speaking graduate students of theology. PhD thesis, University of Toronto.
Levelt, W. (1989) *Speaking: From Intention to Articulation*. Cambridge, MA: Bradford Books/MIT Press.
Li, X. (1988) Effects of contextual clues on inferring and remembering meanings of new words. *Applied Linguistics* 9, 402–413.
Liu, N. and Nation, I.S.P. (1985) Factors affecting guessing vocabulary in context. *RELC Journal* 16, 33–42.
MacWhinney, B. and Bates, E. (eds) (1989) *The Cross-linguistic Study of Sentence Processing*. New York: Cambridge University Press.
Meara, P. (1996) The dimensions of lexical competence. In G. Brown, K. Malmkjaer and J. Williams (eds) *Performance and Competence in Second Language Acquisition* (pp. 35–53). Cambridge: Cambridge University Press.
Milton, J. and Meara, P. (1995) How periods abroad affect vocabulary growth in a foreign language. *ITL Review of Applied Linguistics* 107–108, 17–34.
Mondria, J.A. and Witt-de Boer, M. (1991) The effects of contextual richness on the guessability and the retention of words in a foreign language. *Applied Linguistics* 12, 249–267.
Mori, Y. (2002) Individual differences in the integration of information from context and word parts in interpreting unknown kanji words. *Applied Psycholinguistics* 23, 375–397.
Morrison, L. (1996) Talking about words. A study of French as a second language learners' lexical inferencing procedures. *Canadian Modern Language Review* 53, 41–67.
Murphy, M.I. (2003) *Semantic Relations and the Lexicon: Antonymy, Synonymy, and other Paradigms*. Cambridge: Cambridge University Press.
Nagy, W. and Anderson, R. (1984) The number of words in printed school English. *Reading Research Quarterly* 19, 304–330.
Nagy, W.E., Herman, P.A. and Anderson, R.C. (1985) Learning words from context. *Reading Research Quarterly* 20, 233–253.
Nagy, W.E. and Herman, P.A. (1987) Breadth and depth of vocabulary knowledge: Implications for acquisition and instruction. In M.G. McKeown and M. Curtis (eds) *The Nature of Vocabulary Acquisition* (pp. 19–35). Hillsdale, NJ: Erlbaum.
Nagy, W.E., McClure, E.F. and Mir, M. (1997) Linguistic transfer and the use of context by Spanish-English bilinguals. *Applied Psycholinguistics* 18, 431–452.
Nassaji, H. (2003) L2 vocabulary learning from context: Strategies, knowledge sources, and their relationship with success in L2 lexical inferencing. *TESOL Quarterly* 37, 645–670.
Nassaji, H. (2004) The relationship between depth of vocabulary knowledge and L2 learners' lexical inferencing strategy use and success. *The Canadian Modern Language Review* 61, 107–134.
Nation, I.S.P. (1990) *Teaching and Learning Vocabulary*. New York: Newbury House.
Nation, I.S.P. (2006) How large a vocabulary is needed for reading and listening? *The Canadian Modern Language Review* 63, 59–81.

Nation, P. and Coady, J. (1988) Vocabulary and reading. In R. Carter and M. McCarthy (eds) *Vocabulary and Language Teaching* (pp. 97–110). New York: Longman.
Nemser, W. (1998) Variations on a theme by Haastrup. In D. Albrechtsen, B. Henriksen, I.M. Mees and E. Poulsen (eds) *Perspectives on Foreign Language Pedagogy* (pp. 107–117). Odense: Odense University Press.
Newton, J. (1995) Task-based interaction and incidental vocabulary learning: A case study. *Second Language Research* 11, 159–177.
Odlin, T. (1989) *Language Transfer*. Cambridge: Cambridge University Press.
Odlin, T. (1997) Bilingualism and substrate influence: A look at clefts and reflexives. In J. Kallen (ed.) *Focus on Ireland* (pp. 35–50). Amsterdam: John Benjamins.
Odlin, T. (2003) Cross-linguistic influence. In C.J. Doughty and M.H. Long (eds) *The Handbook of Second Language Acquisition* (pp. 437–486). Malden, MA: Blackwell.
Odlin, T. (2005) Cross-linguistic influence and conceptual transfer: What are the concepts? *Annual Review of Applied Linguistics* 25, 3–25.
Palmberg, R. (1985) How much English vocabulary do Swedish-speaking primary-school pupils know before starting to learn English at school? In H. Ringbom (ed.) *Foreign Language Learning and Bilingualism* (pp. 89–97). Åbo: Åbo Akademi.
Palmberg, R. (2008) On lexical inferencing and language distance. *Journal of Pragmatics* 12, 207–214.
Paribakht, T.S. (1985) Strategic competence and language proficiency. *Applied Linguistics* 6, 132–146.
Paribakht, T.S. (2005) The influence of first language lexicalization on second language lexical inferencing: A study of Farsi-speaking learners of English as a foreign language. *Language Learning* 55, 701–748.
Paribakht, T.S. and Tréville, M.C. (2007) L'influence lexicale chez des locuteurs de français et des locuteurs de persan lors de la lecture de textes anglais: effet de la lexicalisation en première langue. *The Canadian Modern Language Review* 63 (3), 399–428.
Paribakht, T.S. and Wesche, M. (1993) Reading comprehension and second language development in a comprehension-based ESL program. *TESL Canada Journal* 11, 9–29.
Paribakht, T.S. and Wesche, M. (1996) Enhancing vocabulary acquisition through reading: A hierarchy of text-related exercise types. *The Canadian Modern Language Review* 52 (2), 155–175.
Paribakht, T.S. and Wesche, M. (1997) Vocabulary enhancement activities and reading for meaning in second language vocabulary acquisition. In J. Coady and T. Huckin (eds) *Second Language Vocabulary Acquisition: A Rationale for Pedagogy* (pp. 174–199). New York: Cambridge University Press.
Paribakht, T.S. and Wesche, M. (1998) "Incidental" and instructed L2 vocabulary acquisition: Different contexts, common processes. In D. Albrechten, B. Henriksen, I.M. Mees and Poulsen (eds) *Perspectives on Foreign and Second Language Pedagogy* (pp. 203–220). Lund: Odense University Press.
Paribakht, T.S. and Wesche, M. (1999) Reading and "incidental" L2 vocabulary acquisition: An introspective study of lexical inferencing. In M. Wesche and T.S. Paribakht (eds) *Incidental L2 Vocabulary Acquisition: Theory, Current Research*

and Instructional Implications. Special Issue: Studies in Second Language Acquisition 21, 195–224.

Paribakht, T.S. and Wesche, M. (2006) Lexical inferencing in L1 and L2: Implications for learning and instruction at advanced levels. In H. Byrnes, H. Weger-Guntharp and K.A. Sprang (eds) *Educating for Advanced Foreign Language Capacities: Constructs, Curriculum, Instruction, Assessment* (pp. 118–135). Washington, DC: Georgetown University Press.

Parry, K. (1993) Too many words: Learning the vocabulary of an academic subject. In T. Huckin, M. Haynes and J. Coady (eds) *Second Language Reading and Vocabulary Learning* (pp. 109–129). Norwood, NJ: Ablex.

Parry, K. (1997) Vocabulary and comprehension: Two portraits. In J. Coady and T. Huckin (eds) *Second Language Vocabulary Acquisition: A Rationale for Pedagogy* (pp. 55–68). New York: Cambridge University Press.

Pitts, M., White, H. and Krashen, S. (1989) Acquiring second language vocabulary through reading: A replication of the *Clockwork Orange* study using second language acquirers. *Reading in a Foreign Language* 5 (2), 271–275.

Poulisse, N. (1993) A theoretical account of lexical communication strategies. In R. Schreuder and B. Weltens (eds) *The Bilingual Lexicon* (pp. 157–189). Amsterdam: Benjamins.

Pulido, D. (2003) Modeling the role of second language proficiency and topic familiarity in second language incidental vocabulary acquisition through reading. *Language Learning* 53, 233–284.

Qian, D. (1999) Assessing the roles of depth and breadth of vocabulary knowledge in reading comprehension. *The Canadian Modern Language Review* 56, 282–308.

Read, J. (1993) The development of a new measure of L2 vocabulary knowledge. *Language Testing* 10, 355–371.

Read, J. (1998) Validating a test to measure depth of vocabulary knowledge. In A. Kunnen (ed.) *Validation in Language Assessment* (pp. 41–60). Hillsdale, NJ: Erlbaum.

Read, J. (2000) *Assessing Vocabulary*. Cambridge: Cambridge University Press.

Read, J. (2004) Plumbing the depths: How should the construct of vocabulary knowledge be defined? In P. Bogaards and B. Laufer (eds) *Vocabulary in a Second Language: Selection, Acquisition and Testing* (pp. 209–227). Amsterdam: John Benjamins.

Richards, J. (1976) The role of vocabulary teaching. *TESOL Quarterly* 10, 77–89.

Ringbom, H. (1987) *The Role of First Language in Foreign Language Learning*. Clevedon: Multilingual Matters.

Ringbom, H. (1992) On L1 transfer in L2 comprehension and production. *Language Learning* 42, 85–112.

Ringbom, H. (2007) *Cross-linguistic Similarity in Foreign Language Learning*. Clevedon: Multilingual Matters.

Saragi, T., Nation, I.S.P. and Meister, G. (1978) Vocabulary learning and reading. *System* 6, 72–78.

Schmidt, R. (1990) The role of consciousness in second language learning. *Applied Linguistics* 11, 129–158.

Schmitt, N. (1998) Tracking the incremental acquisition of second language vocabulary: A longitudinal study. *Language Learning* 48 (2), 281–317.

Schmitt, N., Schmitt, D. and Clapham, C. (2001). Developing and exploring the behaviour of two new versions of the Vocabulary Levels Test. *Language Testing* 18, 55–88.

Schouten van Parreren, C. (1989) Vocabulary learning through reading: Which conditions should be met when presenting words in texts? *AILA Review* 6, 75–85.

Seidenberg, M. (1995) Visual word recognition: An overview. In J. Miller and P. Eimas (eds) *Speech, Language, and Communication* (pp. 137–179). San Diego, CA: Academic Press.

Singleton, D. (1994) Learning L2 lexis: A matter of form? In G. Bartelt (ed.) *The Dynamics of Language Processes: Essays in Honour of Hans W. Dechert* (pp. 45–57). Tübingen: Gunter Narr.

Singleton, D. (2006) Lexical transfer: Interlexical or intralexical? In J. Arabski (ed.) *Cross-linguistic Influences in the Second Language Lexicon* (pp. 130–143). Clevedon: Multilingual Matters.

Sjöholm, K. (1993) Patterns of transferability among fixed expressions in L2 acquisition. In B. Kettemann and W. Wieden (eds) *Current Issues in European Second Language Acquisition Research* (pp. 263–275). Tübingen: Gunter Narr.

Sjöholm, K. (1998) A reappraisal of the role of cross-linguistic and environmental factors in lexical L2 acquisition. In K. Haastrup and Å. Viberg (eds) *Perspectives on Lexical Acquisition in a Second Language* (pp. 135–147). Lund: Lund University Press.

Soria, J. (2001) A study of Ilokano learners' lexical inferencing procedures through think-aloud. *Second Language Studies* 19, 77–110.

Sternberg, R.J. (1987) Most vocabulary is learned from context. In M.G. McKeown and M.E. Curtis (eds) *The Nature of Vocabulary Acquisition* (pp. 89–105). Hillsdale, NJ: Lawrence Erlbaum.

Sternberg, R.J. (2003) *Wisdom, Intelligence, and Creativity Synthesized*. Cambridge: Cambridge University Press.

Sternberg, R.J. and Powell, J.S. (1983) Comprehending verbal comprehension. *American Psychologist* 38, 878–893.

Svensson, H.L. (2003) Lexical inferencing – A strategy for comprehension and/or learning? MA thesis, University of Copenhagen.

Swain, M. (1985) Communicative competence: Some roles of comprehensible input and comprehensive output in its development. In S. Gass and C. Madden (eds) *Input in Second Language Acquisition* (pp. 235–253). Rowley, MA: Newbury House.

Swain, M. (1995) Three functions of output in second language learning. In G. Cook and B. Seidlhofer (eds) *Principle and Practice in Applied Linguistics: Studies in Honour of H. G. Widdowson* (pp. 125–144). Oxford: Oxford University Press.

Swain, M. and Lapkin, S. (1995) Problems in output and the cognitive processes they generate: A step towards second language learning. *Applied Linguistics* 16, 371–391.

Swain, M. and Lapkin, S. (1998) Interaction and second language learning. Two adolescent French immersion students working together. *Modern Language Journal* 82, 320–337.

Tréville, M-C. (1990) *Good Friends: The use of English Cognates for learning French*. Aylmer, Québec: Les Edition Varro.

Viberg, Å. (1998a) Lexical development and the lexical profile of the target language. In D. Albrechtsen, B. Henriksen, I.M. Mees and E. Poulsen (eds) *Perspectives on Foreign and Second language Pedagogy* (pp. 119–134). Odense: Odense University Press.

Viberg, Å. (1998b) Cross-linguistic perspectives on lexical acquisition: The case of language-specific semantic differentiation. In K. Haastrup and Å. Viberg (eds) *Perspectives on Lexical Acquisition in a Second language* (pp. 175–208). Lund: Lund University Press.

Walters, J. (2006) Methods of teaching inferring meaning from context. *RELC* 37, 176–190.

Weinreich, U. (1953) *Languages in Contact*. The Hague: Mouton.

Wesche, M. (1994) Input and interaction in second language acquisition. In C. Gallaway and B. Richards (eds) *Input and Interaction in Language Acquisition* (pp. 219–249). Cambridge: Cambridge University Press.

Wesche, M. and Paribakht, T.S. (1996) Assessing L2 vocabulary knowledge: Depth versus breadth. *The Canadian Modern Language Review*, 53 (1), 13–40.

Wesche, M. and Paribakht, T.S. (1998) The influence of task in reading-based vocabulary acquisition: Evidence from introspective studies. In K. Haastrup and Å.Viberg (eds) *Perspectives on Lexical Acquisition in a Second Language* (pp. 19–59). Lund: Lund University Press.

Wesche, M. and Paribakht, T.S. (1999a) Introduction. In M. Wesche and T.S. Paribakht (eds) *Incidental L2 Vocabulary Acquisition: Theory, Current Research and Instructional Implications. Special Issue: Studies in Second Language Acquisition* 21, 175–180.

Wesche, M. and Paribakht, T.S. (eds) (1999b) *Incidental L2 Vocabulary Acquisition: Theory, Current Research and Instructional Implications. Special Issue: Studies in Second Language Acquisition* 21.

Wesche, M. and Paribakht, T.S. (2000) Reading-based exercises in second language vocabulary learning: An introspective study. *The Modern Language Journal* 84, 196–213.

Wolff, D. (1994) Importance of procedural knowledge in second language comprehension, production and learning. In G. Bartelt (ed.) *The Dynamics of Language Processes: Essays in Honour of Hans W. Dechert* (pp. 213–227). Tübingen: Gunter Narr.

Yu, L. (1996a) The role of cross-linguistic lexical similarity in the use of motion verbs in English by Chinese and Japanese learners. EdD thesis, University of Toronto.

Yu, L. (1996b) The role of L1 in the acquisition of motion verbs in English by Chinese and Japanese learners. *The Canadian Modern Language Review* 53, 190–218.

Zahar, R., Cobb, T. and Spada, N. (2001) Acquiring vocabulary through reading: Effects of frequency and contextual richness. *The Canadian Modern Language Review* 57, 541–572.

Index

Page numbers in *italics* refer to figures.

AILA Congress, Finland xii
Albrechtsen, D. *et al.* 14, 22, 26-7, 37-8, 42, 50, 73, 164, 166
analytical processing 23
analytical skills 27-8, 29
Ard, H. and Holmburg, T. 36
associative networks *see* connectionism
attempts at lexical inferencing 10-11

Bensoussan, M. and Laufer, B. 8, 10, 11
Bialystok, E. 7
bilingual *vs* monolingual processing in reading 33-4
breadth of vocabulary knowledge 14
Brown, G. and Yule, G. 4

Carton, A. 6, 7, 8, 19
Chinese/English 23, 34-5, 39, 41
class membership cues 7
closely related languages 36-9
cognates 36-7
cognitive processing
 – and connectionism 22
 – framework 23-4
 – and retention 17
cognitive theory 24-6
comprehension 4-6
 – and acquisition outcomes 24-6
 – -oriented frameworks 22-4
conceptualization of lexical inferencing 18-29, 49-50
connectionism 21-2
cross-linguistic issues
 – closely related languages 36-9
 – commonalities 157
 – distantly related languages 39-42
 – knowledge sources (KSs) and shared processing tendencies 68, 107-9, 140-3
 – language distance 34-42, 51, 116-17, 156-7, 165-6
cross-linguistic study (study V) xvii
cues 6, 7, 8, 11, 12, 19, 23, 49, 141-2

 – *see also* knowledge sources (KSs)
culture
 – knowledge and language distance 35-6, 71-2
 – and social influences 160-1
 – unfamiliar 12

Danish/English 8, 14, 26-7, 29, 37-8, 42, 50, 71, 110
de Bot, K. *et al.* 10, 19-20, 49
declarative and procedural knowledge 26-9, 49, 140
depth of vocabulary knowledge 13-14
discourse as a knowledge source 76, 77, 141-2, 148, 149
distantly related languages 39-42

Ellis, N. 21-2
English/
 – Chinese 23, 34-5, 39, 41
 – Danish 8, 14, 26-7, 29, 37-8, 42, 50, 71, 110
 – Finnish/Swedish 35-6, 37, 40
 – Spanish 36, 39, 50
 see also English/Persian/French *under* knowledge sources (KSs); research study; success; trilingual study summary, discussion and implications
English Reading Comprehension Test 56
evaluator component of cognitive processing 23
extralingual cues 6, 19

'false friends' 37
Finnish/Swedish/English 35-6, 37, 40
first language (L1) development 3-4
formal schemata 77, *82*, 93, 94, 97, 98, 99, 108, 112, 145
French *see* English/Persian/French *under* knowledge sources (KSs); research study; success; trilingual study summary, discussion and implications
future research issues 162-3

190

Index

Gass, S. 24
generator component of cognitive
 processing 23
Ghahremani-Ghajar, S. and Masny, D.
 39-40, 70

Haastrup, K. 4, 8, 11, 12, 18-19, 22-3, 27,
 28-9, 37, 38-9, 71, 73, 142, 144, 164
Haynes, M. 5, 11
Henriksen, B. 13, 14, 22, 25-6, 155
high-quality lexical inferencing 28
higher-level processing 27-8
holistic processing 23
Huckin, T. and Bloch, J. 23-4
Hulstijn, J.H. 10, 17, 21, 25

incidental *vs* instructed vocabulary learning
 (study II) xiv-xv
initial development of word knowledge *see
 under* success
input processing 24-5
interactional processing 23
interlingual cues 6, 19
intra-lingual cues 6, 19
intra-word awareness 29

Jiang, N. 37, 41

knowledge
 – declarative and procedural 26-9, 49, 140
 – linguistic and non-linguistic/world 76,
  77-84, 141-2, 149
knowledge sources (KSs) 18-19, 77-84
 – importance of study 68-9
 – L1 influences on use in L2 (English/
  French/Persian) study
   findings 76-107
   issues 68-73
   research methodology 74-6
   summary and discussion 107-12, 144-5
 – multiple use 72-3
 – 'nativeness' *vs* 'non-nativeness' 68
 – processing tendencies shared across
  languages 68, 107-9, 140-3
 – proficiency in text language 109
 – readers
   role of language proficiency 69-70
   use of initial *vs* post-initial 102-5
   use of single *vs* multiple 100-2
   use of sub-types 88-94
   use of types 84-8
 – synthesis of use
   across five conditions 94, *95*
   distinguishing L1 from L2 inferencing 97

in L1 and L2 inferencing 96-7
 L1 proficiency and text language
  effects 99-100
 transfer effects 97-9
 – target word features 73
 – taxonomies 76, 77
 – text language influences 112
 – transfer effects 70-2, 97-9, 147-9
 – word class 105-7
Koda, K. 5, 21, 28-9, 33-4, 35, 36, 37, 40, 70

language distance 34-42, 51, 116-17, 156-7,
 165-6
Laufer, B. and Hulstijn, J.H. 17
lemma construction 19-21, 49
lemma mediation hypothesis 41
Levelt, W. 19-20, 21, 49
lexeme 20, 21
lexical inferencing
 – conceptualization 18-29, 49-50
 – definitions 3-6, 8
 – early studies 6-8
 – influencing factors 10-18
 – processes 18-29
 – research approaches 9-10
lexical profile 34
lexical network knowledge 14-15
lexicalization hypothesis 20-1, 42
lexicalization status 15, 50, 57-61, 115-16, 145
lexicalized words 59
lexically linked frameworks 18-22
Li, X. 8, 11
linguistic and non-linguistic/world
 knowledge 76, 77-84, 141-2, 149

metalinguistic control component of
 cognitive processing 23
moderating variables 7
monolingual *vs* bilingual processing in
 reading 33-4

Nagy, W.E. *et al.* 3-4, 6, 39, 50
Nassaji, H. 14, 15, 24
Nation, I.S.P. 13, 14, 15, 54-5, 56, 61, 153,
 159, 164
'naturalistic' *vs* 'manipulated'
 methodologies 9
Nemser, W. 37, 42
non-lexicalized words 58-9
non-linguistic/world knowledge 76, 77-84,
 141-2, 149

Odlin, T. 5, 33, 34
oral communication 143

orthographies and phonological
  information 40
parallel activation 40-1
parallel distributive processing *see*
  connectionism
Paribakht, T.S. 5, 13, 15, 16, 18-19, 20-1, 38-9,
  41, 42, 49, 50, 63, 71, 140-1, 143, 159, 165-6
– and Tréville, M.C. 11, 15, 18-19, 38-9, 50, 71-2
– and Wesche, M. xii, xiii, xiv, xv, 10, 11, 13,
  15-16, 18-19, 24, 56, 57, 73
Persian/English 39-40, 42
  see also English/Persian/French *under*
  knowledge sources (KSs); research
  study; success; trilingual study
  summary, discussion and implications
phonological information and
  orthographies 40
procedural and declarative knowledge 26-9,
  49, 140
pseudo target words 60-1
punctuation 77, *82*, 92, 97, 98-9, 100, 145

Qian, D. 14

reactivation 17-18
Read, J. 14
reading comprehension *see* comprehension
reading only (study III) xv-xvi
reading plus (study IV) xvi
reading theory 22-3
receptive knowledge 151
research (English/Persian/French) study
– choice of languages 52
– data analysis 63-4
– design 51
– expectations and approach 53
– instruments 56-7, 61-3
– issues 161-3
– methodology 54-63
– participants 54-6
– procedures 61-3
– questions 52-3
– shared journey xi-xii
– target words and texts 57-61
  see also knowledge sources (KSs);
  success; trilingual study summary,
  discussion and implications
retention and success 15-18, 50, 124-34,
  151-4
Ringbom, H. 35-6, 152, 160

second language (L2)
– development 4

– proficiency 12-13
– vocabulary knowledge 13-15
segmental understanding 29
selective combination 7, 28
selective comparison 7, 28
selective encoding 7, 28
sentence(s) 76, *77*, 141
– grammar 77, 79, *81*, 92, 93, 96, 97, 98,
  99-100, 102-4, 107, 108, 144, 149
– meaning 77, *78-9*, 92, 96, 97, 98, 99, 100,
  101-4, 107, 108, 141-2, 144
shared processing tendencies 68, 107-9,
  140-3
Sjöholm, K. 35, 36, 40
Spanish/English 36, 39, 50
spatial cues 7
speech production model 19-20, 49
Sternberg, R.J. 3-4, 7, 11, 16, 28
style/register 77, 78, *83*, 93, 94, 97, 98, 102,
  104, 108, 145
success 11-12, 145-6, 150-1, 158-9
– and initial development of word
  knowledge (English/Persian/French)
  findings 119-34
  issues 115-16
  research methodology 116-19
  summary and discussion 134-7
– L1 inferencing 119-20
– L2 inferencing 120-1
– language distance 116-17
– lexical development 136-7
– lexicalization 115-16
– lexicalized *vs* non-lexicalized L2 target
  words 121-3
– previous vocabulary knowledge 115
– relationship to vocabulary knowledge
  128-34
– and retention 15-18, 50, 124-34, 151-4
Swedish/Finnish/English 35-6, 37, 40
symbol-to-sound relations 40
synthesis skills 27-8
  see also knowledge sources (KSs);
  synthesis of use

task-induced involvement and retention 17
temporal cues 7
text language effects/influences 99-100,
  109, 112, 149-50
think-aloud protocols 75
topic familiarity/unfamiliarity 12, 166-7
training 163-5
transfer effects 33-4, 50, 154-5, 160
– knowledge sources (KSs) 70-2, 97-9, 147-9
trilingual study summary, discussion and

implications
- differential receptive L2 vocabulary knowledge and outcomes 154-7
- implications for L2 reading and vocabulary instruction 163-7
- L1 influences on L2 processes and outcomes 146-54
- L1 transfer 154-5
- L1 vs L2 differences 144-6
- L1 vs L2 use in knowledge sources 144-5
- L2 learning context 155-6
- outcomes 157-61
- research issues 161-3
- shared cross-linguistic aspects of knowledge sources (KSs) 140-3

unfamiliar/familiarity 12, 166-7

Viberg, Å. 34
vocabulary knowledge 13-14, 115, 128-34, 151-7
Vocabulary Knowledge Scale (VKS) xiv, 56-7, 61-2, 162
vocabulary learning in a comprehension-based L2 course (study 1) xiii-xiv
Vocabulary Levels Test 14, 15, 56, 61-3, 153
vocabulary measures 13, 14

Wesche, M. 24
- and Paribakht, T.S. xii, 13, 16, 24, 25, 56
word analysis skills 27-8, 29
word association test (WAT) 14
word class 105-7
word-form 25, 147-8
word(s) 76, 77, 141, 144-5
- collocation 77, 78, 81-2, 88, 91, 97, 98, 99, 100, 145, 147
- morphology 77, 79, 80, 88-92, 96, 98, 99, 100, 107, 108, 109, 111-12, 148-9
world/non-linguistic knowledge 76, 77-84, 141-2, 149
writing systems 39-40

Yu, L. 34-5